MICHAEL JOHN LACHIUSA

MICHAEL JOHN LACHIUSA: A CRITICAL COMPANION

Joshua Robinson

methuen | drama

LONDON · NEW YORK · OXFORD · NEW DELHI · SYDNEY

METHUEN DRAMA
Bloomsbury Publishing Plc
50 Bedford Square, London, WC1B 3DP, UK
1385 Broadway, New York, NY 10018, USA
29 Earlsfort Terrace, Dublin 2, Ireland

BLOOMSBURY, METHUEN DRAMA and the Methuen Drama logo
are trademarks of Bloomsbury Publishing Plc

First published in Great Britain 2025

Series design by Holly Capper
Cover image © The Washington Post / Contributor/Getty Images

A catalogue record for this book is available from the British Library.

A catalog record for this work is available from the Library of Congress.

ISBN: HB: 978-1-3505-0876-7
         PB: 978-1-3505-0877-4
       ePDF: 978-1-3505-0879-8
      eBook: 978-1-3505-0878-1

Series: Critical Companions

Typeset by Integra Software Services Pvt. Ltd.
Printed and bound in Great Britain

To find out more about our authors and books visit www.bloomsbury.com
and sign up for our newsletters.

CONTENTS

Contents

ACKNOWLEDGMENTS

My work on Michael John LaChiusa extends back to my PhD program at Indiana University and has followed me at both of my academic appointments at Southwestern College and University of Southern Indiana. So, it seems only right that I would begin by thanking my committee, Ansley Valentine, Shane Vogel, Ronald Wainscott, and Stacy Wolf, for offering guidance and support throughout this process. A special thank you to my committee chair Jennifer Goodlander for her feedback, support, and generosity in guiding this project to fruition and for continuing to support my development as a teacher and a scholar since my graduation from the program. I would, of course, be remiss not to mention the incredible support I have had from Dom O'Hanlon in walking me through the publication of my first monograph. I am, indeed, in your debt.

Over the course of this book's development, I have been fortunate to have presented portions of my research at several conferences, including the Mid-America Theater Conference, Comparative Drama, ASTR, The Musical Theatre Forum, and the Song, Stage and Screen conference. Much of the feedback I received at these events directly influenced the final product. I've also met some incredible scholars in the field who have had a profound impact on this text. I would especially like to thank Stacy Wolf for first mentoring me and continuing to be a constant resource. Thanks also to Doug Reside, whose advice and guidance helped to establish the structure of this project, as well as Elizabeth Wollman, who was never too busy to answer a question via Facebook.

This project was supported by a generous fellowship from the New York Public Library, which funded a short-term residency in New York City during which I had ample time to peruse Michael John LaChiusa's papers and the recorded archive of his NYC productions. I am deeply indebted to the selection committee as well as Doug Reside who bent over backwards to be sure I had access to the collection as well as Annemarie van Roessel, who organized the trip. In addition, the staff at the Theatre on Film and Tape collection was incredibly accommodating and supportive. A heartfelt thank you to Wendy Norris, Brendan Leonard, Steve Massa, and Melisa Tien for dealing with my constant requests and schedule changes, always with a smile.

Additionally, I was fortunate to receive ample financial support from the Indiana University Department of Theatre, Drama, and Contemporary Dance throughout my program and through the completion of this project. In particular, I would like to thank Jonathan Michaelson and Linda Pisano for providing as much financial support as possible for conferences and research trips as well as the department as a whole for supporting me throughout the duration of my program. Also, I received significant financial support from my new academic home, University of Southern Indiana, to attend conferences, share my work on LaChiusa, and get invaluable feedback. My new colleagues have been particularly supportive of my work, most especially Paul Weimer, Shan Jensen, and Josh Stallings. Additionally, I have had the fortune to be continually inspired by my wonderful students. In particular, I want to thank Via Wagner, whose work on the interview transcripts for this book was invaluable.

I have had the honor of studying and working with the best colleagues in the world, both in my cohort and out. Thank you to Joseph D'Ambrosi, Greer Gerni, Huihui Huang, Anna Holman, and Andres Lopez for your input, support, and friendship. In particular, my cohort was an amazing source of encouragement. Thanks to Jihay Park for being a fantastic office mate and a truly heartfelt "thank you" to Whit Emerson, who was not only a colleague and friend but also became a part of my chosen family, along with his wife and our honorary cohort member Amanda Li, who offered her expertise as a musician as well as her friendship at several key points when the process became tough.

On the subject of chosen families, there are three folks without whom this never would have happened. To my "sister" Krista Smith, whose constant love and loyalty have made me a better person and whose experiences in academia have helped immensely in navigating the past five years. I couldn't imagine achieving anything without her standing next to me. To my "brother" John Bronston, the real musical theatre scholar in the family, who was my first teacher and mentor. Without John, I would never have even discovered the musical *Hello Again* on our first trip to NYC and thus my journey with Michael John LaChiusa would never have begun. I am particularly indebted to his refusal to let me slide when he read a passage in my dissertation that didn't make sense or that needed revision. So much of this book is indebted to him, and his constant guidance has made me a better scholar and a better human. And also, to my husband, Shaun Altneu, whose endless support and patience made getting through a PhD program and a new career possible. Shaun's belief in me helped me to see possibilities that I had not considered for myself and his love is the foundation that made this book possible. I am forever changed because of him.

Finally, I would like to dedicate this book to the memory of my mother, Juanita Louise Robinson, who passed away in the middle of my program. My mother was in a constant war with her own health throughout her life and her perseverance was a bright example to me whenever things would get rough. I miss her, but I know that she was with me, in some way, throughout the entire writing of this book.

INTRODUCTION: "CURIOSITY": LACHIUSA AND THE EMERGENCE OF "THE NEW MUSICAL DRAMA"

In August of 2005, musical theatre composer, lyricist, and librettist Michael John LaChiusa published a polemical editorial in that month's issue of *Opera News*. Entitled "The Great Gray Way," LaChiusa declares the American musical "dead" or, more to the point, "un-dead."[1] He goes on to posit that the recent trend in musical theatre, a trend he labels "faux-musicals," relies more on nostalgia than innovation: "All sense of invention and craft is abandoned in favor of delivering what the audience thinks a musical should deliver."[2] While the real impetus for LaChiusa's essay was to encourage critics and writers to look outside of Broadway to see that the American musical was alive and kicking, his arguments about what makes a "real musical" are far more memorable. For LaChiusa, a real musical contains "Lyric, music, libretto, choreography—all [these elements] work in equal parts to spin out the drama."[3] Additionally, a real musical "makes perfect symmetry" out of the disparate elements and sources that comprise musical theatre creation and "is organic in all its parts. It's equal parts intelligence and heart. It can never be realistic theatre, only realistic in its humanity."[4] These are the standards that, in 2005, LaChiusa found lacking among the various titles playing on Broadway, though he makes special mention of the musicals *The Producers* and *Hairspray*, both of which he labels as "faux musicals" because they are engineered to the audiences' craving for nostalgia and, in his opinion, display theatricality without actually being "theatre." The theatre community was dumbfounded; it was rare for someone working in the field to be so openly critical of his peers, particularly going so far as to name the shows he felt were at fault. Marc Shaiman, the composer and co-lyricist of *Hairspray*, took to various theatre chat boards to share his response to "The Great Gray Way," a response that made strong statements about the nature of LaChiusa's work, particularly his 1999 musical, *Marie Christine*. While the bickering back and forth is interesting, there is a more important takeaway from LaChiusa's essay, which is concerned with the ways in which the Broadway musical creates frequently formulaic work in order to maintain commercial viability. More importantly, LaChiusa points to regional and off-Broadway nonprofit theatres as the places where musical theatre can find an alternative, thereby proposing a broadening of the landscape which historians and critics use when looking for developments in the American musical.

The article also suggests that LaChiusa's works were somehow separate and different from the work of some of his contemporaries, suggesting that his aim as a musical theatre writer was somehow operating under different rules, standards, and expectations. But the question of LaChiusa's uniqueness is a more complicated issue, intersecting with the historical narrative of the American musical and problematizing standards of representation, identity, and legitimacy on the musical stage. In particular, his project becomes a type of vanguard for "The New Musical Drama" movement, which aims to continue the tradition of a "chamber musical" or an "art musical" that foregoes the spectacle typically inherent in musical theatre in favor of a narratively complex, musically sophisticated product. What are the factors, then, that differentiate Michael John LaChiusa's work as well as the work of his contemporary musical dramatists also associated with "The New Musical Drama" movement as implied in his essay "The Great Gray Way"? This question serves to guide this project, exploring the ways and means that LaChiusa's works have made unique, far-reaching contributions to the musical, particularly in our current moment when musical theatre's visibility and cultural relevance have increased. Additionally, its considerations of race, gender, and sexuality have become more nuanced and complicated, as exemplified in Broadway successes such as *Fun Home*, *Hamilton*, *Dear Evan Hansen*, and *Hadestown*.

Defining "The New Musical Drama"

Before moving forward, it is important to explicate and define the term "The New Musical Drama." In her book *Directors and the New Musical Drama*, Miranda Lundskaer-Nielsen employs the term "musical dramas" to refer to musicals that "combine the fundamental traditions of Broadway musical plays and concept musicals … with dramaturgical and staging approaches from developments in nonmusical drama."[5] In particular, Lundskaer-Nielsen is interested in musicals that come out of the "musical play" tradition that dates back to shows like *Show Boat* (1927) and *The Cradle Will Rock* (1937), a tradition that is often labeled "the art musical" and is relabeled "the concept musical" in the 1970s. Lundskaer-Nielsen sees the "musical drama" as providing an alternative to the megamusical tradition imported from Europe, then reincarnated with large American corporations such as Disney. Lundskaer-Nielsen doesn't condemn the megamusical; rather, she suggests that the "musical drama" presents an alternative to the megamusical and that the two exist in a type of plurality in the musical theatre world. As such, Lundskaer-Nielsen calls for a reconsideration of theatre in the late 1980s and 1990s as "a time of broadening horizons, dramatic innovation, and formal experimentation in which the musical became a meeting point for a number of different theatre traditions."[6]

While I use the term "new musical drama" throughout this study, my employment of the term does differ from Lundskaer-Nielsen's use in several key ways. First, while Lundskaer-Nielsen does discuss nonprofit theatres as the site of development for many of these works, the emphasis of her study, and the defining trait of her employment of the phrase "The New Musical Drama," is the directors that take on a differing role from the more traditional expectations of a director of musicals in the development of musical works. For Lundskaer-Nielsen, the contributions of directors like James Lapine, Tina Landau, and George C. Wolfe are the defining factors in differentiating "musical drama" from "megamusical." While I also think these contributions are germane to a consideration of traditions coming out of the 1980s and 1990s into the first part of the twenty-first century, my emphasis on LaChiusa and his methods necessitates that my employment of the term "musical drama" be more writer-centric. This extends to my second departure, in which Lundskaer-Nielsen reaches back to the work of Harold Prince in order to contextualize the directors in her study. This is an apt choice, but, while it works for the parameters of Lundskaer-Nielsen's project, my writer-centric focus means that I will be calling on the work of Stephen Sondheim and other writers, many of whom worked directly with Hal Prince. Third, while Lundskaer-Nielsen limits her employment of the term to the 1980s and 1990s, I extend the term to the present, particularly in consideration of a series of recent Tony Award–winning musicals that carry with them the tradition of the musical drama.

Of course, my greatest departure from Lundskaer-Nielsen's work rests in my subject; she never mentions the work of Michael John LaChiusa in her study, despite the fact that LaChiusa worked with George C. Wolfe and other directors who brought new dramaturgical innovations and standards into the musical. This is perhaps because much of LaChiusa's work has been directed by Graciela Daniele, a director who has been fiercely devoted to the development of new, innovative work, but also comes from the world of choreography. Choreography, rather than dramaturgy, could be said to be the central lens with which Daniele approaches her work. Lundskaer-Nielsen's parameters, which de-emphasize the writer in favor of the director, necessarily leave LaChiusa out. Yet, LaChiusa is in many ways the ideal subject for a consideration of the "musical drama" given his associations with all three of the major nonprofit theatres producing musicals during this period, namely Playwrights Horizons, The Public Theatre, and Lincoln Center Theatre. Additionally, LaChiusa himself positions his work as the alternative not only to the "megamusical," but also to the faux-musical, which he argues is largely dependent on nostalgia.[7] I argue that the work of Michael John LaChiusa is emblematic of "The New Musical Drama" movement and provides a myriad of watershed innovations in the musical theatre form that have served as a foundation for some of the most successful musicals of recent years. This study focuses on seven of LaChiusa's musicals, far less than half of his overall output, as a means of understanding the alternatives LaChiusa sets out for what can constitute musical entertainment.

The Career of Michael John LaChiusa

LaChiusa's career has been long and the shows I focus on span over twenty years. He was born in Chautauqua, New York, in 1962. The eldest of three children, LaChiusa has spoken frequently about his unhappy home life and his strained relationship with his parents, particularly his father. His mother was encouraging of his musical interests and LaChiusa eventually started piano lessons. Despite LaChiusa's reputation for utilizing dense, difficult musical vocabulary, he has had little formal training. "I took piano lessons for three years. My teacher was blind—she had cataracts— but she didn't let me get away with anything. But other than that, I didn't formally study music."[8] Despite this, LaChiusa does recall writing musicals with other neighborhood children. His tendency toward dark material has early roots, given that one of these projects was entitled *The Patty Hearst Story*, a piece LaChiusa characterizes as "sort of like *The Wizard of Oz*, but with guns."[9] LaChiusa graduated from high school early and attended a television journalism program in Boston, Massachusetts, but dropped out after a single semester and moved to New York City in 1980. He attended the BMI Lehman Engel Musical Theatre Workshop in the early 1980s, which he credits for helping him move past writing "camp" songs to more serious material.[10]

LaChiusa began to make a name for himself in the mid-1990s, particularly when The Public Theatre, under the artistic direction of George C. Wolfe, produced *First Lady Suite*. A year later, Lincoln Center Theatre produced *Hello Again*, and many began to wonder about the possibilities of LaChiusa's future output, with some naming him the heir-apparent to Stephen Sondheim. Bud Coleman cites LaChiusa as "one of the promising musical theatre creators who [is] forging new forms."[11] While both *First Lady Suite* and *Hello Again* received positive notices, LaChiusa's next few projects were eviscerated by critics. His much-anticipated collaboration with director Hal Prince, adapting Ingmar Bergman's unproduced screenplay *The Petrified Prince*, which played The Public Theatre in 1995, was highly anticipated and then widely panned. Ben Brantley of *The New York Times* said of the musical and the production:

> This misbegotten production, with songs by Michael John LaChiusa and a book by Edward Gallardo, poses a searing question not unknown in the annals of musical comedy or, for that matter, in Mr. Prince's own oeuvre: how can so much talent, so much flashy stagecraft and so much conspicuous effort come to so very little?[12]

LaChiusa also provided additional material to the Broadway dance play *Chronicles of a Death Foretold* in 1995, earning him his first Tony Award nomination. During the 1999–2000 season, LaChiusa had two productions open on Broadway, the Audra McDonald-vehicle *Marie Christine* and an adaptation of Joseph Moncure March's poem *The Wild Party*, both of which received largely negative reviews. At that season's Tony Awards, LaChiusa came up empty-handed, despite being nominated for three awards. The twin disappointments of *Marie Christine* and *The Wild Party* seemed to dampen the initial enthusiasm regarding LaChiusa's place in the musical theatre landscape. As of this writing, LaChiusa has not had another musical play on Broadway, though he continues to write constantly and has had several shows premiere off-Broadway and in regional theatres across the country. Of his subsequent New York City productions, *Little Fish* (2003), *See What I Wanna See* (2005), *Queen of the Mist* (2011), and *First Daughter Suite* (2015) all received favorable notices in *The New York Times* and other publications. His continued artistic successes in this realm have firmly placed LaChiusa and his work in the seemingly "high-brow" world of nonprofit developed musical theatre, where artists are able to take risks that seem to be unviable in the commercially motivated Broadway market.

Struggles for "The New Musical Drama"

The fact that LaChiusa's work has found its primary home in off-Broadway nonprofit theatres isn't shocking considering that "The New Musical Drama" was born and developed in the off-Broadway nonprofit theatres that still maintain a significant presence in New York City. There was a moment, however, that seemed to suggest "The New Musical Drama" had found a pathway to commercial viability when Jonathan Larson's musical *Rent* transferred its developmental off-Broadway production, produced and developed by New York Theatre Workshop, to the Nederlander Theatre on Broadway in April of 1996. The musical had been in the news, not just for its racially diverse cast and its frank depictions of sex and AIDS but also because Larson tragically died from an aortic dissection on the morning before *Rent*'s first preview performance off-Broadway.[13] *Rent* was a runaway success on Broadway, playing for over twelve years and over 5,000 performances. *Rent*'s success signaled good news and bad news for the future of "The New Musical Drama." On the one hand, *Rent* proved that artistically ambitious works could find life in the commercially driven market of Broadway musicals again. On the other hand, Larson's death left the unofficial movement without a leader, creating a vacuum in the market. Critics and journalists looked to the writers of "The New Musical Drama," particularly LaChiusa, Jason Robert Brown, Adam Guettel, and Jeanine Tesori, to fill the void created by Larson's death.

Unfortunately, in the years immediately following Larson's death and *Rent*'s meteoric rise, the work of "The New Musical Drama" writers struggled to maintain the standard set by *Rent*'s commercial viability. As previously discussed, both of LaChiusa's major Broadway productions, both backed by major New York City nonprofits, failed with most critics and at the box office. After receiving rapturous reviews for her 1997 musical *Violet*, developed by Playwrights Horizons, Tesori found that there were no producers willing to take a chance on moving the show to Broadway. Brown's *Parade* opened at Lincoln Center a year before LaChiusa's *Marie Christine* to largely dismissive reviews. From 1997 to 2005, it seemed that there was no place on Broadway for musicals that were taking risks. In 2005, Guettel finally scored a success with Lincoln Center Theatre's production of the musical *The Light in the Piazza* which would go on to win six Tony Awards and play a successful fourteen-month run. "The New Musical Drama" would pick up steam over the next few years as shows like *Spring Awakening* and *Next to Normal*, both developed by major New York City nonprofits and both featuring unlikely source material for a musical, tasted both artistic and financial success. Things have continued to improve for "The New Musical Drama" on Broadway. Many of the recent Tony Award winners for Best Musical can all be potentially defined as extending from the "musical drama" tradition. Musicals such as *Fun Home, Hamilton, Dear Evan Hansen, The Band's Visit,* and *Hadestown* were all developed by nonprofit theatres and all featured stories and scores that were not the norm for commercially successful musical theatre.

It would be impossible to determine how or if LaChiusa's work directly impacted the development of the above titles. While one of the titles, the musical *Fun Home*, features a score by Tesori, providing a direct link between "The New Musical Drama" and the current Broadway market, the other titles are from newer writers who did not come up through the mid-1990s movement that was intent on providing an alternative to the megamusical. Yet, it does seem likely that LaChiusa's work, particularly his methods of writing and adaptation, helped to open the door to viability for these recent "musical dramas." While I don't mean to suggest that selecting difficult material for musical adaptation makes LaChiusa unique, nor do I mean to suggest that his methods aren't shared by other writers in his cohort, his body of work as a whole does prove to be emblematic of "The New Musical Drama" movement. In particular, LaChiusa's work has remained largely in the nonprofit sector, suggesting that his work continues to engage with the bureaucratic structures that gave birth to the movement. I also don't mean to suggest that *Marie Christine* and *The Wild Party* are flawless works that fell victim to their time of production. Rather, I am interested in looking at the career and output of LaChiusa as a means of recontextualizing the role of nonprofit developed musical theatre, particularly given these works are afforded the opportunity to take greater risks since their development is somewhat shielded by the safety of the nonprofit system in many ways.

Description of the Book

In order to analyze LaChiusa's oeuvre, I lean heavily on other scholars' writings in the fields of Musical Theatre Studies. As previously mentioned,

I utilize the term "The New Musical Drama," a term that is coined by Lundskaer-Nielsen. Her work in contextualizing the "art musicals" and "chamber musicals" of the 1980s and 1990s has helped to place constraints on my project, particularly in terms of discussing these various writers and shows in an academic way. Lundskaer-Nielsen's study historicizes the roots of the "musical drama," pointing back to the early 1980s and Playwrights Horizons' development of *March of the Falsettos*, a one-act musical that would form the first half of *Falsettos*, which premiered on Broadway more than a decade later. She starts her study here largely due to James Lapine, who had previously worked in more experimental forms of nonmusical theatre off-Broadway. Lundskaer-Nielsen points to this collaboration as a starting point for the new relationship between the dramaturgically based director and the writer. While her connection between the movement and this new relationship is apt, I am more concerned with the role of the writer working within the relative safety of the nonprofit theatre system, though directing and directors come into the purview of my project with some frequency. Rather, it is Lundskaer-Nielsen's emphasis on the establishment of an alternative musical theatre that eschews the commercial interests of the megamusical and corporate-backed Broadway shows that I find have particular relevance to LaChiusa's body of work. While it is these shows, developed on the margins of the New York City theatrical market, that are Lundskaer-Nielsen's focus, it is important to note that she doesn't associate these two approaches, one commercial, one noncommercial, as antagonistic. Rather, she advocates for a type of plurality in which both the British model of the megamusical and the more experimental works being developed in nonprofits coexist.[14] In a similar vein, I analyze LaChiusa's work not as a superior, "highbrow" brand of musical theatre but rather as an alternative that might have coexisted with the Broadway fare of the period.

Throughout this study, I have tried to be consistent in my use of the phrase "The New Musical Drama," despite the fact that Lundskaer-Nielsen uses "musical drama," "chamber musical," and "art musical" somewhat interchangeably. Additionally, for the purposes of this project, I use the following criteria in order to define examples of "The New Musical Drama," using Lundskaer-Nielsen's work as a foundation. First, I limit the definition by only including works that were developed in nonprofit theatres. To further clarify, I am only considering musicals that had "first class" productions with a nonprofit as a sole or coproducer. This necessarily limits the use of the term and differentiates these pieces from other "musical dramas" that were developed solely for commercial interests. Second, I utilize Lundskaer-Nielsen's starting point, namely the development of *March of the Falsettos*, but extend her study to consider works that are being produced as of this writing.[15] While this designation expands the literature for consideration to a time span of almost forty years, it also helps to make legible the changing role in producing models that have, in recent years, encouraged more experimental forms of musical theatre to make the leap from off-Broadway nonprofit to commercial Broadway production. The third criterion, which is much more difficult to define, concerns the artistic impetus of each project. I have chosen to focus this definition on examples of musical entertainment that have, in some way or another, broken with the standard, traditional mode that categorizes much of commercial Broadway entertainment. I admit that this is a very subjective criterion, and I freely concede that this makes an already subjective project even more subjective, but I will try to pose some additional constraints that help to make the limits of this designation more apparent. In general, I have chosen to focus on musicals that have dealt with unlikely materials for adaptation, that have attempted to utilize music not exclusively identifiable as part of the Broadway musical vocabulary, as well as musicals that have attempted structural innovations in the form. Some of the examples discussed here only satisfy two of these three conditions, and some only one. Despite that, I use them as a general guideline in order to bring these works into conversation with the works of LaChiusa, whose output tends to satisfy all three of these elements. In order to further explain this idea, it may be useful to set forth guidelines on my methods of textual analysis.

My textual analysis of the works presented in the study is hugely indebted to the work of Bruce Kirle, who places an emphasis on the "open" nature of musical theatre texts. Leaning on Roland Barthes, Kirle proposes that musicals are inherently "unfinished business" or constant works-in-progress because musicals are products of popular culture; since social and political viewpoints and lenses change over time, the ways in which musicals are "read" is ever-changing.[16] One of the most relevant examples of this idea is the changing response to the musical *Chicago*, a modest success in its original run, largely dwarfed by the success of *A Chorus Line* in the same season, but a runaway hit when it was revived on Broadway in 1996 that is still running as of this writing. The idea of women murdering their partners or husbands has clearly become more palatable twenty years later. I take this cue to understand that many of the issues discussed throughout my analysis of LaChiusa's work are being read from a contemporary lens and that I am privileging my reading of the text, sometimes over authorial intent.

Kirle also points out the privileging of the written text in analysis of musical theatre, an idea that becomes further problematized by the fact that musicals are intensely collaborative and authorial intent can often be obscured or even lost completely.[17] Kirle cites the example of the original Broadway production of *Pippin*, in which Stephen Schwartz and Roger O. Hirson's original concept for the musical, a concept closer in tone to Schwartz's *Godspell*, was largely lost in the stylized, dark concept extrinsically applied to the piece by iconic director-choreographer Bob Fosse.[18] In light of this, I have frequently brought into the conversation other artists, including directors and performers, whose work on LaChiusa's musicals have given them a type of authorial claim. In some cases, most notably Chapters 1 and 5, I have attempted to give close readings of staging and performances as a means of deconstructing the ways in which both direction and performance imbue the pieces in question with additional levels of meaning. Admittedly, as these are my deconstructions of the staging and performance, the end result is, once again, very subjective.

Given LaChiusa's tendency to play with linearity and time, I have chosen to honor that instinct by avoiding the temptation to structure this study chronologically. Rather, I have chosen to bookend the work with each of the two shows by LaChiusa that opened on Broadway in the 1999–2000 season. Additionally, given LaChiusa's ability to bring in disparate traditions and concepts into his work, I have also utilized a wide variety of frameworks and academic disciplines in order to shape each of the studies contained in these four chapters. The first chapter, "'Miracles and Mysteries': 'Mongrel America' and the Genre of *Marie Christine*," uses another essay by LaChiusa published in *The New York Times* to explore the ways in which the idea of the word "mongrel" echoes and reverberates throughout the musical *Marie Christine*. In order to fully explore this idea, I bring the musical into conversation with several Musical Theatre Studies scholars, as well as some musicologists, most notably Scott McMillan, Geoffrey Block, and John Bush Jones. At the end of the chapter, I attempt to explore the meaning imbued on a production by both performance and staging by giving written deconstructions of Audra McDonald's vocal performance of the song "And You Would Lie / I Will Give" as well as a deconstruction of Graciela Daniele's staging for the number "Prison in a Prison." While I lean on Musical Theatre studies and musicology in Chapter 1, in Chapter 2, I look at R. G. Collingwood's idea of "historical imagination" in exploring the musicals *First Lady Suite* and *First Daughter Suite*. These musicals, written over twenty years apart, give remarkable insight into LaChiusa's role as a dramatist-historian, particularly given his own historical obsession with the lives of First Ladies. In order to explore this association, I utilize education scholar Lynn Speer Lemisko's reading of Collingwood, which breaks the idea of "historical imagination" into three components: re-enactment, interpolation, and interrogation. While Lemisko's writing is specifically reorienting Collingwood's theories for the classroom, I find that they also have significant relevance when considering the methods of the dramatist in setting historical moments.

The third chapter looks back at the history of the "Musical Drama" by linking one of LaChiusa's most ambitious projects, the musical *Giant*, to another adaptation of an Edna Ferber novel, the monumentally important *Show Boat*. This chapter links these two shows, and other titles in the American musical canon, by looking at definitions of "The American Dream" that appear throughout the narrative of these musicals. In the fourth chapter, I extend the consideration of dramatization by looking at two LaChiusa shows based on canonical source material. The first piece, *Hello Again*, is an adaptation of Arthur Schnitzler's *La Ronde*. The second, the musical *See What I Wanna See*, is adapted from three short stories by the famed Japanese modernist writer Ryūnosuke Akutagawa. The musical is presented in the form of three one-acts, though one of these acts is split into two and performed at the beginning of each of the other two. I bring both of these works into conversation with various theories of adaptation, namely Linda Hutcheon's idea of "palimpsestuous pleasures" and Jane Barnette's concept of "geographies of adaptation." By utilizing these two frameworks, I explore the ways in which LaChiusa's adaptations enter a larger conversation about the relationship between adaptation and musical theatre history. In the final chapter, I look at LaChiusa's adaptation of Joseph Moncure March's *The Wild Party*. In particular, I bring the musical into conversation with the work of Critical Race Theory and Theatre Studies, particularly the work of Harvey Young and Angela C. Pao, in order to understand the ways in which a casting change from an actress of color to a white actress led to differing degrees of legibility in the performance of the musical. In particular, I hinge my analysis of this idea on an extremely close reading of the staging of the original production by George C. Wolfe. In exploring the ways that both written and performed texts change with changes in casting, I also return to the ideas of Kirle in reifying the musical as an inherently "open" form. The conclusion of this study briefly looks at some of the successes of "The New Musical Drama" over the past decade, particularly focusing on four titles from the past four years.

Because I have established the subjective nature of this work, it may also be useful to discuss elements of my training and how they have impacted my approach to an analysis of LaChiusa's oeuvre. I have been trained in the critical side of American Studies, an interdisciplinary field that has undergone many changes in the past few years. To be more specific, my training has included an emphasis on Critical Race Theory, Queer Theory, and Queer-of-Color Critiques. I mention this so that I can more fully explain the rationales present throughout this study. Additionally, my work is also entrenched in Marxist materialism and other leftist orientations. In particular, my critique of the commercial platform of the Broadway musical is heavily influenced by my orientation toward cultural materialist critique. Finally, I would like to point out that, while I am a musician, I am not trained as a musicologist and my employment of music theory, my discussions of vocal technique, and my analysis of certain song forms and structures are informed by my experiences as a musician. Although I do engage with various musicologists throughout this study, I want to be clear that my central orientation is as a Theatre Studies scholar and my analysis of music is closely linked to an analysis on each work as a piece of theatre.

LaChiusa's engagement of issues of race, his project to deconstruct the normative assumptions of the American musical, and his positioning against the commercial constraints of the Broadway musical have all proved fertile ground for exploration of "The New Musical Drama." My first exposure to LaChiusa's work was in high school when a friend and I randomly selected the Original Cast Recording of *Hello Again* as one of the many recordings to serve as a soundtrack to my first road trip to New York City. I remember how enraptured I was by LaChiusa's use of harmonic density, his use of recitative, and his employment of various styles and pastiche. But, most importantly, I was fascinated by his ability to weave character and music together in the service of storytelling. I mention this because, as will soon become clear, I have written a study of LaChiusa's work that is more concerned with his abilities as a storyteller than as a composer, a lyricist, or a librettist. While I give ample attention to all three writing elements employed by LaChiusa, it is his ability to combine them into a cohesive storytelling device that fuels the analysis in this study.

CHAPTER 1
"MIRACLES AND MYSTERIES":
"MONGREL AMERICA" AND THE
GENRE OF *MARIE CHRISTINE*

By all accounts, the 1999–2000 Broadway season was meant to be the season of Michael John LaChiusa. After numerous delays, both *Marie Christine* and *The Wild Party* were set to open on either side of the turn of the century. In a profile regarding the promise of the coming season, Brantley identified LaChiusa as "one of the more intriguing descendants of the School of Sondheim ..." and expressed high expectations for both titles, particularly Audra McDonald's anticipated performance in *Marie Christine* which Brantley described as an "event."[1] The excitement for *Marie Christine* is well documented; both McDonald and LaChiusa did an extraordinary amount of press, scoring several cover stories in magazines throughout the arts world. McDonald, fresh from her third Tony Award in the featured actress category for the musical *Ragtime*, would finally be appearing in a leading role in a new Broadway musical. Her critically acclaimed first solo album, featuring works from the "new school" of musical theatre composers, featured "Way Back to Paradise" from *Marie Christine* as the title track. And LaChiusa, who had tasted critical praise (*Hello Again, First Lady Suite*) and scorn (*The Petrified Prince*), was finally making a full Broadway debut as composer, lyricist, and dramatist. In addition, the musical's premise, a relocation of Euripides' *Medea* to turn-of-the-century New Orleans and Chicago, was both intriguing and provocative.

Shortly before the musical opened in 1999, LaChiusa published an op-ed in *The New York Times*. Entitled "I Sing of America's Mongrel Culture," LaChiusa's article explores the designations between "musical" and "opera" and muses on the state of the American Musical.[2] While the article is a far cry from the polemical bent of his essay "The Great Gray Way" in *Opera News*, "I Sing of America's Mongrel Culture" does merit a close analysis, particularly as it attempts to classify the musical *Marie Christine* as a celebration of the "mongrel" nature of American art and society. LaChiusa makes an argument that writers should avoid the Eurocentric strictures that associate opera as a "pure" form and instead exploit European traditions by incorporating them with other performance techniques and genealogies.[3] He firmly states that no one has come up with suitable criteria to distinguish musical theatre from opera and discounts the commonly held assumption that opera is primarily concerned with music alone. Additionally, he confesses to being "a cultural raider of sorts" by borrowing from a plethora of performance and musical styles and incorporating them into a single form. The end of the essay foreshadows his argument from "The Great Gray Way," but in more gracious tones. He laments that producers are less willing to take a chance on "unconventional" pieces, simply stating, "We have to get older. We have to grow up. And so does the American musical."

While the article seems to speak generally to the intervention LaChiusa's work makes in the American musical, his employment of the term "mongrel" is remarkable for a number of reasons. In most current published dictionaries, the word "mongrel" has a single definition, referring to a mixed-breed dog, but the word's history is far more complicated than that. The word dates back to the late fifteenth century and is derived from the obsolete word *mong*, meaning "mixture," and the old English *gemong*, which means "mingling." More tellingly, these roots were in turn derived from a Proto-Germanic verb *mangjan*, meaning "to knead together."[4] Merriam Webster's definition of the word "mongrel" helps us to make a connection between the word's roots and its use by LaChiusa. Giving two definitions, the dictionary defines the word as;

1. An individual resulting from the interbreeding of diverse breeds or strains.

2. A cross between types of persons or things.[5]

Although these definitions are justified by their inclusion in the Merriam-Webster dictionary, they are often excluded from other listings because the term, when used in descriptions of humans, has been deemed offensive for quite some time. In particular, the word can be used as an insult to another person, especially when it is used to describe impurity and illegitimacy. This is problematic, particularly given Marie Christine, the heroine of LaChiusa's piece of the same name, is herself of mixed-race and her children, fathered by the white Dante, are also mixed-race. LaChiusa's invocation of the term is surprising, given its offensive nature and its applicability to his title character. But LaChiusa's op-ed isn't interested in the racially insulting nature of the word. Instead, he sets up the terms *mongrel* and *pure* in a type of binary in which he characterizes the celebration of disparate traditions co-mingled in the former and identifies the dangers in the latter word. "Pure is a word that frightens me. We are mongrels in a mongrel country," he writes. His employment of the word takes on cultural meaning, representing the myriad influences and traditions that are present in American culture. But the word "mongrel" also performs additional labor, particularly in terms of defining LaChiusa's methods as a writer as well as understanding the structural and character conceits of the musical *Marie Christine*.

In this chapter, I argue that *Marie Christine* represents an intentional "mongrelizing" effect in its development, adaptation, and performance that marks the piece as inherently different from most other Broadway fare at the turn of the last century. In particular, I utilize both the word's contemporary and archaic definitions. In the more contemporary invocation, the word "mongrel" helps to explain the process of *Marie Christine*'s development, the process of the piece's adaptation, and the tactics utilized in staging and performing the musical. The word's more archaic form also applies to the piece, though it is used to refer to Marie Christine and her children pejoratively. The concept of "mongrel," its association as a hybridization of multiple cultures, forms, and techniques, also helps to situate LaChiusa's work and mission within the context of commercial musical theatre while also providing a useful rubric for understanding and identifying "The New Musical Drama" movement.

While *Marie Christine* is, in many ways, working around and against expectations for what is "producible" on Broadway, it shares many of these qualities with other contemporaneous titles. In his article, LaChiusa also cites *Floyd Collins* with music and lyrics by Adam Guettel and book by Tina Landau, and *Violet* with music by Jeanine Tesori and book and lyrics by Brian Crawley as examples of sophisticated off-Broadway musicals utilizing unusual subject matter.[6] He is also careful to identify these musicals, and others like them, as "sophisticated" as opposed to "elitist," stating "no one needs a degree in music theory to appreciate their scores."[7] In the 1998–9 season, Lincoln Center Theatre, who produced *Marie Christine*, also offered Jason Robert Brown and Alfred Uhry's musical *Parade*. Like *Marie Christine*, *Parade* presented a mongrelization of Eurocentric operetta conventions with more contemporary musical trends. The possible impact of *Parade*'s financial failure on the Broadway production of *Marie Christine* is discussed later in this chapter.

This chapter hopes to define the ways in which the term "mongrel" helps to categorize different aspects of the musical *Marie Christine* and, in turn, explore the ways in which the word aids in categorizing LaChiusa's place among his peers associated with "The New Musical Drama." First, the chapter briefly synopsizes the musical *Marie Christine* and discusses the facts of its brief Broadway run. Second, I discuss the various interpretations of the show, and its genre, by critics. Third, I look at the structure of the musical itself and explicate the difficulty critics and audiences had in defining its form. In order to explore the ways in which *Marie Christine* intermingles with the forms of musical theatre and opera, I look at John Bush Jones's differentiation between "social musicals" and "diversionary" musicals as well as Scott McMillin's intervention into the argument regarding the musical's "integrated" form. Finally, I deconstruct two moments in the original production of *Marie Christine* to better illustrate the ways in which the musical was inherently perceived as "mongrel" in performance. In particular, I look at Audra McDonald's vocal performance of "And You Would Lie / I Will Give" in Act I and Graciela Daniele's staging of the Act II number "Prison in a Prison."

I would also like to note that, throughout this chapter, I will be referring to *Marie Christine* as a musical. In some ways, this may appear disingenuous as much of what follows is concerned with troubling the labels of "musical theatre" and "opera." In order to assume some level of consistency, I have resorted to the label "musical" simply because the show opened on Broadway in a Broadway theatre. Also, *Marie Christine* was marketed by Lincoln Center Theatre as a musical and was reviewed as a musical by theatre critics, not music critics.[8] While this justification is, in some ways, arbitrary, it will hopefully lend clarity to the discussion. As for LaChiusa's stance on labeling the piece? he states, "When people ask" "Is it an opera?" I'm inclined to say, "Does it matter? Were you entertained? Were you moved?"[9]

Marie Christine on Broadway[10]

Marie Christine began previews at Lincoln Center's Vivian Beaumont Theatre on October 28th, 1999. Its official opening was December 2nd, 1999. Michael John LaChiusa is credited as the sole writer, responsible for music, lyrics, and book. The production was directed and choreographed by Graciela Daniele with musical direction by David Evans and orchestrations by Jonathan Tunick. Lincoln Center produced the musical on its own, despite having worked with an outside producing entity called Livent Inc. on the Broadway production of *Parade* the season prior. Toni-Leslie James provided the costume designs and lighting was designed by Jules Fisher and Peggy Eisenhauer. The scenic design, executed by Christopher H. Barreca, featured a fairly open ground plan. The Vivian Beaumont is Broadway's only "thrust" theatre. The thrust is circular which extends out into the audience and connects a larger playing space upstage. Upon entering the theatre, the audience was greeted by a large set of risers at stage left, evoking the hillside theatres of Ancient Greece. At stage right, a platform was suspended above the stage, housing an auxiliary percussionist who would play a series of hand drums and other percussive instruments throughout the show. The drummer, dressed in Caribbean garb, likely represented Marie Christine's connection to her Caribbean-born mother as well as her African roots. The upstage playing area was raked. Furniture moved in and out of the playing area to establish different settings.

Marie Christine begins with the ensemble wandering around the circular thrust of the Vivian Beaumont stage. They are all speaking or singing random thoughts and ideas and it is clear that these are denizens of some prison or asylum. In the center of the madness stands a hooded figure who is confronted by three women of the ensemble, all African American and dressed in all black. They inquire about the woman's crimes and the woman reveals herself, stating, "My name is my mother's name. Marie Christine. Marie Christine."[11] Marie begins to recount her story, though it is largely in fragments and memories that are not always told linearly. The space comes alive as Marie Christine reveals that she learned the secrets "of Mother Africa" from her mother. Although she doesn't identify these secrets, it becomes apparent that both Marie and her mother are voodoo priestesses. After revealing this information to her interlocutors, Marie sings about the first time she met Dante, a Caucasian ship's captain and father of her children, in the haunting "Beautiful."[12]

The audience sees a flashback to Dante's first meeting with Marie. The two are drawn to each other and Marie begins to share her story with Dante, particularly that she is of mixed ancestry and born out of wedlock, though her father did provide for her welfare and for that of her brothers, Paris and Jean. Marie's brothers insist that she acts like a proper woman of Creole society, but Marie confesses to her maid Lisette that it "isn't always a pleasurable thing to be a woman."[13]

The action returns to Marie and Dante's first meeting. Dante shares stories from his time on the seas as Marie confesses her secret gift to him. Marie succumbs to Dante's charms and the two make love under a tree. Marie's mother appears, admonishing her daughter for falling for a white man in the song "Miracles and Mysteries."[14] Marie defies her brother's protestations and moves Dante into an apartment in her house on the grounds of the family estate. Word is traveling that Marie has a "bird inside the house" and her brothers demand that she get rid of Dante. Marie goes to find Dante and spies him trying to sleep with her maid Lisette. Dante informs Marie that he has to go back to Biloxi to pay his crew. She demands that Dante take her with him and offers him the key to her brother Jean's study, where Dante will find a safebox with her mother's gold and jewelry. The two plan the robbery to coincide with Jean's engagement party three days later.

As Dante leaves, Marie, holding a ribbon, confronts Lisette. Marie accuses Lisette of trying to inform Dante as well as her brothers that she is carrying Dante's child. She cuts pieces off of the ribbon; each cut renders Lisette's limbs numb until she falls onto the floor. Marie and the three prisoners then sing a remarkable piece of music, "And You Would Lie / I Will Give," in which Marie determines that she will do anything, even kill, for Dante.[15] Jean's engagement party commences, and Dante is discovered trying to rob the safe box from Jean's study. A fight ensues between Dante and Paris. Marie, recovering a dropped dagger, stabs her brother Paris, killing him. Dante and Marie flee, and the act ends with Marie placing Dante's hand on her stomach, hinting to him that she is carrying his child.

As Act II opens, the three prisoners inform us that Marie and Dante sailed for five years up and down the coast before settling in Chicago. They now have two sons. The action then cuts to a saloon managed by Magdalena and her husband. Dante enters, and the audience learns that he is running for City Alderman. However, rumors are spreading that Dante is keeping a mixed-race mistress and two children on the outskirts of town. Dante's campaign is being funded by Charles Gates; a wealthy man who decides to have Dante marry his daughter in order to silence the rumors. Dante meets Marie and informs her of the marriage and also demands his children. Marie refuses and reminds Dante that she has killed for him, including an incident in New York, and that she has powers that she can use. Dante exits and Magdalena, mistress of the saloon, enters Marie Christine's shack. Magdalena reveals that her real name is Lucy Mott and that, if Marie hands over her children to Dante, she can work to get them back. In exchange, Magdalena asks Marie Christine to use her powers to help her conceive a child. Marie is uncertain, and Magdalena leaves her.

Marie's thoughts become consumed with Helena, Gates' daughter and Dante's future wife. During the number "Prison in a Prison," Marie invades Dante's thoughts and literally inserts herself between Dante and Helena as they make love.[16] Marie is interrupted by McMahon and Leary, two cronies that work for Charles Gates. The men try to intimidate her, causing Marie to ask, "Do I threaten your master?" Gates then appears and states that he is not threatened by Marie at all. He says that he will bring harm to both Marie and her children if she doesn't cooperate by handing the boys over to Dante and by leaving town. The men leave and Marie is visited by her mother and those she has harmed. They all sing "No Turning Back," informing Marie that she has gone too far and cannot give up now.[17] Marie arranges a meeting with Dante on his wedding day and informs him that she is releasing her children to his care. She asks if the children can present Helena with a gift, a necklace that Marie claims belonged to her mother. The necklace is contained in the safe box from the first act. Dante takes the children to present the gift to Helena. Magdalena then enters with the boys and recounts their meeting with Helena to Marie. She then informs Marie that she has found a place for her to go on the outskirts of the city. Marie gives Magdalena a small satchel and says its contents will help Magdalena have children "as many as your arms can hold."[18] Marie then says she is taking the children to bathe and prepare them. As she exits, Dante storms in, informing Magdalena that the necklace was poisoned, burning Helena alive and reducing her body to ashes. Marie enters, and Dante confronts her, demanding his children. Marie is silent. Dante goes offstage and sees that his children have been drowned. The ensemble sings a finale version of the song "I Will Give" as Marie is consumed by an explosion of light.

"Mongrel" Effects on Critical Reception

Critical response to the Broadway production of *Marie Christine* highlights the very tensions between the terms "opera" and "musical theatre" that LaChiusa was challenging in "I Sing of Mongrel America." In a mixed review, Ben Brantley of *The New York Times* embraces the musical's mongrel nature, both in terms of the breadth of its score, which Brantley describes as "swirling" and "complex," and the vocal tactics of the musical's leading lady Audra McDonald, who Brantley defines as exercising a range "from the operatic to gospel."[19] Elaborating on the nature of LaChiusa's score, Brantley writes that the composer "is working from the disparate, clashing strands of

American culture."[20] For Brantley, it is LaChiusa's libretto that is mostly at fault for the show feeling "unfinished" and "fuzzy" when its leading lady isn't singing. In particular, Brantley finds the scenes that are meant to establish the social/racial order and hierarchy of New Orleans have very little impact. In his final summation, Brantley notes that LaChiusa's musical may still provide an innovation into the form of the musical: "If this production fails to make a persuasive case for Mr. LaChiusa's ability to shape a complete, satisfying musical, it definitely points to new possibilities for defining character within the genre."[21]

Brantley's review, while reinforcing several of the elements from LaChiusa's "mongrel" thesis, doesn't deal directly with warring definitions of "musical" and "opera." A month later, critic Terry Teachout published his own review of *Marie Christine* in *The New York Times*, entitled "A 'Musical' That's Really an Opera." Teachout mentions LaChiusa's essay, though he mischaracterizes LaChiusa's argument, stating that LaChiusa firmly identifies *Marie Christine* as a musical.[22] Teachout classifies *Marie Christine* as an opera for several reasons. First, he notes that around two-thirds of the piece is sung with the dialogue sequences largely underscored by the orchestra. He then notes that only one song in the piece, "Way Back to Paradise," is self-contained, allowing for applause in the traditional musical theatre sense in which a song "ends" and is "buttoned" to allow for applause, a distinction that has fallen out of favor in more contemporary opera. He also notes the musical's dense, complicated harmonic language and the fact that it doesn't contain "a trace of Hammersteinian uplift."[23] The crux of Teachout's argument is that LaChiusa's suggestion that the term "opera" is elitist and Eurocentric is rooted in LaChiusa's own desire to be considered popular. He goes so far as to pair LaChiusa with Stephen Sondheim and Adam Guettel as a group of composers who refuse to accept that their works are operas. Teachout's argument hinges on the contemporary moment in which *Marie Christine* opened. In particular, he finds fault with the marketing decision to present *Marie Christine* and other pieces with sophisticated scores as musicals, particularly since such designations group these titles with Broadway fare like *Beauty and the Beast* and *Footloose*, both of which were playing at the time of *Marie Christine*'s opening. His final comment on the subject manages to both celebrate and disparage LaChiusa's work: "Is *Marie Christine* worthy of being produced alongside these works [operas]? I believe so—but we'll never be sure until Michael John LaChiusa shakes off his morbid fear of being branded elitist and allows it to be marketed as the excellent opera that it is."[24]

If Brantley's review highlights the ways in which *Marie Christine* exemplifies a "mongrel" approach in the score as well as the performance of McDonald while Teachout's review highlights the ways in which the musical's "mongrel" moniker is an attempt to resist the elitist designation of opera, then kalamu ya salaam's essay, appearing in *Lincoln Center Theatre Review* in the fall of 1999, attempts to highlight the dramatization's reliance on "mongrel" racial identities and their inherent racism. salaam is an activist, poet, and teacher who resides in New Orleans. His scathing review of the musical *Marie Christine*, published well before the show officially opened, accused the piece of reinforcing the notion that "it's in the blood," forcing a white supremacist view that there is a biological and psychological difference between black and white bodies.[25] He goes on to claim that the play "glorifies the white male penis and its desire for the 'color struck' mulatto female vagina."[26] He also characterizes the piece as dealing in the "tragic mulatto" character trope that is the stuff of white male "rape" and "racist fantasy." His most derogatory comment questions the need for any consideration of *Marie Christine*: "i could go point by point through the play—the assumptions, the mixing of time periods, the ignoring of historical accuracy—but to argue at length only dignifies an object that does not deserve serious scrutiny."[27]

While it is shocking and strange that Lincoln Center Theatre decided to publish the essay in their quarterly magazine, particularly given the issue in which it appeared was completely devoted to promoting their production of *Marie Christine*, salaam's essay encourages several questions worth exploring. In an intensely polemical response, LaChiusa questions *Lincoln Center Review*'s decision to publish salaam's review as grossly unfair to Lincoln Center and the musical's collaborators.[28] In a letter to the administration of Lincoln Center Theatre, LaChiusa concedes salaam is entitled to his own opinion but later refutes most of salaam's observations as a misreading of the play, particularly in terms of the "tragic mulatto" trope. He also makes a clear designation between the characters of the play, some of which are white supremacists, and the author's own political stance. "Several of the characters in the play may indeed be white supremacists but that does not mean the author condones their philosophy or shares their psychology," he states in the letter's second paragraph.[29] Provocatively, LaChiusa also challenges salaam's assertion that "if american history proves nothing else, it proves that white men are going to be white men" as hypocrisy by pointing out the fact that the comment reifies the essay's stated issue with the idea that "it's in the blood."[30] LaChiusa goes so far as to accuse salaam of propagating a late twentieth-century black supremacist slant.[31]

Although LaChiusa's outrage is understandable, the argument between salaam's essay and LaChiusa's response letter to Lincoln Center Theatre does highlight the ways in which the "mongrel" approach invites a variety of readings regarding the intentions and tactics used in the writing, adaptation, and performance of the piece. If the claim by LaChiusa that *Marie Christine* in particular and his body of work in general are all celebrations of the mongrel nature of American culture is held as a defining characteristic of the musical's machinations, then it can be argued that all of the musical's various elements are part of LaChiusa's "mongrelizing" project that impacts the piece's categorization as well as the musical's impact in terms of performance and direction.

The Trouble with Labels

When critics and journalists posed that Michael John LaChiusa may be the great hope for Broadway at the turn of the century, it is likely that they were talking in very specific terms about the Broadway musical. In some ways, critical confusion regarding the classification of *Marie Christine* may have been fueled by a sense of betrayal, particularly given LaChiusa's own hesitancy in labeling the piece. If the theatre intelligentsia were looking to LaChiusa to bring about a new form of the American musical, there may have been disappointment when many decided that he had delivered an American opera instead. While the semantical argument regarding what *Marie Christine* is (or isn't) may seem pointless, it does in fact point to a long-form tension that has always been present in the form. Traditional narratives of musical theatre history suggest that the American musical is a populist form. This certainly was true in the 1980s and 1990s when production costs soared to unfathomable heights, forcing most Broadway shows to run for several years before returning an investment to producers. Because of musical theatre's populist bent and its roots in "lowbrow" forms of entertainment like minstrel shows and vaudeville, the form has always found itself at odds with its "highbrow" cousin, the European opera. This warring between distinctions has been evident in several moments throughout musical theatre history.

Porgy and Bess opened at the Alvin Theatre in 1935 for a very modest run of 124 performances. The piece, produced by the Theatre Guild and directed by Rouben Mamoulian, is considered by many to be a masterwork, though it also garnered harsh criticism both at the time and presently. While some critics wrote quite favorable reviews of the piece when it opened, particularly Robert Garland, the chief theatre critic at *New York World-Telegram*, the black response was far less adulatory. In an article discussing African American responses to the 1935 production, musicologists Ray Allen and George P. Cunningham cite a rebuttal published in the *New York World-Telegram* that plainly states, "No Negro could possibly be fooled by *Porgy and Bess*" and cites several other complaints from African American musicians and critics, principally that Gershwin "has composed an opera about Negroes rather than a Negro opera."[32] While reviews of the piece run the gamut of positive and negative notices, they are remarkably consistent in referring to the show, which opened in a Broadway theatre for a Broadway audience, as an opera.

Part of this designation of "opera" likely stems from the marketing of the show. The Gershwin brothers and playwright DuBose Heyward subtitled their piece as "An American Folk Opera." So, in some ways, the tension had already been set by the authors themselves. In recent years, the term "An American Folk Opera" has come under sharp criticism. In another essay, musicologist Ray Allen discusses the ways in which the piece's subtitle reveals much about the triangulation of tradition, race, and national identity "at a crucial moment when the country was struggling to define who its folk were and how folk heritage(s) could form the foundation of a common American identity."[33] Allen asserts that the piece, which is about African American life and is performed by African American performers, suffers from the "folk opera" designation principally because all of the piece's creators are white. Despite the authors' attempt to classify the piece as opera, the show has played a number of Broadway revivals, with three engagements playing Broadway in the 1940s alone. The debate raged on when director Diane Paulus, playwright Suzan-Lori Parks, and *Marie Christine*'s Audra McDonald announced that they were collaborating on a revamped version of the piece at American Repertory Theatre in Cambridge, Massachusetts, where Paulus served as artistic director in 2011.

The production, which characterized itself as an attempt to make the piece more comfortable as a Broadway musical, added new scenes, punched up dialogue, invented biographical details, and altered the ending to be more upbeat and hopeful.[34] Several artists and critics published blistering responses, most notably composer-lyricist Stephen Sondheim, who took particular issue with a statement by Paulus regarding the nature of operas and musicals. Paulus articulates a distinction between opera and musical theatre in terms of character development. In Sondheim's polemical analysis of the production announcement, he points out that Paulus declares "that in opera you don't get to know the characters as people."[35] Additionally, he refers to Paulus' condescending attitude toward the audience in a statement about the character of Bess: "I'm sorry, but to ask an audience these days to invest three hours in a show requires your heroine be an understandable and fully rounded character." She is backed by McDonald, who states that Bess "is often more of a plot device than a full-blooded character." Sondheim's legitimate objections aside, both Paulus, who has gone on to stage canonical operas, and McDonald, who is a Julliard classically trained singer, seem to make the assertion that previous versions of *Porgy and Bess* have suffered from a lack of character development stemming from its classification as an opera. If this statement is taken broadly to help designate musical theatre from opera, then it would seem that both Paulus and McDonald classify opera as inherently less concerned with character as a dramatic device, while musical theatre thrives on it. Additionally, American Repertory Theatre stated with total clarity that the new treatment of *Porgy and Bess* was an attempt "to make it more palatable for Broadway audiences accustomed to musicals."[36]

There are important points of comparison here between the debate over *Porgy and Bess* and the debate which emerged from reviews of *Marie Christine*. In Brantley's review, he praises LaChiusa and McDonald for their fully realized, complicated characterization of the title character while also expressing dismay that she seems to be the only developed character within the piece.[37] Brantley's criticism of the piece's lack of character development would seem to fall in line with Paulus' critique of characterizations in operas. Further, both debates seem to find their roots in the ways in which producers and creators chose to market their pieces. The writers of *Porgy and Bess* chose to clearly market the show as an opera, a decision that Paulus and her collaborators contest with their 2011 treatment. Conversely, Lincoln Center Theatre was very clear about labeling *Marie Christine* "a new musical" even though the show's creator was a bit more ambivalent about the designation. Both titles have been praised (and critiqued) for their musical complexity. Both have also faced blistering critiques from people of color regarding their dramatizations of a racialized narrative. One major difference between the two titles is evident in their production histories. While *Porgy and Bess* has become a staple of opera companies around the world, *Marie Christine* has only had two subsequent productions, one at

Columbia University and another at the BoHo Theatre in Chicago as of this writing. No opera company has mounted *Marie Christine* to date despite the fact that LaChiusa has written several libretti for contemporary operas. Part of this may be fueled by Gershwin's designation as a classical composer, whereas LaChiusa, despite his work in opera, is firmly characterized as a writer of musical theatre.

Other titles have sparked debate over their classification. *Candide* opened on Broadway in December of 1956. While it would only play seventy-three performances in that run, a heavily revised version, replacing Lillian Hellman's book with a new one by Hugh Wheeler and featuring additional lyrics by Sondheim, played ten times the length of the original run in 1974. That version, which would be revised a third time to make the show more suitable for opera houses, would become a staple of opera companies across the globe. Sondheim and Wheeler's *Sweeney Todd; The Demon Barber of Fleet Street*, which only played a modest 557 performances during its original Broadway run, would also challenge categorization as opera companies began to produce the work. Even Sondheim has been inconsistent with labeling his work, stating at one point that *Sweeney Todd* was a musical because it opened in a Broadway house, then later deciding that the piece was "a dark opera." Yet, while all three of the above-discussed titles had their supporters and detractors, the debate invoked over their categorization was nowhere nearly as fierce as that surrounding *Marie Christine*. While these reviewers were, in some ways, encouraged into the debate by LaChiusa's statements in "I Sing of Mongrel America," their sentiments over the show's intended audience were strongly stated, leading some critics to believe that it was the producer's categorization of the show as a musical that resulted in its poor reception and brief run. For a full understanding of this debate, and to further define the ways in which LaChiusa is creating a "mongrel" work of art by borrowing from both traditions, a discussion of more theoretical arguments regarding designation may be helpful.

Scholars, critics, and journalists are always hesitant to place a firm dividing line between the conventions of opera and musical theatre. In a 2000 "Critic's Notebook" entry for *The New York Times*, Anthony Tommasini boldly declares that there is a very simple distinction between opera and musical theatre; in opera, the music has the upper hand whereas in musical theatre, it's the text.[38] Tommasini goes on to declare that while many Broadway songwriters managed lush, memorable melodies, they were all generally in service to the lyrics. In some ways, LaChiusa himself has touted the same distinction when discussing his writing. In an interview in *Opera News* in 1999, shortly before the opening of *Marie Christine*, LaChiusa initially counters the idea of the text's dominance: "I don't separate the importance of the libretto from the score- and the two elements often seem to be at war with each other. One way to keep the play and the music on equal footing is the lyric."[39] LaChiusa begins by proposing that the score and text are of equal importance in the composition of a musical, but then elaborates and, in a sense, contradicts himself by saying that it is the lyrics that maintain the equal importance between libretto and score. It is also noteworthy that the interviewer forwards LaChiusa's idea of mongrelization by suggesting that LaChiusa is "one of a new breed of songwriters who are blurring the lines between opera and musical theatre."[40]

But there is significant evidence that music *does* take priority over text in *Marie Christine.* As Teachout suggests in his review of *Marie Christine*, roughly two-thirds of the musical is sung with only short stretches of dialogue interspersed that are largely accompanied by orchestration.[41] And his estimation is correct; out of the sixty-nine pages in the musical's libretto, roughly one-third, or twenty-four pages, are dialogue and they are all largely underscored. For many, this suggestion is enough to classify *Marie Christine* as an opera. Several critics have gone so far as to say that this classification even extends its definition to titles usually associated as musicals, including *Les Misérables, Phantom of the Opera*, and even *The Who's Tommy.* But the amount of music doesn't sufficiently define a piece as operatic so much as the importance of the music in telling the story of the opera according to Tommasini. Here again, there are conventions of the operatic tradition's importance on music that are utilized by LaChiusa. One of the most obvious is found in the show's initial conception.

While the idea for *Marie Christine* was born out of a discussion between LaChiusa and director/choreographer Graciela Daniele during a rehearsal break from *Hello Again* combined with LaChiusa's discovery of Louis Tallant's *Voodoo in New Orleans*, which highlighted the life of Marie Laveau, part of the musical's inception was an opportunity to write a role for Audra McDonald. LaChiusa first encountered McDonald at auditions for *Hello Again.* She was deemed too young for the role of the Young Wife in *Hello Again* at the time, but LaChiusa has stated many times that he knew immediately he wanted to write for McDonald's singular talents. The vocal demands of the role, the massive range for the title character, the vocal stamina required to navigate a single performance, and the various vocal styles that have to be employed placed significant emphasis on McDonald (and her alternate Sherry Boone) as a vocalist, a focus more often associated with opera repertoire than musical theatre, evidenced by the verbiage that an opera singer usually "sings" a role while a musical theatre performer generally "plays" a role. This emphasis is reified by Brantley's review, in which he suggested, "One tends to feel lost and lonely when Ms. McDonald isn't onstage, and I found myself wishing that *Marie Christine* had been presented as a musical monologue."[42] McDonald found the role so vocally demanding that she would only commit to doing six performances a week, and never twice in one day.[43] The vocal demands are also a part of the show's dramaturgy, which requires its heroine to constantly take on herculean tasks. In this way, the show also brings to mind another title which some have suggested is an opera, Andrew Lloyd Webber and Tim Rice's *Evita.*

Another factor that tends to suggest *Marie Christine* follows in the opera tradition is the seriousness of the material and the weight of its larger-than-life situation. Euripides' *Medea* is certainly the stuff of operatic proportions. It has inspired at least one operatic adaptation, Luigi Cherubini's French-language opera *Medée*, which premiered in 1797. *Marie Christine* maintains many of the weightier elements of the *Medea* storyline: a woman betrayed by her lover and the father of her children, sorcery, and, most infamously, infanticide. But it furthers this sense of weightiness by also complicating the *Medea* character's story arc with the issue of race. Marie Christine's own mixed ancestry, combined with her love for her white lover, adds an additional layer of seriousness and social commentary to an already serious story. Most historians locate the roots of musical theatre in more comedic modes, particularly European operetta, burlesques, and vaudeville. The heavy, sometimes humorless nature of *Marie Christine* certainly stands in opposition to that lineage, though serious material has bred many pieces identified as musicals throughout the twentieth century and beyond. The lack of humorous material here is a point worthy of serious consideration. Other than the Act II opening number "Cincinnati," there are very few opportunities for any sort of laughs in *Marie Christine* and the aforementioned number is difficult to land as the audience hasn't been given permission to laugh in the musical's first act. Scholar John Bush Jones points to this fact in his negative assessments of both LaChiusa's *Marie Christine* and Jason Robert Brown and Alfred Uhry's *Parade*, disparaging both for losing what he identifies as the "playfulness" of most socially minded musicals.[44]

This "lack of playfulness" may be one of the very distinctions between opera and musical theatre that is being "blurred" or "mongrelized" by LaChiusa. While the suggestion that *Marie Christine* is humorless comes across as a negative critique, it would be more appropriate to state that the *observation* of the piece's lack of humor puts it in line with the grand tragic operas like *Tosca*, *Turandot*, and *Aida*. The piece certainly contains less humor than many of the other musical titles mentioned above that are often considered to be operas, such as *Porgy and Bess* and *Sweeney Todd*. This turn toward the serious, darker elements of human interaction that is indicative of tragic opera seems to be one of LaChiusa's more successful tactics in writing a "mongrel" piece of theatre.

While several of the expected conventions of opera are utilized in *Marie Christine,* there are also plenty of musical theatre conventions present in the piece. In an effort to contextualize and organize his argument, Jones categorizes musical theatre titles into two categories: musicals that contain social relevance and "diversionary musicals" which he defines as "mindless fluff."[45] While Jones is dismissive of *Marie Christine* in general, he does label it "the last of the twentieth-century's socially relevant musicals."[46] Jones' analysis of the musical is a surface consideration at best, but he does accurately highlight the "solemnity" of *Marie Christine* and other titles that could be grouped together in "The New Musical Drama" movement. These titles deviate from the form's more historical expectations, particularly in terms of the "playfulness" found in titles like *West Side Story*, *Cabaret*, and *Urinetown*. Quoting Sondheim, Jones suggests that these writers are beginning their work with "themes" as opposed to "story" or "character."[47] This statement is problematic, particularly since Sondheim's argument could certainly apply to the writing of *Company*, *Follies*, and other titles in his oeuvre. But Sondheim's comment inadvertently connects the work of "The New Musical Drama" with the genealogy of the concept musical, a genealogy that safely makes room for the designation of *Marie Christine* as a musical. Sondheim intends to critique these works for their thematic inceptions, but instead helps to solidify the line that connects Sondheim's work with that of one of his adherents, in this case, LaChiusa. And there is no doubt that the inception of *Marie Christine* was largely thematic. In a statement used for an application for a grant from the National Endowment of the Arts, LaChiusa shares that the idea for *Marie Christine* came out of a discussion with Daniele regarding whether *Medea* could be musicalized.[48] While the score was written, and the title role conceived, for McDonald, it was the concept of *Medea*-as-musical that began this journey.

While definitions of the American musical are vast and varied, there is a generally held assumption that most musicals post-*Oklahoma!* can be categorized with the term "integrated." Although history often characterizes *Oklahoma!* as the birth of the integrated musical, it would be more accurate to label it as a watershed moment in which various elements from previous shows that would later be identified as elements of integration were packaged and marketed in a way that could give weight to the term "integrated." Musicologist Geoffrey Block, who specializes in the works of Richard Rodgers, has attempted to define what makes a musical "integrated" by isolating principles that are discussed in the various works of both Rodgers and Oscar Hammerstein II. These five principles include: songs advance the plot, songs flow directly from the dialogue, songs express the characters who sing them, dances advance the plot and enhance the dramatic meaning of the songs that precede them, and the orchestration parallels or advances the action.[49] This is an idea central to the work of conductor Lehman Engel who ran the BMI Musical Theatre writing workshop in New York City where LaChiusa was a student. Lehman defines the musical as "A form which seeks to integrate drama, music, and dance."[50] While it is possible to take issue with Rodgers and Hammerstein's strict adherence to these principles, they do give a useful rubric for evaluating a title's adherence to the "book musical" tradition. On the whole, *Marie Christine* does adhere to Block's "Principles of Integration." Numbers like "Before the Morning," "C'est Lamour" and "Bird Inside the House" advance the plot while others like "The Storm" and "Tell Me" flow directly out of dialogue sequences. Numbers like "I Will Give" and "Miracles and Mysteries" help to define and clarify character while dance sequences like "Finale of Act I" and "Prison in a Prison" emerge organically out of action and story. And certainly, the musical's ubiquitous orchestration and accompaniment becomes a type of character in the proceedings.

But it would be wrong to assume that only the "integrated" definition is useful for defining, or rather, delimiting the musical. Other scholars have taken issue with the term "integration" from a historical and theoretical standpoint. Scott McMillin has suggested that the term "integration" robs the musical of its special nature as it implies a sameness in the writing as well as in the various ways an audience receives a work. For McMillin, when a musical is working, it isn't the smoothness of unity but "the crackle of difference …" that causes an emotional response.[51] Using the myriad collaborators and contributors that make a musical come to life as a starting point, McMillin suggests that the various elements of a show don't create an integrated whole as much as they represent a "cohesion" of elements that are inherently different. For McMillin, musicals provide examples of two types of "time": "book time," which is the natural unfolding of events derived from the libretto, and "lyric time" which interrupts "book time" with songs and dances.[52] "Lyric time" is experienced differently by the audience than "book time," largely because of the use of repetition in lyrics and melody and the emotional responses to musicality and vocal performance. McMillin's intervention is to disrupt the "integration" theoretical approach, which he connects to the Wagnerian concept of *Gesamtkunstwerk,* by introducing the idea of "cohesion" of different elements as a principle more in line with Brecht's "Epic Theatre."

At first glance, McMillin's approach may seem antagonistic to classifying LaChiusa's work in general and *Marie Christine* in particular as a musical. McMillin directly and specifically calls out the intermingling of operatic traditions in contemporary musicals. "There are musicals today that try to become operatic, as though the musical were a lower form that should strive for an elevated state, and this strikes me as a confusion of genres," he explains.[53] This would seem a direct repudiation of LaChiusa's idea of a "mongrel" musical. Further, McMillin's distinction between "book time" and "lyric time" in many ways rules out a musical like *Marie Christine* that is mostly sung, as is many of LaChiusa's other works. But a closer look reveals that LaChiusa-as-writer is very aware of the plurality of time that McMillin locates in the musical. In several instances throughout the show, LaChiusa uses a shift from a dialogue scene into music to establish a flashback, a time shift that is both literal and, in McMillin's terms, theoretical. In an early scene in the musical's first act, Dante confesses to Marie Christine that he is broke, that there are men who owe him money, and the money that he is owed is, in turn, owed to powerful men. It is in this dialogued scene that Marie decides to confess to Dante that she has gifts and powers she can use. "I come here to the Lake. And people come to me for help," Marie exclaims as the setting moves back in time and Marie highlights other cases in which people have come to make use of her powers in the number "C'est Lamour / To Find a Lover."[54] This sequence confirms McMillin's proposal regarding the difference of "book time" and "lyric time." In the scene, Dante's situation is spelled out and Marie offers her help in addition to a secret about her talents. The dramaturgical work is done and the plot has been advanced. The number, which does flow out of the dialogue in the Rodgers and Hammerstein tradition extrapolated by Block, gives us an opportunity to see Marie put her talents to use. While the information obtained in the number is interesting and even illuminating, it is dramaturgically unnecessary. Instead, the number relocates the audiences' orientation from "book time" to "lyric time" by offering a musical sequence that elevates the ideas and themes from "book time" while also demanding a different emotional response from the audience.

Another example not only features a literal relocation of time, but also of place. Deep in the second act, Marie gets lost in her thoughts after the departure of Magdalena. Using her powers, she relocates herself into Dante's mind while he is making love to Helena in the number "Prison in a Prison." In a narrative often concerned with the literal, this moment in the musical deserves special attention. By inserting herself into Dante's thoughts, Marie literally inserts herself into the physical act of love making, often cutting off Helena's movements and replacing Helena's body with her own. Marie threatens Dante in the lyric:

In the warmth of her bed
In the heat of her breath
I'll come to you.
Through the mirror of her eyes
Through the sweat on her skin
I'll come to you.

I will kiss your breast
I will draw your blood
I will take you down
I will not let go–
I will not let go–
I will not let go–[55]

The lyric of the song itself exemplifies many of the elements of McMillin's "lyric time." While many of LaChiusa's songs would be classified as "through-composed," "Prison in a Prison" is strophic in form, following a strict verse/chorus format.[56] Additionally, the number utilizes the sequencing of melodically similar material in both verses and both choruses, despite the fact that LaChiusa has stated that he isn't fond of using sequences.[57] Because both lyrical and musical ideas are repeated, the number confirms McMillin's assertion that the use of repetition helps to differentiate "lyric time" from "book time." Additionally, this format resists the "integration" style approach that would suggest that the number must have dramaturgical relevance. The idea of Marie's threats is reiterated in various ways but all communicating the same idea. The lyric relies heavily on repeated phrases. In the first stanza, the first three lines set up the expectation of repetition. Both the first lines begin with the words "In the" while the third line sets up a later repetition of the lyric "I'll come to you." The rest of the stanza carries on the work set out by the first half by repeating the words "Through the" in the next two lines, then repeating the phrase "I'll come to you" in the final line of the stanza. The second stanza goes even further with repetition. All six lines of the stanza begin with the words "I will" with the final three lines repeating the single phrase "I will not let go–." All of these repetitions of lyric, combined with the strophic nature of the melody, help to relocate the sense of "time" from "book time" to "lyric time." Daniele's staging of the number, which also helps to highlight the examples of difference cited by McMillin, is discussed in the next section.

While none of these conventions of opera or musical theatre offer a clear-cut distinction between the two genres, the various discussions by scholars and journalists do help in understanding the differing elements that are expected of each form. By his own admission, LaChiusa is seeking to borrow from a variety of traditions, celebrating the "mongrel" backbone of American culture. So, it is unsurprising that some dramaturgical and musical elements of *Marie Christine* are indicative of European opera, despite LaChiusa's complaints about opera being elitist. Conversely, much of the musical vocabulary of the score borrows from several traditions, from jazz, to gospel, to traditional musical theatre, separating it from the so-called "purity" of the Eurocentric opera aesthetic. And in terms of dramaturgy, much of LaChiusa's piece is at home in the scholarly conversations that are attempting to define the American musical, whether the emphasis is on the traditional "integration" argument articulated by Block or the more Brechtian approach of duality of time offered by McMillin.

"Mongrel" Performance: Analyzing the Work of McDonald and Daniele

While the critical reception and the writing of *Marie Christine* both provide examples of the labor of the mongrelized form, it is crucial to understand the ways in which LaChiusa's collaborators also contributed to both the show and his larger project, even if he was credited as the sole writer. In the book *Unfinished Show Business,* scholar Bruce Kirle argues that musicals are never entirely "finished" because they are "read" by audiences watching the show in a theatre.[58] Kirle goes further by rejecting the historical insistence on studying musical theatre based on the text and score, suggesting that performance and direction are necessary elements of a production's history and are crucial in understanding how a particular show played at a particular moment.[59] While Kirle's view intervenes in commonly held assumptions that privilege the writers when discussing theatre, musical theatre, and opera, his stance that performance and direction are legible attributes with which to analyze the musical forces a reconsideration of that stance. If the musical is a constantly changing entity and its collaborations are only readable in a theatre, then the performance and direction of *Marie Christine* must come in to play when discussing the work's classification as "mongrel." With Kirle's suggestion in mind, this last section of the chapter focuses on two musical numbers from *Marie Christine*. The first, "And You Would Lie / I Will Give," focuses on the vocal performance of Audra McDonald as an example of mongrel performance. Utilizing my notes from the archival tape of the original production in conjunction with the Original Cast Recording of *Marie Christine*, I focus on the ways in which McDonald changes vocal and stylistic tactics to further the identification of the musical as "mongrel." Second, I look at the staging and choreography of the song "Prison in a Prison" as a means of describing the practical ways in which director/choreographer Graciela Daniele was an equal collaborator in the "mongrel" project.

The career of Audra McDonald has been celebrated and, in turn, well documented. She is the only person in history to have won Tony Awards in all four of the performance categories eligible to her as assigned by gender. Additionally, she holds the record for the most Tony Award wins for an actor. In addition to her work on the Broadway stage, McDonald has enjoyed a celebrated career as a recording artist and film actress. By the time of her performance in *Marie Christine*, her first time in a leading role on Broadway, the then 29-year-old singing actress had already won three Tony Awards: two in the Featured Actress in a Musical category and one in the Featured Actress in a Play category. While McDonald's aim was always a career in musical theatre, she was trained as a classical singer at the Julliard School. McDonald developed *Marie Christine* through all of its major readings, including a large, six-week workshop produced by Lincoln Center in 1996. Therefore, her contribution to the show cannot be overstated. McDonald's classical training, combined with her familiarity of different musical styles and vocal techniques, is in evidence throughout her performance in the theatre as well as the Original Cast Recording. While it would be impossible to analyze the entire vocal performance here, I do highlight the vocal performance in "And You Will Lie / I Will Give" for several reasons. First, the number has major dramaturgical import as it is the first unadulterated statement of Marie's devotion to Dante. Second, while the song is through-composed (nonstrophic), the lyric to the song does engage in various points of repetition, making the song an excellent example of McMillin's dual time analysis. Third, and most important to the purpose of this chapter, McDonald utilizes a series of vocal tactics that are only on display during the number in question.

The number comes late in the first act, right after Marie Christine has used voodoo to hurt her maid, Lisette. McDonald's vocals are backed up by the three prisoners, sung by Jennifer Leigh Warren, Andrea Frierson-Toney, and Mary Bond Davis. The number starts with the "And You Would Lie" section, with the prisoners overlapping several lines of lyrics, taunting Marie and admonishing her for the violence she is willing to do in service to Dante. Their section comes to a close in a very chromatic passage with the lyrics "Dangerous / Powerless / Beautiful."[60] When the "I Will Give" section starts, McDonald lets the voice lie comfortably in her lower range, coloring the words with the warmth of her chest register on "I will give you my money," opening into her head voice on the "o" vowel of the word "open" in the phrase "I will open my body."[61] Thus far, the vocal technique is well in line with "Eurocentric" elements of McDonald's classical training. While the lower sections of the first few phrases are lyrically delivered, with McDonald only shading her tone with her chest voice, the mid-staff sections of the phrases are slowly flowering into her head resonance, particularly on the repeated phrase "My love" which slowly ascends the scale. The song is very much in the middle of McDonald's range; the highest note in the short song is E^5. Despite that, McDonald relies on the lyrical qualities of her upper register to color a series of pitches. Throughout the first section of the song, higher pitches creep out of the melody, accentuating words like "open," "brothers," and highest on the word "kill." McDonald's vocals blossom into these words, resting firmly in her classical training. This gradual move from McDonald's chest range into her head voice leads the audience to believe that the song will continue to move up and her vocal technique will continue to live in that classical aesthetic.

Instead, McDonald completely abandons her lyrical, classical sounds and goes into a full chest belt during the initial climax of the song. McDonald uses her head voice one final time, on the word "live" in the phrase, "I will live if you give me."[62] Then, the song repeats the phrase "my love" three times, each phrase moving up the E-flat scale to a C^5, blossoming into a run on the final "love" that extends up to a fully belted E-flat 5. At this point, McDonald has completely abandoned the Eurocentric classical "bel canto" sound in favor of an earthy, raw belt that resonates squarely in the mask. In this way, her more classical technique gives way to a technique more associated with musical theatre, but also indicative of some forms of jazz and gospel. She doesn't abandon this earthier sound either, coming out of the high run into lower phrases. Her belt specifically accentuates certain words, such as "bear" in "I will bear you our children."[63] The final phrases of the song repeat the same text, "my love," four times. McDonald keeps the first two firmly in chest voice, switching to a mix of head voice for the final two phrases. From a vocal technique standpoint, it is likely that McDonald's belt didn't extend up to the F-flat[5] notated in the score. Regardless, the mix of McDonald's head and chest voice work together to create a daring statement, a mixture of acceptance and strength.

McDonald mongrelizes the expectations for vocal performance by using a variety of vocal techniques throughout the performance of "And You Would Lie / I Will Give." Her initial vocal technique rests firmly in musical theatre, then opens up to her more classical training. The climax of the song is delivered in full belt and that belt is sustained through the first part of the coda, surrendering to a mixed technique for the song's final moments. McDonald's vocals bring up a variety of musical associations, from musical theatre, to bel canto, to jazz and gospel. While it is clear that McDonald's vocal choices are a mongrelization of different styles and techniques, it is even more important that they serve to reinforce dramaturgical and character details. McDonald's "mongrel" approach reminds the audience of Marie Christine's Creole status as well as her struggle as she comes to a decision regarding her split allegiance, for her brothers Paris and Jean and her lover Dante. Her navigations between a Eurocentric "classical" sound and her chest belt, more indicative of various popular styles, charts the embodied journey of the character herself, the various cultural influences that are warring within her personal identity, and the social constraints placed on her as a woman in general and as a woman of color in particular. The orchestration works in tandem with McDonald's performance. The percussion for the number is provided by the auxiliary percussionist suspended above the playing area while the principal accompaniment in the orchestration is provided by keyboard and strings. This juxtaposition of European styles with more Caribbean/African rhythms creates both a "mongrel" sound as well as an aural reflection of Marie Christine herself, particularly her mixed heritage and her struggle between the wishes of her brothers and her love for Dante. McDonald's vocal performance works in partnership with the writing in order to present a more complex characterization, a mongrelization of various forces and ideals.

Director and Choreographer Graciela Daniele has a similar background to McDonald in terms of how she trained within her discipline. Born in Buenos Aires, Argentina, Daniele began studying ballet at age seven. She moved to Paris several years later to continue her studies in ballet when she saw a performance of *West Side Story* with Robbins's original choreography. As a result of that experience, she moved to New York City in 1963 in order to study jazz and modern.[64] She studied with Martha Graham and Merce Cunningham and began a career as a Broadway dancer in shows such as *Promises, Promises* and *Chicago*, working with Michael Bennett and Bob Fosse, respectively. Bennet asked her to assist him on the 1971 musical *Follies* by Stephen Sondheim. She made her solo debut as choreographer in 1981 with The Public Theatre's revival of *The Pirates of Penzance*. Daniele is, in many ways, the embodiment of much of what LaChiusa describes as the mongrel idea of America. An American immigrant from South America by way of France, Daniele brings a variety of embodied experiences and identities into her work. Additionally, like McDonald, her training begins with a Eurocentric base that she expands upon by incorporating modern and jazz-based modalities. While the majority of her Broadway credits are as choreographer, she has garnered a great many credits as director and choreographer, largely in off-Broadway nonprofits. Her involvement in "The New Musical Drama" movement charts back to its inception; she was the one first responsible for combining *March of the Falsettos* and *Falsettoland* into a two-act bill at Hartford Stage. Daniele's work itself is a mongrel approach of the more dramaturgically based directors characteristic of "The New Musical Drama" movement as well as the methods emblematic of the 1970s "concept" director-choreographers like Fosse and Bennett. As such, it is often difficult to ascertain where dance ends and musical staging begins in Daniele's work. This is also true of much of her work in *Marie Christine,* particularly her staging of the number "Prison in a Prison."

As discussed earlier, "Prison in a Prison" takes place during a sexual liaison between Dante and his bride-to-be Helena. Marie Christine, alone in her small shack, uses her powers to invade Dante's thoughts while he is making love to Helena. The movement for the number takes place solely on the circular thrust that extends out into the house of the Vivian Beaumont theatre. At the start of the number, the three prisoners are standing, hunched over, at the up-center edge of the circular thrust. Marie Christine is in the upper-right quadrant, breathless. She removes her dress, revealing a black petticoat. She lets the dress fall at stage right and calls out Dante's fiancée's name, "Helena. Helena!"[65] On the second "Helena," the three prisoners slowly straighten their stance and stand at attention. At the same time, Dante and Helena enter the thrust from the stage left entrance, countering Marie Christine across the space. The thrust is washed in a light blue and, along the grating of the thrust, lights shine upward, giving an eerie, ghostly effect similar to those produced by footlights. Marie sings, "Wealthy man's daughter / Slender and treasured" as Dante lifts up Helena, twirling her three times.[66] On the final turn, Helena extends out in Dante's arms, pointing both her hand and foot, extending her body on the phrase "Slender and treasured." At the same time, Marie Christine slowly crosses into the couple. As Marie Christine arrives upstage of Dante, Dante dips Helena forward, Helena extending forward, then moving back up to embrace Dante on the sung line "Whiter than linen / White."[67] On the last word "white," Helena slides down to the floor in front of Dante as Marie Christine moves slightly to upstage left of Dante and the three prisoners slowly side-step around the perimeter of the thrust, landing on the upstage right diagonal.

Dante pulls Helena up, twirls her once, then pulls her in and bends her over toward downstage. Marie echoes the movement, still upstage of Dante, but very close to contact. Marie pulls her left arm back, a movement that seems to force Dante to pull Helena back up to him, face to face. Helena jumps and wraps her legs around Dante's waist. Helena bends her back, her hands touching the floor, indicating penetration has taken place while Marie, right behind Dante, raises up her hands, suggesting that, in some way, she is participating in the sex act. "I will kiss your breast / I will draw your blood / I will take you down," Marie sings as she places her hands on Dante's head, then slides her hands down Dante's chest as Helena pulls back up, then extends back down.[68] Marie keeps moving her hands downward, reaching down to his abdomen as Helena slides down, her face squarely facing Dante's groin. On the repeated phrase "I will not let go—" Marie fully embraces Dante from behind and the two of them begin thrusting as Helena is writhing on the ground.[69] On the first chorus, Dante lowers Helena down to the ground and prepares to mount her, but Marie stops him. She stands to the right of Dante, who is on his knees, and forces his hand to caress her leg. She then throws him toward Helena, who is still lying on the floor. Dante tries to mount Helena again, but Marie pulls him back once again. Dante rests on one knee and Marie once again inserts herself into the lovemaking, this time by sitting on Dante's knee. Dante begins to rub his face on Marie's face, caressing her breasts and moving his hand down toward her skirt. Meanwhile, Helena is lying face down on the ground. While she is still connected in the stage composition, she thrusts up and down on the floor, suggesting that, while she is engaged in the sex act, she is not the focus. At this point, Daniele has employed largely ballet dance vocabulary, though several of Marie Christine's movements have veered into the more jagged shapes of modern dance.

For the second verse of the song, the three prisoners take on the bulk of the vocals, leaving Marie available to be more involved in the movement. As they sing, Helena crawls toward Dante and reaches out for him. Marie counters by moving downstage of Helena, pulling on her waist. Dante twirls Helena, then grabs her arms, extending her out downstage as Marie moves upstage of Dante, grabbing onto his chest again. Dante and Helena break, then move in toward each other, but Marie comes between them. Helena spins out of the configuration, then moves upstage of Dante as Marie takes her place in front of him. Helena then moves downstage of Marie as the prisoners sing "I will not let go—." The three become entangled and Dante begins thrusting violently. He climaxes as the song reaches its zenith. He is flanked by Helena and Marie Christine. The three separate and Helena starts spinning in circles as Marie holds her hand over her head like a puppet master. She appears to be bringing Helena back to Dante, but instead inserts herself, forcing Helena to extend backward as she kisses Dante. Marie Christine removes herself from the situation. Helena and Dante look at each other. They back away from each other, Helena exiting upstage right and Dante upstage left. The prisoners move downstage along the perimeter of the thrust. Marie Christine takes center stage, singing the final lyric, "Prison in a Prison / Christened in My Name."[70]

Daniele utilizes a "mongrel" approach in her staging of the number. In terms of dance vocabulary, she establishes Helena with largely Eurocentric balletic moves, particularly in her line and in the rounded shape of her arms. By contrast, Marie Christine's lines and shapes are more rigid, broken, and angular, calling to mind a more modern dance approach. As the number progresses, as Marie Christine takes more and more control of Dante and Helena's love-making, Marie's dance vocabulary becomes the dominant shape of the entire number, particularly in terms of tempo and duration. Despite this, Helena's arms maintain their rounded, balletic shape. Daniele creates a "mongrel" effect by setting up two differing vocabularies as warring factions, the Eurocentric, white Helena against the mixed-race Marie. This duality, while appropriate for the dramaturgy of the moment, also presents itself as an example of Daniele's own embodied experiences as someone who trained classically prior to opening up her repertoire to more modern and jazz sensibilities. The power structures of this mongrel approach also become apparent in the use of Helena. Helena never instigates a movement throughout the number. Instead, she is largely manipulated, turned about, and commandeered by Dante. Sometimes, these movements are the machinations of Marie Christine, working through Dante's mind. Still, at other times, Marie appears to manipulate Helena's body directly.

Additionally, Daniele "mongrelizes" the space by contrasting stage left and stage right as territories. At the beginning of the number, Marie Christine occupies stage right while Dante and Helena enter hand in hand from stage left. The prisoners are directly upstage center, currently impartial. The beginning of the number is largely staged at stage left, presumably meant to establish Helena's bedroom, though there is no furniture. Marie literally invades their territory during the first verse of the song by crossing from stage right to stage left, inserting herself into the proceedings, and manipulating both the bodies of Dante and Helena. After the first verse, the trio of prisoners moves from their neutral position at upstage center, moving along the perimeter of the thrust to stage right, tipping the balance in favor of Marie's territory. Throughout the course of the second verse, Marie, Dante, and Helena follow suit, slowly moving into the stage right territory. Marie counters the couples, pulls them along, and generally guides their movements into the area of the stage that she controls. However, the final moments of the number, including Dante's climax and his kiss with Marie Christine, happen directly at center, the nexus of the two playing areas. Daniele uses bodies to establish territory, power, and dominance. By positioning each half of the thrust as "owned" territory, Marie at stage right and Dante and Helena at stage left, she creates the opportunity for associated boundaries, initially separated, eventually porous. Marie moves both Dante and Helena away from the Eurocentric "bedroom" they share and into a more exoticized world, her world, in which identities are intermeshed and complicated. By the end of the number, Daniele places the action squarely at center, the ultimate statement of mongrelization between two territories that are seemingly incompatible.

Both the vocal performance of Audra McDonald and the direction and choreography of Graciela Daniele further the argument that *Marie Christine* is representative of a mongrelized type of entertainment. McDonald's mix of classical and popular vocal techniques helps to identify the character of Marie Christine as mongrelized as well as identifying her dilemmas and obstacles. Further, Daniele's mix of ballet and modern, in addition to her techniques of establishing boundaries in the playing space, further reifies the mongrel themes in the dramaturgy of the piece as well as labeling the piece itself as mongrel. While it is often difficult to ferret out the contributions of the various collaborators of a piece of theatre, it is worth considering that McDonald's performance and Daniele's staging both participate in a type of collaborative authorship, working in concert with LaChiusa's theories rather than seeing them as a directive.

"Way Back to Paradise": The State of the Mongrel Musical

As cited earlier in the chapter, LaChiusa has a distrust of the word "pure" and the associations it engenders. "Pure is a word that frightens me," he states.[71] In the wake of the death of Jonathan Larson, Broadway was desperately searching for its new voice, a composer who would innovate and change the form. While LaChiusa answered the call in his own way, his "mongrel" approach created a type of dissonance that may have hindered a full embrace of *Marie Christine* as well as *The Wild Party*, opening later that season. The mongrelization of European opera with a more dramaturgically based style of musical theatre strikes some as a confusing of genres, as McMillin noted in *The Musical as Drama*.[72] Others have suggested that the genres of musical theatre and opera are too closely related to each other, prohibiting any sort of successful amalgam. In an opinion piece in *The New York Times*, classical music critic Anthony Tommasini admonishes the writers who try to fully integrate the two genres: "In some fields fusing different kinds of music is a potentially creative and liberating endeavor. But creators in musical theater and opera are better off working their native turfs. It's fine to pull in other styles and influences as long as you stay rooted in what you, and your art form, do best."[73] Once again, Tommasini mentions his major criterion for the separation of opera and musical theatre—namely, that opera is music-driven while musicals are text driven.[74] That argument has been thoroughly discussed in this chapter, but defining the differences between opera and musical theatre remains an elusive exercise. For LaChiusa, the limits of strictures and definitions don't matter. "Did you like it? Were you moved?" are the questions LaChiusa is interested in.[75] Unfortunately, if we are to accept the assessments of first-night critics, the answer to both of these questions was largely "no" and these negative responses were often predicated on the piece's refusal to adhere to a single genre, likely because the lack of genre definition made audiences uncomfortable because the parameters of the entertainment had not been dictated.

Despite this, critics seemed sure of what genre they were experiencing when watching *Marie Christine*, regardless of the fact that they weren't in agreement as to the identity of that genre. Why does genre matter? Why was classifying *Marie Christine* so important? Why can't LaChiusa's dictum of "Did you like it? Were you moved?" be enough to evaluate a piece of work? While possible justifications have been discussed in this chapter, it is also likely that the theatre community was not yet ready for what LaChiusa was offering. In the conclusion of this study, I will discuss the successes that "The New Musical Drama" has found in the last fifteen years.

While it is unlikely that *Marie Christine* would ever have met the mammoth expectations that surrounded its opening, it is difficult to ascertain why it managed little staying power at all. Subsequent productions have been far less frequent than other titles by LaChiusa, likely because of the piece's difficult casting, particularly the vocally demanding title character. *Marie Christine* was the most expensive production in Lincoln Center Theatre's history at the time and the financial demands of the piece, combined with the significant losses accumulated from the musical *Parade* the season before, may have compromised Lincoln Center Theatre's ability to produce the title effectively. At one point during the process, LaChiusa was asked to downsize the casting requirements for the show. In response, LaChiusa submitted an email with a possible plan to downsize the cast to twenty, but also pushed back on the potential cuts: "If we're talking integrity, what's the difference between [hiring stars] and turning my score into coleslaw? … Next time you guys want me to write a ten-character musical, just tell me you want that."[76] In the end, Lincoln Center relented, and the Broadway company had thirty-one ensemble members. Production issues aside, a musical about a mixed-race woman killing her children to get revenge on their father was always going to be a tough sell, regardless of the caliber of talent involved.

LaChiusa's work, along with the efforts of leading lady Audra McDonald and director-choreographer Graciela Daniele, created the possibility for a more mongrelized form of Broadway entertainment, resting on the legacies of *Porgy and Bess* and others. Interestingly, the 1999–2000 Broadway season offered a variety of musical options, including other musicals that could be said to be "mongrel." *James Joyce's The Dead* by Richard Nelson and Shaun Davey, based on the short story of the same name, transferred to Broadway from Playwrights Horizons in January of 2000, running nearly three times the brief run of *Marie Christine*. The chamber musical, featuring a score of almost entirely diegetic Irish parlor songs, didn't integrate opera conventions so much as those more commonly associated with straight plays, leading to some critics labeling the piece a play with music. While *James Joyce's The Dead* came up through the same nonprofit systems that produced *Marie Christine*, the musical *Aida* came from the behemoth producers of Disney Theatricals. With a score by Elton John and lyrics by Tim Rice, *Aida* marked Disney's first Broadway foray into developing a musical not based on one of their film properties. Pertinent to our purposes, *Aida* represents an even greater co-mingling of the genres of opera and musical theatre, particularly given the Verdi opera as source material. *Aida* ran for over four years despite the fact that many of the dramaturgical issues expressed in regard to *Marie Christine* were just as prevalent in *Aida*, though the scores couldn't be more different.

Despite *Aida*'s massive success, Broadway productions of "The New Musical Drama" did not fare well at the turn of the century. Screen-to-stage adaptations, such as *Footloose*, tended to rule the economics of Broadway, in conjunction with an upswing in revivals of classic titles such as *The Music Man* and *Kiss Me, Kate.* Whether or not a different time and a different market would have been friendlier to the Broadway debut of *Marie Christine* is anyone's guess and isn't the purpose of this chapter. Instead, the ways in which LaChiusa forwarded a "mongrel" option for the American musical, as codified in his opinion piece in *The New York Times*, become essential in understanding both LaChiusa's work as well as the work of many of his peers in the so-called "movement." Additionally, LaChiusa's "mongrel" philosophy gives us a useful framework for exploring the success of "The New Musical Drama" in more recent seasons.

CHAPTER 2
"A HOUSE THAT WILL NEVER BE A HOME": HISTORICAL IMAGINATION AND CREATIVITY IN *FIRST LADY SUITE* AND *FIRST DAUGHTER SUITE*

In several ways, LaChiusa's work tends to deal in history, positioning LaChiusa as a dramatist-historian who utilizes elements of R. G. Collingwood's "historical imagination" in order to dramatize historical moments. This idea is exemplified in the construction of both *First Lady Suite* and *First Daughter Suite*, both of which are structured into four individual one-acts. Many of LaChiusa's pieces favor one-act forms and vignettes. His first major debut in New York City was a collection of one-act musicals, now licensed under the title *Lucky Nurse*. Two of these one acts, *Agnes* and *Eulogy for Mister Hamm*, were responsible for winning LaChiusa his first major grant award, the Richard Rodgers Development Award.[1] Although the grant funded a developmental staged reading of the first two one-acts in 1986, the entire bill wouldn't be fully staged until December of 1991, when Playwrights Horizons produced them for fourteen performances.[2] For LaChiusa's next project, he turned to one of his obsessions: the lives of America's First Ladies. LaChiusa has labeled himself a "First Lady-ologist" and claims to have over 400 various books on the lives of America's First Ladies.[3] He began by writing *Over Texas*, a one-act musical that imagines a conversation between Mary Gallagher, Jackie Kennedy's personal secretary, and Evelyn Lincoln, John Kennedy's personal secretary on Air Force One right before the plane touches down in Dallas on November 22nd, 1963. LaChiusa would add two more one-act musical dramas as well as a fourth brief "olio" scene, culminating in the musical *First Lady Suite*. While *Over Texas* did debut solo at a one-act festival at Ensemble Studio Theatre in 1991, the entire work would eventually be fully produced by The Public Theater in late 1993. LaChiusa remarked at the time that, while he had expanded into three acts and one olio focusing on four First Ladies, he fancied continuing the piece with other stories of First Ladies: "I'd still like to do Nancy Reagan," LaChiusa stated in an interview with Barry Singer.[4]

LaChiusa would eventually get around to Nancy Reagan when his companion piece, *First Daughter Suite*, premiered at The Public Theatre in 2015, over twenty years after the premiere of *First Lady Suite* in the same theatre. LaChiusa stated in interviews that, while certain themes and musical motifs echo throughout the piece, it shouldn't be considered a sequel: "I didn't want *First Daughter Suite* to be a sequel—there were more stories to tell and this was a new platform," he stated in an interview prior to the release of the musical's original cast recording in March of 2016.[5] While it is true that *First Daughter Suite*'s four one-acts rely on a different set of themes and ideas, it is nearly impossible to consider one piece without thinking about the conversation it engages in with the other. While *First Lady Suite* relies largely on images of flight, *First Daughter Suite* is all built around images of water. These ideas are stated directly in each respective musical's opening number.[6] Yet, while each opening number focuses on a different image, the songs do share musical vocabularies and the melodic line to each song is almost identical, furthering the notion that, while *First Daughter Suite* may not be a sequel to *First Lady Suite*, it is certainly a companion piece. Other elements help to mark the similarities and differences between the two titles. *First Lady Suite* presents its stories in reverse chronological order, beginning with *Over Texas* and Jackie Kennedy, moving back to Mamie Eisenhower in the comedic *Where's Mamie*, moving back to Bess Truman in the brief *Olio*, before finishing with Eleanor Roosevelt in *Eleanor Sleeps Here*. In contrast, *First Daughter Suite* moves forward, starting with Pat Nixon in *Happy Pat*, then combining the stories of Rosalynn Carter and Betty Ford in *Amy Carter's Fabulous Dream Adventure*, moving to the aforementioned Nancy Reagan in *Patti by the Pool*, before finishing with the haunting *In the Deep Bosom of the Ocean Buried* which includes both Barbara and Laura Bush. Despite the differences in the flow of time, both musicals present ideas of historical imagination, thereby showcasing LaChiusa as a type of creative historian.

In this chapter, I argue that both *First Lady Suite* and *First Daughter Suite* utilize the method of historical imagination, marking LaChiusa's work as historical vis-à-vis his creative employment of historiography. While I'm not suggesting that LaChiusa is the only musical theatre dramatist to engage in historical imagination, his massive knowledge of his subjects, namely First Ladies, makes his work an essential point of consideration for exploring how musical theatre as a whole participates in the process of historical imagination. Historical imagination has a long history throughout the musical theatre canon, with musicals such as *1776, Annie, Sunday in the Park with George,* and, more recently, *Hamilton* all engaging in various degrees of imagined and reimagined vignettes from history. LaChiusa's output serves as a fascinating venue for considering these processes, particularly given that his work bridges the "golden age" model of musical theatre writing with the more experimental works that have found commercial viability in today's market. Historical imagination has played a role in several of LaChiusa's works. In *Hello Again* and *See What I Wanna See,* both of which are discussed in detail in Chapter 4, LaChiusa historicizes various periods throughout the history of New York City. His 2011 musical *Queen of the Mist* utilizes the archive surrounding the life of Annie Edson Taylor, the first woman to successfully go over Niagara Falls in a barrel at the turn of the twentieth century, in order to imagine her life both before and after the momentous event. And his massive musical *Giant,* based on the novel by Edna Ferber and discussed in Chapter 3, chronicles a Texas ranch from the 1920s through the 1950s. All of these examples help to label the work of LaChiusa as works of historical imagination.

Historical imagination is a term coined by philosopher, historian, and archaeologist R. G. Collingwood. Collingwood brings historical inquiry into conversation with the field of phenomenology, specifically the view of phenomenology that focuses on the primacy and importance of perception, by discussing the role of perception in the work of the historian.[7] Collingwood goes on to advocate the use of "historical imagination" in the work of the historian: "The imagination, that 'blind but indispensable faculty' without which, as Kant has shown, we could never perceive the world around us, is indispensable in the same way to history: it is this which, operating not capriciously as fancy but in it's *a priori* form, does the entire work of historical construction."[8] Collingwood makes the point that imagination is not only available to the historian as a tool, it is an essential part of historical exploration. Collingwood reiterates the necessity for imagination in historical inquiry by noting that historical imagination is structural, not ornamental.[9] Collingwood is not necessarily advocating that the historian has no obligation to "facts," but that an element of creativity is permissible and should be encouraged as there are portions of history that cannot be known. The labor of "imagining the past" assumes a certain reliance on empirically produced information, but also gives the historian license to interpret that information and, if necessary, imagine the historical moment in question.[10]

Collingwood's provocative stance has provided a framework for several works of historical inquiry, one of the most notable being George Chauncey's massive study of gay men in America in the first half of the twentieth century, *Gay New York*, which uses the concept of historical imagination to process information about the lives of gay men during a period in which empirical evidence exists, but requires a certain amount of re-enactment, interpolation, and interrogation in order to fully flesh out the narrative.[11] While Chauncey's book isn't relevant to the settings of LaChiusa's *Suites*, his work helps us to understand both the ways in which a musical theatre writer can utilize historical imagination as a dramatist as well as an example of how imagined circumstances can still qualify as history. Chauncey utilizes archival material, but also understands that there are several gaps in the historical record largely connected with the precarious nature of putting anything about living as a gay man in the early twentieth century into print. LaChiusa utilizes an archive, largely consisting of biographies, to reconstruct moments in the lives of various First Ladies, but also understands that pieces of information are missing given the secretive nature of the personal lives of both the First Ladies, their President husbands, and their family. As such, both Chauncey and LaChiusa must utilize historical imagination in order to realize their respective projects. Second, while Chauncey often makes conjectures and hypotheses regarding what happened in the past, the process of arriving at these conjectures still qualifies as part of the labor of "doing" history, even if the historical suppositions have been imagined rather than archived. LaChiusa also does something similar in his dramaturgical tactics. Most of the stories LaChiusa is dramatizing are personal and private, meaning that he doesn't have access to empirical information when fleshing them out into dramatic works. LaChiusa's license with the historical narratives he is proposing also performs the labor of the historian, allowing him to work within historical imagination that is still rooted in rigorous research and critique. Admittedly, LaChiusa isn't attempting to document events in an empirical way. In fact, his one-acts occasionally develop into fantastical narratives that defy all elements of realism. But even these flights of fantasy are rooted in thorough considerations of the recorded narrative of events.

Both *First Lady Suite* and *First Daughter Suite* are noteworthy in the specific methods in which they employ historical imagination. First, the musicals imagine events that are rooted in the mundane, for the most part, alternating with moments of historical importance. Second, while all of the pieces that comprise the two musicals are rooted in historical fact, LaChiusa takes significant license with his imagination, sometimes dramatizing events that are rooted in history but developed in fantasy. Third, the very nature of his subjects, the various First Ladies in question, begs a sense of history from the audience. The project marks itself as inherently historical because of our strong association with presidential families and history. Indeed, much of American history is structured around the various administrations in power during a historical moment. Therefore, both of the *Suites* operate both as musical theatre and as history, despite the fact that much of the history being presented is imagined.

In order to explore these ideas, I have decided to bring different acts from each musical into conversation with each other utilizing different aspects of Collingwood's conception of historical imagination in order to further explicate how these two musicals are related works that comment on the nature of First Ladies. For the sake of clarity, I do move through each work in the order in which the acts are presented, though it turns out that this process also provides a useful thematic framework for consideration of each of the acts. First, I consider Collingwood's idea of "re-enactment" in historical imagination to look at *Over Texas* from *First Lady Suite* and *Happy Pat* from *First Daughter Suite*. In particular, I look at how these depictions of historical moments of crisis both comment on the ways in which First Ladies and their staff and families are dramatized at moments before or during these tumultuous circumstances. Second, I consider the ways in which Collingwood's concept of interpolation is at work in the two most fantasy-based acts in each musical, *Where's Mamie?* and *Amy Carter's Fabulous Dream Adventure*, both of which feature fantastical elements that violate the realism more commonly associated with historical dramas and musicals. I use these acts to explore the ways in which historical imagination can encourage reconsiderations of the realist impulse in historical representation. Finally, I explore Collingwood's idea of interrogation in order to look at a single one-act, *Patti by the Pool*, from *First Daughter Suite*, which imagines a heated exchange between Nancy Reagan and Patti Davis by the pool of Betsy Bloomingdale in California. I look at this act, which primarily utilizes the method of musical monologue, to understand the ways in which the musical project tries to imagine interpersonal turmoil through interrogative tactics. This consideration isn't complete; in the interest of focus, I have decided not to discuss *Eleanor Sleeps Here*, which takes place during a flight with Amelia Earhart and Lauren Hickok, or *In the Deep Bosom of the Ocean Buried*, which takes place during the height of George W. Bush's second presidential campaign on the anniversary of the death of Barbara's daughter, Robin. I will also be moving past the act *Olio* from *First Lady Suite* as it is largely intended for comedic effect, though its depiction of Margaret Truman's voice recital does make use of historical imagination.

Taken together, I hope to explore the various ways historical imagination gives permission for the exploration of history through the guise of musical theatre, particularly in the work of LaChiusa. In order to more clearly delineate different aspects of Collingwood's theory, I focus on the ideas of "re-enactment," "interpolation," and "interrogation" as a means of making specific connections between Collingwood's ideas and the various one-acts in LaChiusa's *Suites*. These three ideas were extrapolated from the writings of Collingwood by Lynn Speer Lemisko, who utilized these three terms as a framework for introducing historical imagination into the social studies classroom.[12] While I utilize the work of Collingwood, I want to be clear that I am applying these ideas to LaChiusa's work. LaChiusa has not applied the term "historical imagination" to his own work in any of the sources I have consulted. Rather, I am utilizing these theories to help make LaChiusa's employment of historical events as a source material for dramatization more legible. While my employment of Collingwood's "historical imagination" in this analysis is somewhat free-form, the central tenets of the creativity of the historian are kept intact.[13] In addition to my liberal use of this term, I also confess that, in the tradition of LaChiusa's writing of each show, my primary archival evidence comes from non-critical biographies and auto-biographies. Rather than consulting more analytical sources, I have decided to utilize the primary archive LaChiusa used as a historian/dramatist in order to more fully explicate his process and viewpoint.

Re-enacting Historical Crises: *Over Texas* and *Happy Pat*

A consideration of each of the first one-act musicals in *First Lady Suite* and *First Daughter Suite* is aided by Collingwood's employment of re-enactment as a method for historical investigation. As articulated by Lemisko, re-enactment "involves reading documents related to an event, envisaging the situation discussed in the documents as the author(s) of the document envisaged it, and thinking for yourself what the author(s) thought about the situation and about various possible ways of dealing with it."[14] Lemisko invites the historian, through the ideas of Collingwood, to engage with historical evidence and writings by imagining the circumstances that produced the writing. While neither Collingwood nor Lemisko are advocating for theatrical dramatizations of historical moments, the concept, which gives the historian a justification for imagining the intricacies of how historical moments have developed, does find a certain degree of salience when considering theatrical depictions of historical moments.[15] While re-enactment helps to describe the entirety of both of LaChiusa's *Suites*, it is particularly helpful in exploring both *Over Texas*, the first musical in *First Lady Suite*, and *Happy Pat*, the first musical in *First Daughter Suite*. In particular, LaChiusa explores historical moments in the lives of Jacqueline Kennedy and Patricia Nixon by re-enacting the mundane. In *Over Texas*, Jackie Kennedy's personal secretary, Mary Gallagher, strikes up a conversation about her "tom kitten" to her friend and personal secretary to JFK, Evelyn Lincoln.[16] In *Happy Pat*, the scene begins with Pat Nixon speaking to her younger daughter Julie about older daughter Tricia's outdoor wedding that is in peril due to intermittent rain. "In come the chairs and / Out go the chairs / First the sky starts to clear then the clouds reappear / So in come the chairs," Julie remarks to her mother, discussing how the ushers keep setting up and then breaking down the wedding scheduled to take place in the Rose Garden.[17]

These seemingly mundane exchanges help to set up the enormity of events about to take place. In *Over Texas*, the conversation between Mary and Evelyn is taking place on Air Force One as it is about to touch down in Fort Worth-Dallas Airport on November 22nd, 1963, hours before John F. Kennedy's assassination. While Pat, Julie, and Tricia figure out the wedding, an unseen Richard Nixon is taking meetings about the impending publication of "The Pentagon Papers" that would bring about the crumbling of his presidency. The wedding took place on June 12th, 1971; *The New York Times* published their first excerpt of "The Pentagon Papers" on June 13th, 1971. While these major events, most directly impact the men who hold power in the Oval Office, LaChiusa is more interested in the women living in the White House. In his words "a house that will never be a home."[18] While the events themselves are well-documented, the moments before, namely the flight over Texas and the preparations for a White House wedding, are less documented, though the accounts in both Mary Gallagher and Julie Nixon Eisenhower's autobiographies do give LaChiusa a starting place. Both of these pieces utilize the concept of historical imagination by staging a "re-enactment" of events that offer the opportunity for historical conjecture.

Over Texas runs approximately twenty minutes and it is Mary Gallagher, not Jackie Kennedy, who is the protagonist of the story. The musical begins with the mundane chatter of Mary, who is overwhelmed by her first flight on Air Force One. Her conversation mate is Evelyn Lincoln. While Evelyn is industriously typing documents to prepare for JFK's speech, Mary drones on about her "tom kitten" at home who must miss her and her frustrations with the First Lady.[19] Mary decides to take a "kitty cat nap." In her dream, Jackie Kennedy, noted in the libretto simply as "First Lady," enters and engages her in absurd conversation, asking for her hat and gloves which are already in her hands. "Lady Bird" Johnson makes a brief appearance in the dream as well, even though the Vice-President and his wife were on a separate plane, as is typically the custom when the President and Vice-President are traveling. Mary confronts the First Lady, demanding she leave her dream, but the First Lady is largely oblivious. The First Lady sings a massive aria, entitled "The Smallest Thing," in which she details her feelings of both numbness and pain sitting at the side of the President.[20] The second section of the song takes a darker turn as the First Lady predicts, in vague detail, the death of her husband while they are "riding in an open car":

> In the heat
> Of the blood
> Of my husband
> As a million million flashbulbs
> Turn the blood to black and white.
> It sings with all its might:
> The smallest thing.
> The smallest thing:
> My life,
> My life …[21]

The First Lady then realizes her hat and gloves are in her hands and exits as Mary wakes up. Mary is overwhelmed with a sense of foreboding, but she is encouraged and brightened by Evelyn in the song "This Is What We Are."[22] Evelyn convinces Mary to ride in the motorcade, and the act ends with Mary being summoned to the front of the plane by the First Lady.

While *Over Texas* focuses on the First Lady's personal secretary, *Happy Pat*, running around thirty minutes, is directly concerned with the First Lady herself, Pat Nixon, despite the fact that she is appearing in a show entitled *First Daughter Suite*. At the beginning of the piece, Pat is seen smoking, breathing in and out to calm her nerves. Julie enters and asks what they should do about her sister Tricia's wedding. Throughout the scene, Pat Nixon finds herself engaged in conversation with the ghostly presence of her recently deceased mother-in-law Hannah Milhous Nixon, a devout Quaker who still relies on the pronouns "thee/thou/thine."[23] Hannah argues with Pat regarding the way she is bringing up her children, the inadequacies of Richard Nixon as a human being, and Pat's smoking. Eventually, bride-to-be Tricia enters the fray and begins an argument with her younger sister Julie, who is already married. The girls try to speak with their father, but he snaps at them and they return to their mother. Unbeknownst to them, Nixon and Bebe Rebozo were meeting to determine damage control over the leaking of "The Pentagon Papers." Despite Hannah's advice that Pat "surrender," Pat pulls the situation together, encouraging Tricia to decide that "out go the chairs" and that the wedding will go on.[24] LaChiusa leaves the audience with several questions, particularly in terms of Pat's knowledge of what's going on in Nixon's office. Historians have posed that Richard Nixon left his wife largely in the dark about all questions of policy, but LaChiusa leaves the door open to the possibility that Pat understands the necessity for the wedding to happen—the news coverage would likely push the release of "The Pentagon Papers" off of the front pages of newspapers.[25]

LaChiusa's decisions regarding what to dramatize are motivated by a sense of historical imagination, particularly in terms of the mundane. In the beginning of *Over Texas*, Mary becomes fascinated by the idea that there are miniature sewing kits on the plane. This seems like a strange moment to musicalize, but it is inspired by something that was very special to Mary Gallagher. In her autobiography, she discusses the moment that she found the miniature sewing kits on Air Force One and she confesses to accidentally keeping one. She kept this item, seemingly mundane, and it remained in her possession as a reminder of the excitement and horror of the experience in Texas.[26] LaChiusa's emphasis on this moment serves to humanize Mary while also dramatizing a literal touchstone of the historical moment experienced by Mary. The "sewing kit" moment also helps the audience to understand the novelty of the experience of riding on Air Force One for Mary. This idea is forwarded by the "Tom Kitten" section in which Mary goes on at length about how she bets Tom Kitten is "chewing up the house" and "pooping on the rug"—interspersed throughout her musical monologue about Tom Kitten, Mary, almost without continuity of thought, expresses her excitement about "flying over Texas / On a plane with the President— / A real V.I.P.!"[27] Additionally, both Mary and Evelyn consider the prospect of serving "four more years" should the President be reelected. For Mary, this is a daunting idea, particularly given the task of making sure all of Jackie's bills are paid.[28] Mary's ambivalence toward the continuation of her position is contrasted with Evelyn's counterpoint, which shows the audience that Evelyn is entirely devoted to her employer. This idea is summarized when Mary asks, "What is the description / Of my job?" to which she replies "Lots of grief / Everyday," while Evelyn celebrates the opportunity to work even harder for the President. Toward the end of the song, Mary asks, "Could I go back?" in counterpart to Evelyn's "I have to go back."[29] This exchange emphasizes the mundanity of Mary and Evelyn's jobs, namely the requirement for total devotion to their employers, juxtaposed by the literal heights of their position, symbolized by their seats on Air Force One. Additionally, the choice to musicalize Mary in general encourages the idea of historical imagination. LaChiusa takes the creative liberty as historian-dramatist to focus on a historical actor not commonly mentioned in the horrific events of November 22nd, 1963. Collingwood places emphasis on the concept of "re-enactment" which allows the historian to replay events in their mind, based on the various biases and lenses that the mind is subject to.[30] LaChiusa chooses to "re-enact" the pre-crisis moments of Mary Gallagher in order to explore an aspect of political life, in the guise of the day-to-day happenings of a staffer, not often explored by dramatists.

The emphasis in *Over Texas* is less on an actual event than it is on the mundane tasks of its protagonist, but the focus of *Happy Pat* features a prominent moment in the history of the Nixon administration, the White House wedding of Tricia Nixon. This event has been usurped in historical terms by the crisis caused over "The Pentagon Papers," and LaChiusa takes this opportunity to reframe the focus of the wedding and the political situation. Much like *Over Texas*, LaChiusa imagines the moments prior to the crisis as opposed to the actual crisis itself, though the specter of Kennedy's assassination and the release of "The Pentagon Papers" both manage to haunt the proceedings occurring onstage. While there may be nothing mundane about a wedding, there is nothing *more* mundane than seeing to the logistics of a wedding and it is the logistics of the wedding that give *Happy Pat* its dramatic start. While Pat Nixon is considering the crisis at hand, namely whether the chairs go inside or outside, she is also forced to confront a series of questions, chief among them her place in the White House and her relationship with President Nixon.[31] Hannah accuses Pat of never really loving her husband. This idea has basis in historical fact, particularly given how hard Richard had to work to convince Pat to marry him.[32] The dramatization of the mundane allows space for Pat to consider not only her navigation of the crisis with the weather but also her crisis of identity and devotion to her husband.

Both *Over Texas* and *Happy Pat* feature elements of the fantastical, a major indicator that LaChiusa is relying on historical imagination to fill out the dramaturgy of the piece. In *Over Texas*, Jackie Kennedy becomes a type of Cassandra in Mary's dream, whereas in *Happy Pat*, Pat Nixon is literally haunted by the ghost of her deceased mother-in-law. In the middle of *Over Texas*, the First Lady invades Mary's "kitty cap nap" to inquire about the location of her hat and gloves, which she is holding. Throughout the bulk of her stage time, particularly during the haunting aria "The Smallest Thing," the presence of the First Lady in Mary's dream finds multiple moments to reify the piece's consideration of the mundane. "It's the details that count," the First Lady sings while grilling Mary about the location of her hat and gloves. During "The Smallest Thing," the First Lady also repeats the phrase "smile and wave and …" several times, eventually losing the word "smile" as she chants repeatedly "and wave …."[33] The First Lady expresses passionately that there is a mundanity in her own life, even if the version of the First Lady being presented is likely a machination of Mary's subconscious. When the tone of "The Smallest Thing" becomes darker, the First Lady predicts the assassination of her husband. She grabs Mary's arm and their two seats become the back seat of the presidential limousine.[34] As Mary is forced to experience the event through the eyes of the First Lady, she is confronted by the essence of the First Lady's pain as she sings of "The smallest thing" being her life.[35] This "haunting" of Mary's dream not only reinforces the idea of the mundane, it also performs the labor of expressing Mary's frustrations toward her employer. Throughout the initial section of the encounter, Mary takes the opportunity to finally lash out at the First Lady, exclaiming that she doesn't care about the location of her gloves and that she wants to see her family and experience vacations. When pressed by the First Lady, she also expresses her want to never hear or see the First Lady again.[36] While these are things Mary would never say in front of her employer, within the boundaries of her subconscious, she is free to speak plainly about her frustrations with her position and, more importantly, with Jackie herself. These considerations of the mundane, as exemplified through LaChiusa's historiography, position the idea of mundanity as a type of haunting presence.

The haunting in *Happy Pat* is far more literal. Pat is forced to confront a series of questions about her relationship to her husband and her role as First Lady throughout the one-act musical. Many of these questions are teased out by the insistent naggings of Hannah Milhous Nixon, who remains on the periphery of the proceedings both figuratively and literally in Kirsten Sanderson's staging at The Public Theatre.[37] Hannah stays in the downstage vomitories of the space, sometimes sitting in a rocking chair, and barks her criticisms of Pat and Dick from a distance. She chastises Pat for raising her daughters to be "vain and shallow" and insists that Pat call her "mother" instead of "Hannah."[38] Hannah's critiques are not just reserved for Pat but also extend to the absent Richard Nixon. "Richard was the greatest disappointment," Hannah chastises, even stating that he was more disappointing than her two sons who died young.[39] She argues with Pat, stating that Richard is "attracted to the wrong thing," an assertion that Pat refutes. Hannah then states that Richard "wants what he can't have," a statement that Pat admits is true.[40] Throughout the one-act, Hannah keeps insisting that Pat is weak, despite Pat's protestations to the contrary. "Are thee fit for Washington?" she asks Pat, who responds, "I used to think I was."[41] Hannah's criticisms have an effect on Pat, who constantly repeats the refrain "Oh, dear" throughout the act. Her haunting of Pat, as imagined by LaChiusa, is an attack on Pat, as a mother, as a wife, and as a First Lady, all of the identifiers that speak directly to her womanhood as situated in the scene. Despite Hannah's attacks, Pat uses Hannah's words to calm her daughters. "Remember what grandmother Hannah would say?" to which Tricia replies "When life gives thee lemons, make lemonade."[42] As events progress and the question of the wedding's purpose is debated, Hannah becomes even more combative, encouraging Pat to simply "surrender." "Thee failed to keep him from straying …" Hannah admonishes when Julie informs her mother of the leak of "The Pentagon Papers."[43] Hannah repeatedly demands Pat surrender and admit that she has failed:

Thee failed
In thine Marriage,
With thine husband
By thine choices
Thee failed.[44]

Eventually, Pat "defeats" Hannah by shouting, "No!" and making a decision regarding the wedding. "Surrender is the worst of all mortal sin," she states while calming her daughters.[45] Hannah concedes, deciding that she "will go visit Richard now / He will need my advice." Pat retorts, "I'll fight you." "Good," Hannah exclaims as she exits.[46] The entire haunting veers into the fantastical and paranormal, but, like "The Smallest Thing" sequence in *Over Texas*, it is rooted in both fact and character as they are documented in biographies and personal accounts. LaChiusa uses "historical imagination" in order to develop these types of specters, namely Jackie Kennedy and Hannah Nixon, in a way that bridges the imagined and the historical.

A similar notion helps to explain the ways in which both First Ladies are explored in each act. While the focus on Mary Gallagher in *Over Texas* helps to humanize a person not normally brought to mind when considering the assassination of JFK, the characterization of "The First Lady" is dehumanized, broadly speaking. Much of this may be based off the public's surface association of Jackie Kennedy, particularly given how the world came to know her. Prior to the election of JFK to the presidency, the most significant fact regarding Jackie Kennedy consumed by the public was the massive amount of money she spent on clothing, with inaccurate estimates at the time speculating that she spent around $30,000 a year; in fact, it turns out that she spent quite a bit more than that.[47] Eventually, Americans grew to love Jackie Kennedy, thanks in large part to a televised hosted tour of the White House, showcasing the many décor decisions she famously made in order to make the White House "equivalent to the great houses of Europe."[48] Taking these cues into consideration, LaChiusa plays on the assumptions by the public that Jackie Kennedy was base, self-absorbed, and elitist, by positioning her with only superficial concerns in the beginning of her stage time. Even as "The Smallest Thing" transitions into a tale of JFK's impending assassination, The First Lady is still concerned about the smallness of her life, which has been reduced to smiling and waving. The mundane really defines the First Lady, who has little agency in any of the proceedings, particularly given that she is presented as a dream.

By contrast, LaChiusa imagines Pat Nixon as a particularly complicated woman, confronted with varying interests and personal demons. While much of the act is spent watching Pat be tortured by the hovering ghost of her mother-in-law, it is, in the end, Pat's decisions that silence Hannah and get the wedding going. While LaChiusa plays on the public's assumptions of Jackie Kennedy in *Over Texas*, he actively refutes the assumptions made about Pat Nixon in *Happy Pat*. Thanks to her somewhat frozen facial features in the televised Presidential Debates of 1960, Pat Nixon had earned the nickname "Plastic Pat" from both the press and the public, emphasizing a misogynistic viewpoint on the nature of First Ladies and women in general.[49] LaChiusa challenges that assumption by painting Pat Nixon as a complex, fully fleshed-out characters as opposed to the spectral presence signified by Jackie Kennedy. Pat deals with major issues throughout *Happy Pat*. In addition to the issue of her daughter's wedding and deflecting Hannah's taunts, Pat Nixon is forced to deal with the fact that her husband confides information regarding "The Pentagon Papers" to his daughter Julie rather than telling her anything. This is in line with history; historians have commented that Richard Nixon rarely discussed any presidential issues with her.[50] The dramatization of this moment allows the audience to experience the tension Pat Nixon feels, particularly when she finds out that her daughter has been privy to this consequential information while she has not. LaChiusa uses historical imagination, then, by utilizing very different tactics in depicting each First Lady; while Jackie is confined by popular opinion of her as a First Lady and as a woman, Pat Nixon's narrative is built to refute popularly held assumptions regarding her character.

Flights and Sailings of Fantasy: *Where's Mamie?* and *Amy Carter's Fabulous Dream Adventure*

Despite the "hauntings" of *Over Texas* and *Happy Pat*, it is clear that both episodes are largely rooted in historical fact and are presented in a manner that brings to mind American Realism or, perhaps, even "magical realism." The same cannot be said for *Where's Mamie?* from *First Lady Suite* and *Amy Carter's Fabulous Dream Adventure* from *First Daughter Suite*. Both one-acts contain complete flights of fantasy, both literal and figurative. In *Where's Mamie?* Mamie Eisenhower utilizes car, train, boat, and plane as well as time travel to spy on Dwight Eisenhower and his mistress while also helping African American opera singer Marian Anderson aid the "Little Rock Nine." Conversely, *Amy Carter's Fabulous Dream Adventure* takes place in Amy Carter's dream in which she is sailing on the presidential yacht with her mother and current First Lady Rosalynn Carter as well as Betty and Susan Ford, the previous First Lady and First Daughter, respectively. LaChiusa's dramatization of these fantastical stories is rooted in history but they are clearly exercises of his historical imagination. When discussing the different elements of historical imagination, Collingwood confronts the idea of interpolation and its uses to the historian. Interpolation allows for the historian to fill in the gaps that are not produced by archival evidence with conjectures that can be assumed to be part of that historian's block of knowledge.[51] While it is unlikely that Collingwood was endorsing the interpolation of the fantastical into historical exploration, the essence of interpolation is a fascinating framework for analyzing LaChiusa's decision to root history and fantasy in the same dramatizations. While the integration of "The Little Rock Nine" looms over the events of Mamie Eisenhower's birthday, the

Iranian Hostage Crisis of 1980 troubles the mind of twelve-year-old Amy Carter. The machinations of these dramatizations are purely interpolated fiction and, in some cases, completely defy the assumptions of realism that are set up by each of their respective predecessors, namely *Over Texas* and *Happy Pat*, veering into plot devices that are, quite literally, magical. But the background of each fantasy is firmly rooted in character study, supported by historical fact, as well as political events that are having broad effects on both the characters and America as a whole. Working with this idea of interpolation, I explore both of these largely comedic titles as broad extensions of LaChiusa's historiographical project.

Where's Mamie? begins on Mamie Eisenhower's sixty-first birthday. The musical juxtaposes this moment with the integration of "The Little Rock Nine," nine African American students who were forcibly integrated into the all-white Little Rock Central High School that same year. Mamie is left alone on her birthday as her husband Ike is dealing with "a crisis in Little Rock …" leaving Mamie to her own machinations.[52] Mamie gets frustrated waiting for Ike and decides to turn her bed into the presidential limo, in which she decides to drive around Washington, D.C. Then, she decides to go to Little Rock, Arkansas, to try and get "those stupid bigots …" to settle down, this time transforming her bed into a train.[53] Upon arriving in Little Rock, she encounters her friend, African American opera singer Marian Anderson, who implores Mamie to intervene in the crisis in Little Rock. Mamie decides to kill two birds with one stone by sailing a ship back in time to 1944, when General Eisenhower was stationed in Algiers. This gives opportunity for Mamie to have a younger Eisenhower speak with Marian Anderson, which may have an impact on his future decision regarding integration of "The Little Rock Nine." Additionally, it gives Mamie a chance to catch Ike in the act with his mistress and driver. The two sail back in time to Algiers, which is under heavy attack, and manage to subdue and restrain Ike's mistress. Mamie, posing as the chauffeur, blows their cover and Ike realizes what Mamie has done. Mamie introduced Ike to Marian Anderson, who pleads with the future President to intervene in favor of "The Little Rock Nine" when he becomes President. Mamie and Ike reconcile and Mamie and Marian Anderson board a plane back to 1957, Washington, D.C., to begin deploying troops into Little Rock, Arkansas.

Taking place in 1980, the year in which Jimmy Carter and Ronald Reagan would vie for the presidency, *Amy Carter's Fabulous Dream Adventure* chronicles the dream of young Amy Carter. Her dream is set on the presidential yacht and, in addition to her mother and First Lady Rosalynn

Carter, she has also conjured up Betty Ford and her daughter Susan, whom Amy constantly refers to as "The coolest girl / Out of all the girls / Who have ever lived / In the White House."[54] While Amy appears to be the one in control of the progression of the dream, she is slowly manipulated by Susan Ford, who still hasn't gotten over her father's defeat to Jimmy Carter, into taking the presidential yacht to Iran in order to free the American hostages, thereby insuring her father a second term as President. Despite Rosalynn's pleas to stop Amy, she agrees to Susan's plan and the four women head off to Iran. Upon arriving, Susan and Betty Ford go out in disguises, while Amy waits at the yacht. There is heavy fire and Betty returns to the boat, soaked in blood, and dies. A "Revolutionary" enters, speaking lines such as "Hezbollah! Hummus hummus! Baklava! Shish kebob!"[55] Initially, Amy and her mother are afraid for their lives, but Amy recognizes Susan's camera around the Revolutionary's neck, and she confronts Susan, who admits to killing her mother, Betty. Susan then kills Rosalynn Carter and moves in to kill Amy, a task she says she must do before heading back to Washington, D.C., to kill Jimmy Carter so that her father and she can move back to the White House. Amy takes out her Barbie doll and attacks Susan. Death rays come out of Barbie's vagina.[56] Amy kills Susan, then realizes it's her dream, she has agency, and that she can revive all three of the women if she chooses. She does, reconciliations are made, and the foursome head off for a relaxing trip to Puerto Rico.

While LaChiusa is interpolating several ideas into the narrative in each one-act, all of the characterizations are based on various reports about the lives of the women in question. In terms of Mamie Eisenhower, he incorporates her love of the television show *I Love Lucy* that ran on CBS from 1951 to 1957.[57] Mamie was so enamored by the television program that she welcomed the cast to perform at the White House and welcomed Lucille Ball and Desi Arnaz to dine with her and the President after.[58] In fact, it was rumored that Mamie Eisenhower's distaste for Mary McCarthy, wife of the infamous Senator Joseph McCarthy, extended from Lucille Ball's being called to testify before the House Un-American Activities Committee. LaChiusa takes this cue to determine the "madcap" tonal quality of *Where's Mamie?* Other aspects of Mamie Eisenhower find their way into the one-act, sometimes without comment. During the number "My Husband Was an Army Man," Mamie repeats the phrase "Gave him a son" twice. The music, which is a peppy tune set to a militaristic march, suddenly takes on a darker tone. Though there is no direct reference to it in the musical, this likely stems from Mamie Eisenhower's biography. Mamie had two sons, but the first, J. Doud Dwight, died at age three of scarlet fever.[59] While the audience is never told this fact, the music does the work of shading the incantation "Gave him a son" with a menacing, dark tone. LaChiusa also comments on the Eisenhower's philosophy of the role of the First Lady. While it is true that Mamie Eisenhower was utilized by the Republican Party for recruitment of women, and while it is also true that Mamie proved herself to be an undeniable asset on the campaign trail, that was the end of her association with the administration. Edith Mayo, the former curator of "The First Ladies" exhibit at the Smithsonian Museum of American History, states that Mamie Eisenhower only entered the Oval Office four times over the course of Ike's two terms in office.[60] LaChiusa references this throughout the one-act, despite the fact that Mamie does become very involved by the end of the act. His first reference happens directly before the song "My Husband Was an Army Man." After Marian Anderson pleads with Mamie to intervene on behalf of "The Little Rock Nine," Mamie states clearly, "I don't get involved, publicly or otherwise."[61] While she asserts this fact confidently, the subsequent song reveals that staying in the background has taken a toll on Mamie. Near the end of the song, Mamie makes a list of all of the things that have come first in her marriage to Ike:

The army came first, the war came first,
The country came first, the people came first,
Everybody and everything else came first …[62]

This aspect of Mamie may be more rooted in historical imagination, however. All textual evidence suggests that Mamie was comfortable with her role as First Lady and nothing more. Mamie once commented that a wife never went near her husband's command post, suggesting that her time as an Army wife prepared her well for her potentially limited role in the White House. This, of course, points to another interpolation by LaChiusa, given that Mamie does indeed go near her husband's command post when she time travels back to Algiers. Yet, even these seeming inconsistencies point to the historical roots of LaChiusa's dramaturgy, placing the role of historical imagination at the forefront.

While *Amy Carter's Fabulous Dream Adventure* is more centered on two First Daughters, history also operates as a foreground to the dramatizations of Betty Ford and Rosalynn Carter. Betty Ford, in particular, has been well documented, particularly because of the First Lady's willingness to discuss topics that were considered taboo. For instance, Betty Ford was an outspoken advocate of abortion rights, breaking away from the views of both her husband and his party. More importantly to an analysis of *Amy Carter's Fabulous Dream Adventure*, Betty also spoke candidly in a *60 minutes* interview about her daughter Susan, admitting that she had smoked marijuana and that the First Lady didn't care whether Susan engaged in premarital sex. Both of these points are brought up by Amy Carter in the song "Susan Ford," in which Amy lists the many reasons she admires Susan.[63] LaChiusa also incorporates Betty Ford's alcoholism by having her drink several "Billy Beers" throughout the course of the show, a fact that Rosalynn Carter admonishes.[64] Betty Ford's background as a dancer is also on display in the one-act, which opens on Betty dancing about by herself and during Susan's first number, "Mother Likes to Dance."[65] LaChiusa takes similar cues from biographies of Rosalynn Carter. The Carters were and are devout Baptists and many saw the Carter presidency as a move toward aligning the White House with conservative Christian values, despite the Carters' work in various areas of human rights.[66] LaChiusa weaves this idea throughout the one-act, particularly when Betty is drinking and when Amy is bringing up the fact that Betty Ford doesn't care if Susan smokes pot or has sex before marriage.[67] There is also reference in the musical to Rosalynn Carter's work on mental health, given her controversial appointment as chair of the Mental Health Commission.[68] Early in the musical, Betty Ford asks Rosalynn Carter if Susan should see a therapist to deal with her anger about having to leave the White House. "You're the mental health first lady. That's why I ask," she states.[69] While history and biography are the roots of these one-acts, and while both deal with serious issues surrounding the circumstances dramatized, the heart of each of these acts lies in the interpolation of fantastical elements into historical narrative, largely in the form of absurdist comedy.

As is apparent from the brief synopses above, both *Where's Mamie?* and *Amy Carter's Fabulous Dream Adventure* contain elements of absurd comedy. As mentioned above, *Where's Mamie?* brings to mind the style of the hit television show *I Love Lucy*. While this gives the musical one-act a tonal identity, several of the elements of *Where's Mamie?* are completely absurd and impossible, particularly Mamie's ability to time travel with Marian Anderson, thereby violating the more realism-based elements of the television show *I Love Lucy*. Similarly, Mamie's meeting with Marian Anderson by chance on a street in Little Rock, Arkansas, is also completely unmotivated and unjustified, placing the encounter firmly in the school of absurdist comedy. Halfway through *Where's Mamie?* there is a number entitled "In Algiers," which Mamie uses to calm Marian Anderson. The song is positioned as a popular song known to both women. In the stage directions, LaChiusa mentions that the song is an "old favorite" of Mamie's, such as "Bali Ha'i" from *South Pacific*… and mentions "perhaps the number is embellished with choreography à la 'Happy Talk' from the same musical."[70] This association with *South Pacific*, and the suggestion for choreography that mirrors the famous Josh Logan staging of "Happy Talk," is juxtaposed by the sounds of distant explosions around the two women, further painting the scenario with an absurd color.[71] While there is no analog for *Amy Carter's Fabulous Dream Adventure*, there are a number of absurd elements. Throughout the one-act, Amy Carter has complete control over her mother's actions. At one point, Amy demands that Rosalynn eat her book and she does so.[72] Later, she similarly demands that her mother "Put [her] book on [her] head and quack like a duck."[73] Again, Rosalynn obliges. Additionally, Susan's portrayal of the "Revolutionary," complete with offensive Middle Eastern gibberish, presents an absurd element to an act that already seems more tonally like children's play than historical re-enactment. And, of course, Amy's Barbie, whose vagina emits cosmic death rays, is both absurd and reminiscent of children's play. Although Susan kills both First Ladies over the course of the musical's final third, none of it is meant to be taken seriously, evidenced by how quickly and easily each of the women is resurrected by Amy Carter.

Despite the absurdity of each act when analyzed separately, both of these acts display women with varying degrees of agency. While Mamie begins her story decrying how simple and small her life is, it is her decisions to travel to Little Rock, then to Algiers in 1944, that motivates the short musical's narrative. As such, she is in sharp contrast to the depiction of Jackie Kennedy in *Over Texas*. Further, Mamie makes the decision to take Marian Anderson to see Ike in the past, but only because it also gives her an opportunity to confront her husband in the midst of his affair: "You want to change some things, don't you? Well so do I!" Mamie quips to Marian.[74] Mamie makes a comment early in the musical that she knows her place and that she is "No Eleanor Roosevelt," yet she moves forward in *Where's Mamie?* with absolute agency and authority, shaping all of the events of the one-act musical, whereas Jackie Kennedy is presented almost symbolically in *Over Texas*.[75] Conversely, the First Ladies in *Amy Carter's Fabulous Dream Adventure* are constantly controlled by their children. The First Daughters do literally run the show, Amy with her powers of manipulation imbued to her by the dream and Susan with her subtle commandeering of that power. Even after Rosalynn sings the heartwarming "Daughters Of," a wonderful song that adheres to A-A-B-A form in which Rosalynn admits that the life of a daughter of a President isn't necessarily fair and that a "normal" life away from the White House might be nice, Amy counters by demanding that she doesn't want to go back to "boring Georgia!"[76] Also, one of Amy's major reasons for admiring Susan so much is her independence and Betty's permissiveness with her daughter.

> Your mom doesn't care if you smoke pot.
> That's cool.
> Your mom doesn't care if you have sex
> Before you're married.
> That's cool
> Your mom doesn't care
> If you draw nipples on your Barbie …
> Did you draw nipples on your Barbie?[77]

Perhaps even more than Pat Nixon in *Happy Pat*, these women are architects of their own worlds, even if those worlds exist in the confines of a dream.

The term "interpolation" gives a useful framework for considering LaChiusa's two fantasy-based entries into his pair of *Suites*. By using historical evidence as a framework, LaChiusa then utilizes historical imagination in order to effectively interpolate episodes that are non-realism based and that open up fascinating new possibilities for the musical dramatization of historical figures. In *Where's Mamie?* the lack of regard for linearity provides a possibility to counter the claims that Mamie was content in the established limits of her role as both a woman and as a First Lady. Additionally, rooting *Amy Carter's Fabulous Dream Adventure* in the biographies of two First Ladies allows for the employment of historical imagination in crafting a dream adventure that includes a botched rescue attempt. LaChiusa interpolates fantastical elements into each one-act, resulting in a type of absurdist comedy approach that is uncommon in the musical theatre canon. The irony in this idea is that the absurdist tone allows for a more human consideration of women who are also historical figures.

"Screw You and Your Nancy Reagan Red!" Interpersonal Traumas in *Patti by the Pool*

Although Collingwood doesn't use the term "interrogation" itself, he does refer to the "web of imaginative construction," which forces the historian to interrogate the meanings and insinuations behind statements in the historical record while also vetting the source itself.[78] Lemisko uses the term "interrogation" to describe the process by which the historian seriously questions the sources of information and their implied meaning, very much in the style of a lawyer.[79] The idea of interrogating a source becomes particularly useful when exploring the one-act musical *Patti by the Pool*, the third one-act in *First Daughter Suite*, particularly given that much of the musical's playing time is occupied with Patti Davis's interrogation of her mother, Nancy Reagan. In order to create *Patti by the Pool*, LaChiusa draws heavily on two books. The first, *Home Front* written by Patti Davis with Maureen Strange Foster, is billed as a "novel" but features thinly veiled references to Patti's mother and father. The second, an unadulterated autobiography entitled *The Way I See It*, eschews the cover of the novel format and directly implicates the President and First Lady with neglect and child abuse.[80]

LaChiusa interrogates these sources in order to build the antagonistic relationship between Patti and Nancy in *Patti by the Pool*. The musical is set at the pool of Betsy Bloomingdale, a close friend of the President and First Lady. The First Lady has come for a visit and has invited her daughter to spend the afternoon with her poolside. Structurally, much of *Patti by the Pool* takes the form of a musicalized monologue, interspersed with patches of dialogue between Patti and Nancy or Nancy and Anita, Nancy Reagan's Paraguayan personal maid. For the first twenty-two minutes of the musical's roughly twenty-eight-minute playing time, only Patti sings in an extended, nonstrophic musical sequence that calls on a variety of styles and melodic passages, emphasizing the mercurial turmoil that personifies her relationship with her mother. Patti grills her mother on the reason she was invited to Betsy's pool. Nancy assures her that she just wants to see her daughter and it has nothing to do with Patti's recently published novel or its harsh depictions of her and her husband. Throughout the first sequence, a loud, single hammer sound repeatedly emanates from the orchestra every time Patti insults her mother:

How much did you pay for that bathing suit?
(Hammer sound)
Some designer give it to you?
(Hammer sound)
I think you're a little too old for it, frankly.
Me, I'm just not into

Fashion shit
(Hammer sound)
Your kind of thing
It isn't real.
(Hammer sound).[81]

Patti continues to try and antagonize her mother, who simply sits expressionless, her eyes shielded by a large pair of sunglasses. Throughout the course of the one-act, Anita comes in to see to various things for Nancy, from serving Orange Blossoms to fielding phone calls. Throughout, Patti continually asks for a Jack and Coke, a request Anita ignores until later in the act. Patti references several sensitive subjects throughout the musical, including the publication of her book, Anita's indictment for gun-trafficking, as well as the Iran-Contra crisis. Nancy deflects most of these issues by denying them with phrases like "I didn't read it," "She wasn't involved," and "He didn't know anything."[82] While most of the scene is incredibly antagonistic, there are brief moments of release from the tension, most notably when Nancy invites Patti to the ranch for Thanksgiving, an event that she was not previously welcome to attend, presumably in response to the publication of her novel. When Patti brings up the Iran-Contra situation again, Nancy tries to shut down the conversation with "He didn't know anything. That's all you have to say." It becomes clear that the real reason for the meeting was for Nancy to convince Patti to keep quiet. Anita returns and Nancy asks her to finally bring Patti her Jack and Coke. She does so and, after drinking it, Patti "begins to have grotesque convulsions" and "goes suddenly unconscious."[83] Anita reveals that she spiked the drink with "Paraguay nightshade" and that she will be unconscious for three days while Nancy can get ahead of the story.[84] The act ends with Anita singing a lovely, folkish tune about a Mama bird who tries to make her daughter happy, but realizes in the end that she never had what her daughter needed to begin with.

Interrogation is an apt means of exploring *Patti by the Pool* given that the one-act musical is largely an interrogation of Nancy by her daughter, Patti. She begins the interrogation by asking about her mother's clothes and reliance on fashion, then moves into asking her mother to play "Twenty Questions" in which her first question is, "Is it true that before you became the Queen of Washington you were the Blowjob Queen of Hollywood?"[85] Patti continues the interrogation throughout the musical by asking about

Nancy's "Foster Grandparents" program as well as her father's first wife, Jane Wyman, before finally asking, "This Iran-Contra crap. What's Daddy going to do?" the question that brings about the musical's climax.[86] Patti is almost taking a cue from Lemisko's description of the historian-as-lawyer, interrogating her mother, and trying to break her steely resolve with allegations of abuse, neglect, and threats to start sleeping with "a big hunky black man."[87] While the majority of her questions are aimed at irritating her mother, many questions are sincere, despite their flippant delivery. Patti legitimately wants to confront her past with her mother, particularly in terms of physical abuse. Patti makes repeated references to physical abuse throughout the one-act. The first mention of the alleged abuse comes early in the act when Patti is confronting her mother about keeping Anita on despite her indictment in gun-trafficking: "I always thought you had bigger *cojones* than my father. At least you knew how to slap me around as a kid and make it mean something."[88] She alludes to the abuse a short time later, when making fun of Nancy Reagan's "Foster Grandparents" program, she sings:

> Why not adopt some little kid
> Who's starving
> Or beat up
> By her parents.
> Who hate her?[89]

The insinuations return close to the end of the act, shortly before Patti begins convulsing from the ingredients in her Jack and Coke. In her final sung section, many of the lines are accentuated with the word "Slap!" at the end of each phrase. The song eventually devolves into repetitions of the word "Slap!" paired with "No Mommy."[90] Patti's abuse is at the forefront of her mind during the entire confrontation, regardless of the other issues that are present. The character herself takes on the role of Collingwood's interrogator because she wants answers about her parents' treatment of her, past and present.

Of course, all of Patti's questions are coming from LaChiusa's interrogation(s) of Patti's writing, particularly the aforementioned *Home Front* and *The Way I See It*. Both books contain allegations of abuse by Patti Davis. LaChiusa's invocation of the abuse theme could be said to be a direct extension of his interrogation as to the validity of such claims. The results are somewhat ambiguous. While Patti's claims are presented largely without comment, from LaChiusa or from the character of Nancy, the musical's final number, "Anita's Song," weaves a tale of a mother bird whose baby bird keeps changing her mind about what she needs. In the end, Anita sings:

A mama wants her children
To be happy.
Happy for as long as they may live.
But she cannot always give them
All they want.
And what they really want
She may not know how to give.[91]

The song creates a fascinating juxtaposition as it is being sung while Nancy Reagan looks over the unconscious body of her daughter sprawled out on a lounge chair. While the majority of the song seems to side with the mother bird, the song's final section almost seems to implicate the mother bird in the neglect of her child, suggesting an acceptance of the regrets regarding how the mother bird has behaved as a parent. LaChiusa's inclusion of this song at the end of the piece would seem to suggest that his interrogations have arrived at an ambiguous conclusion regarding the validity of Patti's claims of abuse. This is exacerbated by Nancy's refusal to respond to the various insinuations throughout the one-act musical. While it seems clear that the audience is supposed to find their surrogate in the character of Patti, it is unclear whether they are supposed to side with her arguments completely, without question. Instead, LaChiusa-as-interrogator asks the audience to also participate in the process of interrogation and judge the various arguments presented by Patti through their own perspectives and biases. As such, the audience is placed in the same position as LaChiusa in terms of evaluating Patti's claims without the benefit of Nancy's perspective on them, leading to a type of ambiguity in the audience's relationship to the musical, albeit an intriguing ambiguity.

LaChiusa's interrogation is not limited to the character of Patti. Despite her largely reticent presentation in *Patti by the Pool*, LaChiusa is just as interested in evaluating the behaviors of Nancy Reagan. Although the bulk of the musical's text and music belongs to Patti, Nancy retains the power entirely throughout the one-act's running time. This is evidenced in several ways, chief among them being her unchanging facial expression throughout Patti's interrogations. Most of Nancy's lines are delivered during Anita's appearances. Almost all of these lines involve giving orders to Anita or commenting on the spotless appearance of Betsy's pool. Nancy is keeping all of the spokes in the wheel turning, despite the healthy dose of criticism she is receiving from her daughter. Additionally, a scene late in the musical depicts Nancy on the phone with Secretary of State James Baker. Over the course of the phone call, she demands that Baker dismiss two key members of the Reagan administration, declaring, "No, there's no need to talk to Ronnie about this …"[92] More importantly, she takes the phone call right after Patti's realization that she has been invited to the pool and to Thanksgiving to keep her mouth shut. LaChiusa's dramatization of these aspects of Nancy's character seems to extend from his interrogation of Nancy's role within her family life and as well as within the Reagan administration. Even while attempting to relax by the pool, she is able to give orders to the maid, dismiss members of the administration, and comment on the appearance of the Bloomingdale home, all while deflecting the interrogatives and insults being hurled at her by her daughter.

This extension of the interrogation of Nancy also influences the structuring of the musical. As previously stated, the majority of the musical's sung passages are reserved for Patti. In fact, Nancy only sings one phrase in the entire one-act. After Patti is rendered unconscious, Nancy drones on about the fabulous parties Betsy Bloomingdale has hosted at her home. She then sings the simple phrase "Oh, my friends!" before musing on the possibilities of moving near the Bloomingdale's after Reagan's second term is finished. This positioning of Patti as the primary musical character almost associates a desperation in terms of music, calling to mind McMillan's differentiation between "book time" and "lyric time" discussed in detail in Chapter 1.[93] Because Nancy exists almost entirely in "book time" while most of Patti's comments are delivered in "lyric time," the association of Patti's fanciful, mercurial nature is made even more evident, particularly given the wide array of various themes and influences utilized in the score to the one-act. By contrast, Nancy's orientation in "book time" paints her as steadier and more secure. Because most of her lines are short, excepting her exchanges with Anita, Nancy is painted as concise, controlled, and in-control. LaChiusa uses her position in "book time" in order to keep Nancy seemingly composed and, as a result, thoroughly in charge of all of the proceedings in the piece.

LaChiusa's interrogation of the sources available also leads him to interesting observations regarding the nature of the relationship between Nancy and Patti. Most of the one-act is filled with tension, extending from Patti's interrogation of her mother. However, this pervading tension does alternate with moments of vulnerability in which Patti and, seemingly, Nancy both let their guards down. Despite her being disinvited from Thanksgiving, Nancy broaches the possibility of Patti coming to the ranch for the holiday. "You really want me to come for Thanksgiving?" Patti asks. "You always make him smile," Nancy responds.[94] This dropping of the "wall" between Nancy and Patti is brief, but shows a moment of tenderness, regardless of Nancy's actual motivation in extending the invitation. The wall returns, however, when Patti interprets a comment from Nancy as accusatory, prompting Nancy to encourage Patti to "let go of the past."[95] A second moment happens near the end, when it seems that Patti has agreed to come for Thanksgiving. Nancy is elated that Patti has accepted the invitation, exclaiming, "Thanksgiving at the ranch! All of us together again. Like old times. Your father will be so happy. He needs a break from Washington. He needs to be with people who love him. Us girls."[96] Patti allows herself to be caught up in the moment, even cracking a joke with her mother at the expense of her younger brother, Ron Jr. Again, the moment is brief, and a question from Patti regarding the Iran-Contra scandal sends things spiraling out of control again. LaChiusa's interrogation of his sources lends itself to an exploration of the possibility of intimacy between Nancy and Patti. Patti's craving for a loving relationship with her mother comes through in these brief moments, despite her largely antagonistic approach throughout the majority of the musical. While LaChiusa's positioning of Nancy Reagan leaves her motivations purposely obscured, there is a certain amount of warmth coming from Nancy's invitation for Patti to join her family for the holiday. LaChiusa's choice to feature these moments provides the one-act with an empathy despite its largely interrogative nature. While it is unclear at the end of the act whether Nancy and Patti will find common ground, LaChiusa's interrogation seems to reveal the impulse toward reconciliation lies in both women.

In his employment of what Lemisko calls "interrogation," LaChiusa manages to dramatize a series of conclusions and observations, despite the fact that many of these conclusions are ambiguous. His choice to lean toward ambiguity, in essence a conclusion with no conclusion, speaks to his prerogative as artist in sharing the results of his interrogation. Interestingly, LaChiusa actually spells out his prerogative to approach history in this manner within the text of the one-act. In a sequence in which Patti is defending her book, she comments on her right to use her life as inspiration: "Yeah, there might be similarities because that's a writer's <u>prerogative:</u> to take her life's experiences, the people she knows, her parents, things like that, and <u>fictionalize</u> them. I only <u>fictionalized</u>," she exclaims.[97] This statement applies to Patti's book *Home Front* but could also apply to LaChiusa, who has determined what elements of the narrative are apt for dramatization, extending from his interrogation of the sources involved. LaChiusa exercises his prerogative by determining the tone, manner, and dramaturgy of how his historical characters are presented on the stage.

LaChiusa and the Dramatist-Historian's Prerogative

The concept of "prerogative" goes far in both exploring LaChiusa's process as a "dramatist-historian" and explaining how the idea of historical imagination aids in that explanation. It is obvious to state that it is within the artist's prerogative to write what they want and adapt in the way they see fit but understanding possible justifications for that employment of prerogative helps make the process more legible. This prerogative is far-reaching, often violating the perceived continuity of both *First Lady Suite* and *First Daughter Suite*. The exclusion of the Clinton administration and First Lady and future Senator, Secretary of State, and presidential candidate Hillary Clinton is one such example. The pieces together consistently cover all of the First Ladies in some manner, reaching back to Eleanor Roosevelt and moving forward to Laura Bush, making LaChiusa's decision to skip Clinton more noticeable. LaChiusa has said that he didn't want to dramatize Hillary Clinton because her "story isn't over yet," a particularly apt statement given that Hillary Clinton's second bid for the White House would come after the opening of *First Daughter Suite*.[98] LaChiusa makes a similar assertion regarding the possibility of dramatizing Michelle Obama.[99] While this exclusion jeopardizes the continuous narrative implied by these twin investigations of First Families, it also speaks to the prerogative of LaChiusa himself, who has determined that he should ignore a narrative because the results of its dramatical potential have not yet played out. Additionally, the concept of the writer's prerogative shows up repeatedly across the two *Suites*, in terms of how to frame the First Ladies, which auxiliary characters should be emphasized, and what moments generated the most artistic potential for dramatization, decisions that could be considered a bit of a gamble when dealing with beloved figures, such as Nancy Reagan, whose story is certainly darker than what is on the surface. LaChiusa has commented particularly on his thought process in dramatizing a slice of the Reagan era: "Where did that ambivalence and hostility come from, when the picture the Reagan family presented was of a perfect American family? How can I find compassion for these people?"[100]

The gamble did pay off. Both the *Suites* garnered LaChiusa some of the strongest reviews of his career. Ben Brantley of *The New York Times* designated the production of *First Daughter Suite* a "NY Times Critic's Pick," stating:

> But Mr. LaChiusa, also being a gifted composer with a deep purple streak, has set these speculations [of First Ladies] to music and let melody and imagination lead him into altitudes where caged songbirds can soar. Unaccustomed to the freedom of such heights, Mr. LaChiusa's characters often become intoxicated and dizzy. It is a vertigo likely to be shared by this production's audience.[101]

Historical imagination, considered broadly, provides a useful framework for understanding several musicals dealing with historical narratives that are emblematic of "The New Musical Drama" movement. The musical *Floyd Collins*, with score and lyrics by Adam Guettel and book and additional lyrics by Tina Landau and produced off-Broadway at Playwrights Horizons in 1996, dramatizes the plight of Floyd Collins, a man trapped inside a cave in Kentucky during the winter of 1925. While the musical is fairly faithful in terms of the historical record regarding Collins plight and subsequent death, the text of the show does place an emphasis on the re-enactment of the media circus that erupted around the entrance to the cave as rescue attempts continued to fail. Additionally, Guettel and Landau interpolate a somewhat fantastical element into the show's final moments, in which Floyd confronts God about what death is like before finally succumbing to it. The 1998 musical *Parade*, with music and lyrics by Jason Robert Brown and a book by Alfred Uhry, took similar cues from the idea of historical imagination, particularly in terms of the explosion of activity that occurred in Atlanta surrounding the trial of Leo Frank, a Jewish man from Brooklyn falsely accused of the murder of a young girl in the pencil factory where he is foreman. The musical leans heavily on the historical record, but definitely takes creative liberties, particularly in humanizing the relationship between Frank and his wife, Lucille, charting their journey from married strangers to partners. More recently, the megahit *Hamilton* presents a very faithful interrogation of Ron Chernow's biography of the nation's first Secretary of Treasury while interpolating ideas of a racialized utopia into the musical's casting concept while also adding the anachronistic sounds of hip-hop and R&B to the musical's re-enactment of the life of Alexander Hamilton.

LaChiusa's engagement with history also extends into his other long-form works, such as the previously discussed *Marie Christine* and *The Wild Party*, discussed in Chapter 5. In *Marie Christine*, LaChiusa engages with the history of Creole culture while also exploring the historical landscapes of both New Orleans and Chicago. In *The Wild Party*, LaChiusa and co-book writer George C. Wolfe look at the history of vaudeville while also directly engaging in 1920s cultural, social, and racial history. To say that historical imagination is a useful rubric for understanding the entirety of LaChiusa's canon is overstatement, but his engagement with ideas rooted in the tradition of historical imagination is rich, ubiquitous, and varied.

CHAPTER 3
"HEARTBREAK COUNTRY": FINDING THE "AMERICAN DREAM" IN *GIANT*

Much of what is written about Michael John LaChiusa's work positions his oeuvre as completely forward focused. Indeed, much of what LaChiusa is doing attempts to challenge long-held conceptions about what makes a musical work, particularly in his choice of material to adapt. But there are several factors that suggest that LaChiusa's work looks to the past as much as it looks ahead to the future of the form. To begin with, part of LaChiusa's primary training in musical theatre writing comes from three years spent at the historic BMI Lehman Engel Musical Theatre Workshop in New York City, where LaChiusa was taught by Maury Yeston, Richard Enquist, and Lehman Engel himself in his final year teaching for the program before he passed away.[1] Much of what Engel taught has been passed down in his book *Words with Music; Creating the Broadway Musical Libretto* and his other writings, all of which position Engel as a bit of a traditionalist in his take on what makes the Broadway musical work. And, while LaChiusa often favors more free-form song structures in his work, echoing his admiration of modernists such as John Adams, Ned Rorem, and Phillip Glass, he is just as much a student of the great masters of song forms, such as the Gershwins', Richard Rodgers and Oscar Hammerstein II, and, of course, Stephen Sondheim.[2]

While much of this book is concerned with LaChiusa's innovations and interventions into the form of musical theatre, it is also fitting to explore the ways in which his works participate in conversations with the forms and titles that came before. Looking at titles that incorporate themes reminiscent of the pursuit of the "American Dream" into the fabric of their construction, it becomes more evident that LaChiusa's work is participating in a long-form conversation about the nature of American culture and how it can be adapted and musicalized. In particular, I devote most of this chapter to investigating LaChiusa's work on the musical *Giant*, an adaptation of Edna Ferber's epic novel which spans significant time periods and investigates different aspects of the "American Dream" within the context of its score and libretto. This title offers a myriad of opportunities for exploration in terms of their engagement with the "American Dream." This is familiar terrain for the American musical, as highlighted by Howard Kissel in his updated and revised version of Lehman Engel's text in *Words with Music*, highlighted above.[3] In fact, the musical *Show Boat*, a musical rife with considerations of the "American Dream" is that considered by many to be the inception point for the "serious musical," was also an adaptation of an Edna Ferber novel. *Giant* interacts and engages with themes relating to the pursuit of the "American Dream" in ways that situate the musical into a lineage of other musicals that trade in the same tropes.

Before proceeding, it would be helpful to define and delimit the term "American Dream." Definitions and histories of the term are boundless, but it is well summarized in the work of scholar Jennifer Hochshield as a set of "tenets about achieving success."[4] To support her definition, she quotes President Bill Clinton in saying that "if you work hard and play by the rules you should be given a chance to go as far as your God-given ability will take you."[5] While Hochshield's discussion is useful in delimiting the term, it is also helpful to understand the plural nature of the phrase. Scholar Michael Schudson, in his discussion of Jim Cullen's *American Dream: A Short History of an Idea that Shaped a Nation*, posits that, while the term "American Dream" is consistently referred to in the singular, it is more commonly thought of in the plural.[6] This opens up the defining terms of the "American Dream" while also maintaining some adherence to Hochshield's summation of the dream as a series of tenets applied to achieving success in the American idiom. For the purposes of this chapter, I utilize Hochshield's definition while also allowing for a series of interpretations of that definition, particularly in terms of what measures are being used to define success. For the characters in LaChiusa's *Giant*, success is sometimes monetary, sometimes defined in terms of fame, but is often defined in terms of propagating the next generation and ensuring a sense of commitment to ideas surviving generational evolution.

Schudson also notes that much of what ties up the "American Dream" is a reference to the Declaration of Independence, in particular the phrase "life, liberty, and the pursuit of happiness."[7] Because the word "happiness" can have as many manifestations as there are people in the world, this allows for a broad consideration of what makes the "American Dream" or, more to the point, "American Dreams" so varied. In *Giant*, there are a number of dreams, including the dream of establishing an American family, the passing down of legacy from one generation to the next, and the dream of progress which is presented in a myriad of ways. All these dreams are pursued with a variety of successes and failures. With that in mind, it would be appropriate to say that it is the *pursuit* of the "American Dream" in musical theatre that ties *Giant* to other titles employing explorations of Americana throughout the history of the form.

In this chapter, I bring the work of LaChiusa into conversation with some iconic musicals throughout the history of musical theatre, primarily reaching back to Kern and Hammerstein's *Show Boat*, as well as more recent titles such as Roger Miller's *Big River* and Ahrens, Flaherty, and McNally's *Ragtime*. In discussing these titles, I argue that LaChiusa's work in general, and *Giant* in particular, interacts with musicals featuring depictions of pursuits of the "American Dream." In the first section of the chapter, I will look at the production history of *Giant* and explore its plot in detail. Next, I will discuss the themes that resonate from *Show Boat* to *Giant*, placing special emphasis on the depictions of the "American Dream." Finally, I look briefly at connections between some of LaChiusa's other works, such as the musical *Queen of the Mist*, and the "pursuit of happiness" that fuels the American obsession with the "American Dream."

Before proceeding, it is important to distinguish *Giant* from most of the other titles discussed in this book. While LaChiusa is responsible for all written elements of most of his shows, and most of the shows discussed here, *Giant* is an exception as he collaborated with book writer Sybille Pearson, LaChiusa's colleague in the Graduate Musical Theatre Writing Program at NYU. Since this is a rare case of LaChiusa only being responsible for the lyrics and score, it may seem unfair or disingenuous to include *Giant* in a study that has relied on LaChiusa as the primary dramatist composing and writing his works. In this case, I rely on Rebecca Applin Warner's book *The Musical Theatre Composer as Dramatist* to justify looking at LaChiusa's contributions to *Giant* from a dramaturgical standpoint. Warner discusses the need for all elements to come together, primarily "music" and "drama," to construct what she calls a "musico-dramatic work," and while the major thrust of her book is concerned with finding language that the creative team can employ to discuss dramaturgical elements of the score without a thorough background in musicology, her emphasis on the composer as a contributor to the dramaturgical elements of the show is useful in exploring the nature of the relationship between the book writer and the composer/lyricist.[8] While my emphasis here will be on the work of the score and lyrics, there may be times when it is difficult to separate out which contributions are the book writer's and which contributions are solely in the realm of the work of the lyricist and composer, particularly given that *Giant* is an adaptation of a novel. Therefore, I will be dealing with *Giant* in much the same manner I have discussed other works included in this study, like *The Wild Party*, which had a book written by both LaChiusa and George C. Wolfe.

Giant in Perspective

The musical *Giant* was first staged in 2009 at the Signature Theatre in Arlington, Virginia. In its initial form, the musical was divided into three acts with two intermissions, with a running time of nearly four and a half hours.[9] The production was directed by Jonathan Butterell and featured Betsy Morgan and Lewis Cleale in the cast. A 2011 reading occurred in New York City, this time with Michael Greif replacing Butterell as the director. Both the Dallas Theatre Center and the Public Theatre would present the musical in a co-production in 2012, with the piece premiering in January in Dallas and in October in New York City at the Public Theatre. For the Dallas production, the show was heavily edited and structured into two acts with one intermission. This production would begin performances in New York City at the Public Theatre on October 26th, 2012, with many of the same cast members from the Dallas production. For the production at the Public, Brian D'Arcy James would take over the role of Bick from Aaron Lazar, and Michelle Pawk, who had appeared in the Signature production, took on the role of Luz from Dee Hoty.

The musical spans nearly thirty years and begins in a flash-forward to the 1950s. While Polo, a vaquero, begins the play singing the haunting "Aurelia Dolores" and playing a guitar, we meet Bick and his wife Leslie in a Southwest Texas desert. The tension between the two is apparent as Leslie remarks, "Twenty-seven years and all I know about you is what you need: Your land. Your ranch. Besides being your wife, I don't know what I am to you."[10] The scene shifts back to 1925, and Bick is waiting for his new bride at a BBQ to celebrate their arrival since their marriage. "Aurelia Dolores" explodes into a full ensemble number as we meet a younger Bick. He is joking with the men about waiting on his wife as he sings the Aaron Copland-inspired "Did Spring Come to Texas?" Time flashes back again, this time to Leslie and Bick's first meeting several weeks before in Virginia, where Bick is negotiating the purchase of a horse from Leslie's father. Leslie contemplates Texas and her goals in life in the soaring "Your Texas." Shortly after, Bick calls his sister Luz to inform her that he is going to marry Leslie. Luz is taken aback; she had always thought that Bick would marry Vashti Hake so that their neighboring ranches would become one, but coldly moves ahead with work as she has "No Time for Surprises."

Bick brings Leslie home to Reata, the family ranch, where she is greeted coolly by Luz. Jett, one of Luz's hired hands and a resident on a patch of land at Reata, comes to the house, where Bick reprimands him for not meeting them at the train station. Leslie notices Jett, who lurks in the shadows and notes that Leslie is "Private Property."[11] The next morning, Luz and Leslie have another tense interaction, leading to Leslie going out on the ranch for a walk. She walks far to the outskirts of Reata ranch where she encounters some of the Mexican population of the ranch living in hovels. She becomes overwhelmed in the Texas heat and is rescued by Jett, who drives her back to the ranch house. Leslie is late for the BBQ being given to welcome her and Luz is angry and impatient. Leslie insists on changing before leaving, and Adarene and Heidi, two of the Reata ladies, accompany Leslie up to her room. Vashti Hake is also present and says she will join them in a bit, then sings the country tinged "He Wanted a Girl," in which she expresses her feelings for Bick and flashes back to a playful memory.[12] The ladies re-enter the parlor and Vashti introduces herself to Leslie. During the exchange, we find out that Luz was once engaged to Vashti's father, but the engagement was broken off when her father refused to move their residence to Reata. Luz bursts in the room and declares that, while the others are taking cars to the BBQ, she will ride a horse.

Leslie arrives at the BBQ and meets all the guests. She meets Polo, about whom Bick declares, "Polo's practically part of the family, when he was a boy, he used to sleep outside my father's door."[13] Leslie also meets Angel, whose wife and child she met on the outskirts of Reata. Bick is furious that Leslie went for a walk into town, and while the guests begin to eat, he ushers Leslie up the water tower to have a conversation with her. Leslie fights with Bick about the conditions she witnessed to which Bick responds that "There isn't a ranch in the whole Southwest looks after their Mexicans better than we do."[14] The passion of the fight gives way to their passion for each other as Bick admits that he does have another love, namely the land, in the song "Heartbreak Country." Leslie agrees to try to "learn to love this land."[15] They are interrupted by Jett, who informs them that Luz fell off the racehorse she rode and won't open her eyes. Then Lupe, the servant, sings "Ruega Por Nostoros" as Bick carries Luz's dead body off. The death of Luz puts a strain on Leslie and Bick's already fragile relationship. Tensions are eased with the arrival of Bick's Uncle Bawley, who encourages Bick to "Look Ahead" while the ghosts of Reata, including Luz, encourage him to "Look Back."

The "future" materializes before Leslie and Bick's eyes as the action moves to 1941, the year that Bick is declared "Cattlemen of the Year." They are at a Dallas hotel, and we soon meet Leslie and Bick's children, Lil Luz and Jordy Jr. This scene is also the first substantial mention of the idea of oil and the potential for leasing Reata's land to be drilled. Bick is nervous as he knows his family will vote to lease the land despite his protestations. Leslie tries to distract him with thoughts of a trip to New York City in "Topsy Turvy." Bick is momentarily caught up, but the song ends up having little impact on his mood. At the hotel patio, Jett interacts with Lil Luz where it is revealed that Jett's stretch of land is where oil was found on Reata during the number "When to Bluff / One Day." Jett leaves before Leslie and Bick arrive. During the celebration for Bick, two guests from England bring up some unsavory claims about a William Barrett Travis, the commander of the Alamo. This leads to the unsettling number "My Texas," in which Bick and other members of the party passionately recount a revisionist history of the Alamo battle. The number is repeatedly interrupted by Jordy Jr., who corrects the claims made in the number. The song ends with Leslie, reiterating her melodic theme from "Your Texas," questioning her stances as she feels she's compromised her values while living in Texas. After the party guests head to the bar, Jett has a conversation with Leslie, which is interrupted by a jealous Bick. During the argument, it is revealed that it is Jett's company that is aiming to lease Reata's land for oil drilling. The scene transitions to the family meeting and the "Act One Finale" where Jett is delivering comments to the family to convince them to let him drill. Bick passionately defends the land, but the vote goes against him. Only he and his Uncle Bawley vote in favor of defending the land while the rest of the family votes to lease.

At the top of Act II, two years have passed. Bick decries that "Even here you smell oil. Everywhere! The house, the garden, the god damn tomatoes."[16] Luz enters, and Bick imagines one of their 5:00 am work meetings from before and asks Luz for advice during "Our Mornings / That Thing." Throughout the song, Luz reiterates the "Look Back" theme from Act I as Bick proves himself firmly planted in the past, particularly as he complains about his bookish son. At the end of the number, the action jumps forward to 1944 as Jordy and Lil Luz spend time with their friends, including Angel Obregon Jr., the baby Leslie encountered at the beginning of the show, now eighteen. The young and beautiful Juana cares for the now elderly Polo. Angel reveals that he has enlisted as a Private in the US Army and will be shipping out as soon as he marries Annalita in the number "Jump." The kids exit, but Jordy stays behind to ask Juana to the movies. He confesses that he always sits "in the balcony. I won't sit in whites only."[17] Juana says that she can't go to the movies with Jordy because she must look after Polo. She and Jordy share a tender moment as Juana sings "There Is a Child," in which she confesses that she wants to be a teacher in a Mexican school and details her own mistreatment in her education. The action moves again to five months later as Angel is marrying Analita. The beautiful scene quickly gives way to a funeral, however, as the action jumps to 1945 and it is revealed that Angel died during battle.

After the funeral, Jordy tells his father that he intends to stay at Harvard and then go to Columbia to complete medical school rather than taking over management of Reata Ranch. Bick is furious and threatens to cut Jordy off, when it is revealed that Bawley has been the one paying for Jordy's education. Bick is outraged, even making fun of his son's stutter. The final blow comes when Jordy announces that he is going to marry Juana. Bick exits, exclaiming, "You never had what it takes to be my son."[18] Bick goes to confront Bawley at his campsite in the mountains. During the song "Place in the World / Look Ahead" reprise, Bick and Bawley reconcile, and Bick agrees to stay a couple of days to keep Bawley company.

The action moves forward to 1952 at the Conquistador Hotel, owned by Jett Rink. An interaction among two politicians reveals that Jett has become a major player in Texas politics and has gained significant influence from the money he has made drilling oil at Reata. As Leslie and her family arrive, she is informed that Juana is not welcome at the hotel. Leslie does nothing to defend her daughter-in-law and laments her decision with her friends Adarene and Vashti in their hotel suite. Vashti reveals she's going to be a grandma and that has made her husband, Pinkie, want to have separate bedrooms. She's not ready for that and expresses her displeasure in the number "Midnight Blues," which also features Leslie complaining about her circumstances in her own marriage. After the song, Adarene confesses that she has cancer. The three women sit with their fates as the action switches to the Hotel Grand Ballroom where Jett is making a speech. During the song "The Dog Is Gonna Bark," Jett revels in his conservative politics and makes a statement about protecting the border from Mexico when Jordy rushes the stage over Jett's mistreatment over Juana. Jett's bodyguards beat Jordy brutally as Jett exits. Bick and Leslie go to Jordy as Juana is revealed praying in a church.

The scene changes back to the beginning of the show, with Leslie and Bick confronting each other in the middle of the Southwest Texas desert. They discuss their lives together and Leslie asks Bick why they've never dreamed of what it would be like getting old in the extended musical sequence "The Desert." While neither of them concedes on every point, they do reconcile. The action cuts to Juana and Jordy, who climb up the water tower that Leslie and Bick ascended in the first half of the show. Jordy sings "Aurelia Dolores" to Juana in English. During the "Act Two Finale," Juana and Jordy commit to staying on the land, she as a teacher and he as a doctor in the clinic, as the tune to "Heartbreak Country" gives way to "Aurelia Dolores."

Reviews of the production at The Public Theatre were mixed-to-positive. In his review in *The New York Times*, Ben Brantley praises LaChiusa for having a "wide musical vocabulary," but laments that the leading characters "never seem individualized."[19] Terry Teachout of *The Wall Street Journal* was far more effusive, calling *Giant*, "the most important new musical to come along since *The Light in the Piazza*."[20] Many reviews comment on the show's length and its tendency to include too much of the source material within its narrative. Steven Suskin posits that, while the show wasn't ready for a move to Broadway, he writes that LaChiusa "finally breaks through with a score that is tuneful, expansive and more emotional than intellectual."[21] Some reviews, such as Peter Marks review of the Signature Theatre production of the four-and-a-half-hour version of the show, point out the musical's clear inheritance from the Rodgers and Hammerstein tradition.[22] While *Giant* never did make it to Broadway, it is important to note that many of the reviews mark the production as a sort of milestone for LaChiusa, garnering some of the best reviews of his career.

Look Back: The "American Dream" in *Show Boat* and *Giant*

Shockingly, few of the reviews of *Giant* mention the connection between that show and another adaptation of Edna Ferber's writing, the landmark *Show Boat*, with many reviewers choosing instead to connect the musical to the Rodgers and Hammerstein shows. While critics may not have explored the connections between the two shows, there are plenty of reasons to understand *Giant* as participating in the lineage of the "musical drama" for which *Show Boat* is the beginning. Both novels, and subsequently, both musicals, cover long stretches of time through American history, charting the evolution of two different families in two very different situations. *Show Boat* covers a forty-year time span and is concerned with the lives of the people who work on and near the showboat *Cotton Blossom*. The premiere of *Show Boat* in 1927 is one of those "lightning bolt" moments in the history of the American musical, with some scholars calling it the birth of the musical play, a genre distinct and separate from musical comedy.[23] As such, it already participates in a conversation with LaChiusa's *Giant*, a descendant of the musical play tradition. Additionally, *Show Boat* also went through several cuts, playing over four hours before it came to New York City, much like *Giant*. Further, *Show Boat* brings forward several plot points that echo through the fabric of LaChiusa's works.

It is difficult to come up with a definitive synopsis for *Show Boat* since it has undergone numerous revisions since its 1927 premiere. Several reasons have precipitated these changes, from the length of the show to the problematic depiction of African American characters and issues. Despite these edits and rewrites, there are several plot strains that have survived in the performed text of *Show Boat* even through its most recent Broadway revival in 1993. Most prominent among them is the love story between Magnolia and Gaylord. Stacy Wolf has suggested that heterosexual romance has long been an organizing device for the American musical.[24] Although *Show Boat* has a complicated plot, the romance between Magnolia and Gaylord can certainly be said to be the major plot aspect that organizes the large-scale musical, even as Gaylord is largely absent from the second act. Magnolia and Gaylord meet early in the show's narrative. The beginning of their romance is tentative, employing one of Oscar Hammerstein II's most famous innovations, the "conditional love song" in which love is never expressly confessed in the iconic duet "Make Believe." Shortly after the interaction, Magnolia seeks out her friend Julie, who is the headline attraction on the showboat, to tell her that she's fallen in love. Julie encourages Magnolia to proceed cautiously. Magnolia and Gaylord find themselves swept up in their romance as they are later employed as the leading lady and leading man, respectively, on the showboat after Julie and her husband Steve are fired. Before the Act I curtain, Gaylord proposes to Magnolia, who accepts, and in Act II, the two welcome their child, Kim, into their family.

The number "Make Believe" sets out the romantic pursuit between Gaylord and Magnolia, leading to their own particularized pursuit of the "American Dream." While both characters are expressing their emotions for each other, they do so under the guise of "make believe," allowing both characters to romantically connect while leaving the concept of "love" as something that must be pursued over the course of the musical. As the relationship between Gaylord and Magnolia grows deeper over the course of their taking over as leading man and lady of the Riverboat *Cotton Blossom*, we get a more definite declaration of their feelings during the operatic "You Are Love" at the end of

Act I, though it is important to note that they are largely in their "riverboat" characters during this number. Although the journey for their romance gets turbulent in Act II, the organization of the first act lends itself to focusing on their relationship as one that is taking part in the narrative of the "American Dream," particularly with the birth of Kim.

Heterosexual romance maintains its hold as an organizing device for the American musical, but it also is a key aspect to depictions of the "American Dream." Indeed, heterosexual romance can be considered an essential component of the "American Dream" as it leads to the creation of the heteronormative American family. Therefore, it is not shocking that *Show Boat* gets its narrative thrust from the employment of heterosexual romance, eventually leading to a marriage and the rearing of a child. We can see a similar narrative impetus in the fabric of the musical *Giant*. Although there is no "conditional love song" in *Giant*, there are two numbers that establish the characters of Bick and Leslie while also establishing their romance and its pursuit as an organizing device. During Bick's establishing number, "Did Spring Come to Texas?" the pursuit of romance has already been achieved since Bick and Leslie have already been married. The number itself sets up a romanticized version of both Bick and Leslie's whirlwind courtship as well as Bick's love for the land itself. Narratively, Bick wonders how spring managed to come to Texas in the short time, merely three weeks, that it took for him to meet and marry Leslie. The number itself is heavily influenced by the music of Aaron Copland, particularly *Fanfare for the Common Man*. The lyric itself is a veritable list of all the flora and fauna that seem to come alive in the brush country of Texas. Bick sees the land and all its attributes as an extension of his "American Dream," equating his love of the land with the love for his new bride. In fact, this "love song" is more concerned with the land than it is with Leslie, who isn't mentioned until the song's second verse as something that Bick has had to wait for much as he waited for Christmas morning and his first pony.

It isn't shocking then that Leslie's first number, the beautiful "Your Texas," is also a type of love letter to the land. Leslie juxtaposes the world that she's grown up in and her ambition in that world for what she imagines life to be like in Bick's Texas. The music couldn't be more different from the triumphant, pastoral strains of "Did Spring Come to Texas?" The lush, powerful melody tends to ebb and flow, crashing into a climax every time Leslie lands on the word "Daydreams." The musical language of the two numbers is in opposition, but what ties the two pieces together is the passion with which their composer has imbued their melodies and accompaniment.

There's a sense of wonder in both songs. During "Your Texas," Leslie states, "There's a Great Unknown Just Waiting There / For Those Who Wish to Dream and Dare."[25] This connection of yearning, Bick for the land that he knows and Leslie for the land she doesn't know, ties the characters together in a similar way to Hammerstein's "conditional" lyric in "Make Believe." Neither Bick nor Leslie confesses their love in their establishing numbers, but each has a thematic connection that expresses their love for each other more melodically than lyrically. Their connection lies in the land that Bick knows and can show to Leslie, who has lived a life typical of an East Coast woman of means and wealth.

Giant also follows the structural conceit established in *Show Boat* of confirming the romantic nature of its leads' relationship later in the narrative. While "You Are Love" comes near the end of the first act of *Show Boat*, "Heartbreak Country" comes in the middle of *Giant*'s first act. The number dispenses with the conceit of expressed affection and love and focuses, again, on love for the land. Bick more expressly confesses his split allegiance in the beginning of the song: "I Didn't Tell the Truth / The Moment That I Wed You / That I Had Another Love."[26] He then goes on to admit that he never asked Leslie if she could love the land as well. The theme from "Did Spring Come to Texas?" re-emerges as Leslie makes a promise:

> I'll learn to love this land
> I swear I'll stand beside you.
> You have to give me time.
> Just give me patience
> And the chance to learn what you know.[27]

The most direct affirmation of their feelings for each other comes at the song's end. Leslie asks Bick to "Love Me Just as Hard / As You Love This Land." Bick responds with "I'll Love You Just as Hard / As I Love / This Land."[28] Bick makes this promise while also affirming his feelings of love for Leslie. While Leslie doesn't go so far as to declare her love for Bick, she does ask for his love in turn for learning to love the land.

These propositions of love, even without the exact words "I love you," help to position both Magnolia and Gaylord as well as Bick and Leslie as pursuing romance in further pursuit of the "American Dream." Both couples face a fair amount of opposition to their unions. In *Show Boat*, the opposition comes in two forms: the warnings from Julie and the protestations of Magnolia's mother, Parthy Ann. Prior to the famous number "Can't Help

Lovin' Dat Man," Julie warns Magnolia that Gaylord may be a "no account" and advises Magnolia to proceed cautiously. Further, Parthy Ann protests the romance, and Gaylord's presence on the boat in general, going so far as to faint when Gaylord proposes and after it is revealed that Gaylord was acquitted of murder. Bick and Leslie, on the other hand, face one adversary in their pursuit of romance: Bick's sister Luz. Luz had intended for Bick to marry Vashti and to unite the two ranches. Not only does Leslie's presence make that dream impossible but Leslie's liberal-leaning, East Coast attitude toward ranch life stands in the face of all that Luz holds near and dear to her heart. Even though Luz dies midway through the first act, her specter remains an integral part of the musical's thematic battle over "looking back" and "looking ahead." Luz also comes to represent Bick's split allegiance to both his new wife and to the land itself. Luz is a fellow spirit to Bick in terms of their commitment to the land and the ranch way of life. This means that Luz, not Leslie, can connect with Bick in a profound way. This rift in Bick's relationship with Leslie is felt deeply and impacts their romance, and their pursuit of the "American Dream," throughout the rest of the musical.

Both couples have marital problems throughout their second acts. Gaylord leaves Magnolia alone with their child to raise. Bick and Leslie remain together, but encounter a series of obstacles that, despite their considerable wealth, complicate their pursuit of the "American Dream," particularly in terms of family. Both Jordy and Lil Luz operate outside of expectations for their gender roles. Jordy doesn't want to run Reata after his father retires and resists working on the ranch. In fact, Jordy insinuates that it will be Lil Luz who will run the ranch when the time comes, working against her mother's expectations for her role.[29] Jordy's liberal leanings, his marriage to a Mexican woman, and his ambitions to work in a Mexican clinic are all more in line with his mother's temperament and philosophy, while Lil Luz's ambitions to work the ranch fall more in line with her father. These factors seem to exacerbate the differences in opinion between Leslie and Bick and cause further tensions in their already tumultuous relationship. Despite this, and other pressures, such as Jett's usurpation of Reata for drilling oil, Leslie and Bick do persist in their relationship, even coming to a sense of understanding during the number "The Desert." This, in some ways, mirrors Gaylord and Magnolia's resolution and reinstatement of their feelings for each other in the latter half of *Show Boat* when Gaylord returns to the *Cotton Blossom* and Magnolia forgives him and takes him back after a more than twenty-year absence.

Both couples persist in their pursuit of their "American Dreams" and, at least in terms of keeping their relationships and their families together, experience differing degrees of success despite the challenges set against them. The pursuit of the "American Dream" is much more complicated for the racial minorities present in both *Show Boat* and *Giant*. There is a strict divide between the black and white characters who keep the showboat *Cotton Blossom* running in *Show Boat*. The boat plays to segregated audiences and features an all-white cast, or so it seems. In the middle of the show's first act, it is revealed that Julie is mixed-race and has been passing as white. In one of the show's most provocative moments, a Sherriff comes to arrest Julie and her husband Steve on charges of miscegenation when Steve takes a knife and cuts Julie's hand, swallowing the blood. Steve tells the Sheriff that he has black blood in him and the Sherriff can no longer arrest them for being in a mixed marriage. Julie's "American Dream," which required her to pass as white to enjoy the life of a leading performer on a showboat, is brought to an abrupt end, and by the time we get to the heart of the second act, Steve has left her, and she has become an alcoholic.

The pursuit of the "American Dream" by characters of color in *Giant* is, at least initially, less explicit in the narrative. The show starts with the ballad "Aurelia Dolores" sung in Spanish. The plight of the Mexican Americans living at Reata is more explicitly stated when Leslie goes for a walk on the outskirts of the ranch and encounters the laborers living in squalor. Leslie does as much as she can to improve the lives of those living at Reata and the town of Benedict, including starting a new school, a poetry club, and a library, but the Mexican residents of the ranch town are not welcome at any of the new institutions created by Leslie.[30] Leslie feels constantly confined in her role as the matriarch of Reata ranch. She is caught between her own liberal instincts and her duty to Bick and to the life she has agreed to "learn" at the ranch. She fails to come to Juana's defense when she is thrown out of Jett Rink's hotel and remains largely silent when Jordy confesses to his father that he is going to marry Juana. Leslie's struggles to help give the musical's Mexican characters access to the "American Dream" positions her as a type of failed white savior. She tries, within the constraints of her role, to provide avenues to what she perceives as "betterment" for the Mexican inhabitants of Reata but fails to achieve what she regards as substantial change.

While Leslie's journey only implicitly examines the relationship between characters of color and the "American Dream," the clearest example of a character of color pursuing the "American Dream" comes in Juana, Jordy's eventual wife, who doesn't enter the narrative until the musical's second act. She dreams of being a teacher at the Mexican school in Benedict. Juana rejects Jordy's idea that she should aspire to teach in an English school, making her own type of "American Dream" within the world that she inhabits.[31] Her eventual marriage to Jordy, and the impending birth of her daughter, who will be mixed race, gives Juana a unique perspective of the "American Dream." She advocates for the beauty and opportunity present in her own circumstances rather than dreaming of escaping in the beautiful number "There Is a Child."

> There is a child
> Who's not aware
> There's a world outside
> His little square
> He must be shown
> How beautiful the square he's given is;
> And that he can get out of it
> And see the world is his.[32]

Juana's "American Dream" doesn't divorce her from her given circumstances, but rather embraces them to engage with the world in a very meaningful way. Her pathway to this dream is repeatedly thwarted, first by Bick's initial refusal to accept his son's marriage to Juana, then later in the second act when she is denied a room at Jett Rink's hotel. Despite this, in the musical's final moments, it seems that Juana is the most successful at achieving her version of the "American Dream" as she stands on the water tower, looking out over Reata, and celebrating the fact that she and Jordy will create a new world, and yet another new type of "American Dream" for their unborn daughter.

Narratives of people of color pursuing the "American Dream" are numerous throughout the history of the American musical. At the turn of the century, the musical *Ragtime*, based on the 1975 novel by E. L. Doctorow, is almost entirely organized around the denial of the "American Dream" to Coalhouse and Sarah, the mother of his child. When Coalhouse's car is destroyed by a group of racist firemen, Sarah goes to a rally for the vice-presidential candidate and is beaten to death by Secret Service agents who mistakenly think that she is brandishing a gun. Coalhouse vows revenge for Sarah's death and takes over J. P. Morgan's library, threatening to blow it up.

After being counseled by Booker T. Washington, he surrenders to police but is shot dead. The pursuit of the "American Dream" is important to Coalhouse, as he strives to own a car and raise his young son with the woman he loves. This is encapsulated, quite literally, in the song "Wheels of a Dream."[33] But, unlike the character of Juana, Coalhouse is given a series of obstacles that prove to be insurmountable. The pursuit of the "American Dream" is much more successful for Jim in *Big River*, a musical adaptation of Mark Twain's *The Adventures of Huckleberry Finn*. After a series of challenges, Jim manages to make it out of the bonds of slavery by the musical's end. And in Lin-Manuel Miranda and Quiara Alegría Hudes' *In the Heights*, Nina comes back from college a dropout, unable to reconcile the pressures placed upon her to fulfill the expectations of the "American Dream." While Juana participates in this long-form conversation on the trials of a person of color achieving or losing their own versions of the "American Dream," she also proves to be pursuing a unique version of it, particularly given that she refuses to merely assimilate into the American idiom but wants to take the beauty of her background with her into the larger world.

Juana and Jordy's relationship and their unborn daughter bring about the idea of generational inheritance, even if it is contrary to the type of life that Bick wanted for his son. The idea that the next generation inherits a world better than the one occupied by their parents in their youth is a central tenet of most conceptions of the "American Dream." This is also a concept that reverberates throughout the history of the American musical. In *Show Boat*, Kim inherits her mother's profession and becomes a major stage star. In *Ragtime*, Coalhouse is convinced to stand down by the thought of what his crimes may do to the world his son will inherit. In *Giant*, generational inheritance is constantly appearing throughout the narrative of the musical. First, Bick is keenly aware of the role and responsibility he inherited from his sister and surrogate mother, Luz. Next, Bick hopes to pass the charge of Reata ranch down to his son, Jordy, who rejects the generational inheritance to become a doctor at the Mexican clinic. Finally, Jordy and Juana promise a new type of world for their unborn child as they look out over Reata at the end of the musical. Generational inheritance could be said to be the organizing theme that holds *Giant* together. Part of the function of the "American Dream" is to be able to pass it down to the succeeding generation. This proves true in the narrative of Jett Rink as well, who takes the area of Reata that was given to his father and parlays it into a fortune when he organizes a company to take the oil out of Reata.

Look Ahead: LaChiusa and the American Dream

Both *Show Boat* and *Giant* participate in a conversation on either side of a century divide, considering and debating the nature of the "American Dream" that is a staple of the American musical. In particular, *Giant* explores the idea of heterosexual romance, racial minorities, and generational inheritance as pursuits of the "American Dream," explorations that it shares with its predecessor, *Show Boat* as well as other shows throughout the history of the American musical. This isn't the only title by LaChiusa to explore pursuits of the "American Dream." The chamber musical *Queen of the Mist* has a very different consideration—the pursuit of fame and fortune in the guise of its principal character, Annie Edson Taylor. Based on the historical figure of the same name, Annie would garner temporary fame by becoming the first woman to successfully go over Niagara Falls in a barrel. The musical, which opened in 2011 before *Giant* and garnered generally favorable reviews, charts Annie's course from down-and-out, to temporary celebrity, to the end of her life, which would see her poor, alone, and blind. In Annie's establishing number, she considers the possibilities for her life despite the current challenges she faces. The song "There Is Greatness in Me" harkens back to several other "American Dream"-focused shows with establishing numbers that situate the principal character as someone who is singularly focused on fame, most notably "I'm the Greatest Star" from Jule Styne, Bob Merrill, and Isobel Lennart's *Funny Girl*.[34]

The musical, which focuses on the "American Dream" of Fanny Brice, charts her rise to stardom as a headliner in the Ziegfeld Follies. There are many differences in the narratives of *Funny Girl* and *Queen of the Mist*. First, the outcome of both women couldn't be more different, with Fanny becoming a vaudeville sensation and Annie fading into obscurity. More appropriate to pursuits of the "American Dream," Fanny's life is interrupted and complicated by a heterosexual romance which helps to structure the musical, particularly its second act, while Annie has no romantic pursuits in her narrative. Yet, both characters articulate their unique definitions of the "American Dream" and their pursuit if it in establishing numbers that propel both of their narratives forward and give shape to both musicals. This fact alone gives voice to the idea that LaChiusa's works are constantly in conversation with titles from the past, while also looking forward to new ways to tell stories in musical dramas.

While LaChiusa creates an establishing number that harkens back to a major "Golden Age" title like *Funny Girl*, he also eschews the expectations of musical drama by foregoing a romantic relationship for his leading lady as an organizing device.

In fact, there are just as many attributes of *Giant* that look forward to innovations in the form as those attributes, discussed above, that look back. While there is significant weight to the argument that a heterosexual romance organizes the events of *Giant*, LaChiusa makes quick work of the actual *pursuit* of this heterosexual romance, with Bick's establishing number happening well after his wedding to Leslie. Leslie's number, by contrast, does come earlier in her romance with Bick, but is not really concerned with the pursuit of the romance either in an explicit way. Also, its placement after Bick's number in a flashback undercuts the song's ability to set up the romance between Bick and Leslie as a pursuit at all, given that we already have the information that Bick and Leslie are married. The romance between their son Jordy and Juana is presented more closely to the archetypical musical theatre romantic organizing device present in previous musicals, but the introduction of both characters late in the musical's narrative doesn't allow for their romantic pursuits to be a central organizing device, though much of the musical's second act is concerned with their blossoming relationship. Additionally, the musical's fluid treatment of time, particularly in its first scenes, seems to point to an innovation in the classic assumptions of the form, given that many of the pieces in the American musical theatre canon happen chronologically and the events are largely causal. LaChiusa's work, particularly in terms of considerations of the "American Dream," seems to be looking back and looking ahead at the same time, finding new ways of considering the question of the "American Dream" while concurrently looking to the past and celebrating it.

LaChiusa himself seems to understand his own work as commenting on the "American Dream," or at least on the nature of Americana, given that he used the idea of American stories to structure an evening of his music at Lincoln Center. The concert *Heartbreak Country: Michael John LaChiusa's Stories of America* premiered in February of 2014 and featured songs from eight musicals, including *Giant, Queen of the Mist, First Lady Suite, Marie Christine,* and *Hello Again.* The evening was directed and conceived by Jack Cummings III, the artistic director of The Transport Group, which has a long history of championing LaChiusa's work.[35] The evening focused on the American-ness that is featured in LaChiusa's canon and was presented over a year before LaChiusa would continue to consider the "American Dream" in his follow-up *First Daughter Suite.* The evening closed with Kate Baldwin singing "Your Texas" and "Heartbreak Country" with Andrew Samonsky, further cementing *Giant* in particular as a musical that, much like is stated in one of its most pivotal numbers, is committed to looking back and looking ahead.

CHAPTER 4
"IN SOME OTHER LIFE": ADAPTATION THEORY IN *HELLO AGAIN* AND *SEE WHAT I WANNA SEE*

"This history of theatre is a history of adaptation"—thus begins Jane Barnette in the introduction to her book *Adapturgy: The Dramaturg's Art and Theatrical Adaptation*.[1] While the sentiment may be obvious, there is a certain amount of animus toward adaptations in the contemporary theatre market. Season after season, critics and theatregoers alike decry the lack of "original material" on the stage, particularly demonizing adaptations of famous films. But Barnette's statement is true; the large majority of theatrical offerings are adaptations, or reworkings, of previously drafted material into a new form or media, going as far back as ancient theatre traditions. Barnette's sentiments can be rephrased for the purposes of this study to state that the history of *musical theatre* is also a history of adaptations. As of this writing, the current Broadway season boasts such adaptations as *The Outsiders*, *The Notebook*, and *Water for Elephants*, all adaptations of books and movies. While scholar Linda Hutcheon accurately describes more recent trends as being economically driven, she does seem to ignore the fact that adaptation extends through the entirety of musical theatre history, including such milestones as *Show Boat* (an adaptation of Edna Ferber's novel), *Porgy and Bess* (an adaptation of Dorothy and DuBose Heyward's play *Porgy*), *Oklahoma!* (based on the play *Green Grow the Lilacs* by Lynn Riggs), and even several of the works of Stephen Sondheim and his collaborators (*A Little Night Music*, *Sweeney Todd*, *Merrily We Roll Along*, *Passion*).[2] The allure of adapting previously established material to the musical stage is easy to understand; part of the fun of writing a musical is finding moments within a narrative that can be expanded, elaborated, and reconceived through the use of music. And the range of what can be adapted has always been varied, from plays and films to paintings and photographs. Many of the musicals of the past five years have worked even harder to expand the types of material that can be adapted, particularly *Fun Home*, an adaptation of a graphic novel, *Natasha, Pierre, and the Great Comet of 1812*, an adaptation of a cutting from *War and Peace*, and even the behemoth *Hamilton*, based on Ron Chernow's biography.

The works of Michael John LaChiusa participate in this history of adapting works for the musical stage. Indeed, most of the shows LaChiusa has written are adaptations in some form or another. Many of LaChiusa's works have tackled challenging subject material that may not immediately sound like fertile ground for musicalization. LaChiusa's *Hello Again*, which premiered at Lincoln Center Theatre's Mitzi Newhouse Theatre in 1993, is a musical adaptation of Arthur Schnitlzer's play *Reigen*, more commonly known today by its French title *La Ronde*. Additionally, his musical *See What I Wanna See* is an adaptation of several short stories by the early twentieth-century Japanese writer Ryūnosuke Akutagawa. Because of LaChiusa's tendency to tackle "difficult" material in his choice of what to adapt, theoretical considerations of the nature of dramaturgy may help to elucidate the methods and tactics utilized by LaChiusa, particularly in terms of material that may initially be resistant to the idea of musicalization.

Often, the employment of theory when discussing theatrical works becomes muddied by the emphasis on more amorphous ideas that tend to evade the practical side of "doing" theatre. Barnette's book *Adapturgy*, referenced above, works to connect the ideas of dramaturgy and theatrical adaptation in both a practical and theoretical way. She outlines three different theoretical approaches to adaptation in the second part of her book *Adapturgy*, two of which are particularly salient for consideration of LaChiusa's pieces. First, she looks at the phrase *palimpsestuous pleasures*, cited by Linda Hutcheon in her 2006 book *A Theory of Adaptation*.[3] Hutcheon borrows the phrase from a Scottish poet and reappropriates it as a means of understanding the myriad ways in which an adapted text carries the watermark of the work that inspired it, leading to a palimpsest that retains the markings of previous writings. The audience then experiences a type of pleasure in recognizing the imprints of the source material in the newly adapted work. Next, Barnette explores the ways in which space is assigned and considered in adaptations. Utilizing a concept she calls "Geographies of Adaptation," Barnette considers the ways in which adaptations transform spaces both literal and figurative, both the practical playing space and the "imaginary space" of ideas and cognition.[4]

Utilizing these two approaches by Barnette's to adaptation theory, I argue that the works of Michael John LaChiusa offer innovative pathways for adaptation in the American musical. In order to explore this idea, I will focus on two specific adaptations by LaChiusa. First, I explore one of LaChiusa's earliest critical successes: his adaptation of Schnitzler's *Reigen* entitled *Hello Again*. I will specifically explicate the ways in which this title participates in and encourages "palimpsestuous pleasures" as it proudly shows the imprint of the source material that came before it. Second, I look at the musical *See What I Wanna See*, which resets and adapts three of Akutagawa's short stories, namely the twin monologues "Kesa and Morito," and the stories "In a Bamboo Grove," and "Dragon: The Old Potter's Tale." The relocation of two of these stories, "In a Bamboo Grove" and "Dragon: The Old Potter's Tale" to New York City, helps us to understand the ways in which geographies play a pivotal role in the art of adaptation.

The goal of this chapter is to understand the ways in which LaChiusa's work reflects and expands the long-form history of adaption in the American musical. In order to proceed with that project, I will spend some time defining Barnette's two approaches, namely the idea of *palimpsestuous pleasures* and geographies of adaptation, as well as the thinkers and conversations employed in connection with each idea. Additionally, it is important to note the ways in which his methods and choice of material veer away from the more commercial fare that dominated Broadway at the time of each show's writing. I don't mean to suggest that LaChiusa is somehow unique in his choice to explore unlikely source material. Even the smash hit megamusical *Cats* managed to musicalize an unlikely property. But LaChiusa's choice of material does point to the tendency for many writers in "The New Musical Drama" movement to explore the unexplored in terms of source material. With that in mind, I will conclude the chapter with a brief look at the source material for several current musical theatre titles, particularly the musicals *Fun Home*, *Hamilton*, and *The Band's Visit*. By taking a cursory look at the material for each of these three musicals, I hope to establish that LaChiusa's choices of material and the manner in which he adapted it may have, in some ways, anticipated current methods of adaptation that have found remarkable staying power in the commercial market.

Adapturgy: Two Approaches

Utilizing theoretical considerations of adaptations helps to explain the ways in which LaChiusa's work is working within and around different assumptions of adaptations in musical theatre. Adaptation theory, particularly Barnette's "adapturgy," her term for the amalgamation of adaptation and dramaturgy, helps to explain LaChiusa's dramatic liberties when adapting works, particularly in regard to resettings of place and time. These methods have been employed in various ways by other writers that came before and after the New York City premieres of the two titles explored in this chapter. It may be useful to think of LaChiusa as a type of watershed as opposed to a pioneer, as an artist who has one face toward the past and another to the future. In particular, adaptation theories can be useful in a macro-consideration of LaChiusa's choices of source material. In an interview with Jonathan Frank published on the popular theatre website talkinbroadway.com, LaChiusa briefly explains what Frank calls his "most esoteric tastes in regard to stories": "They kind of find me. I think what I do, Jonathan, is write the shows that fill-in what I feel is missing in the theatrical world; the shows that I want to see as an audience member."[5] LaChiusa's desire to adapt the type of properties that he feels are "missing in the theatrical world" points us to a type of musical theatre activism. Both LaChiusa's methods of adaptation and his choice of material in general can both be better understood within the frameworks of "palimpsestuous pleasures" and geographies of adaptation.

Barnette's discussion of "palimpsestuous pleasures" is closely derived from a discussion that first appeared in 2006 in the work of scholar Linda Hutcheon. Hutcheon, in turn, finds that her discussion of the term is indebted to both Scottish poet and literary critic Michael Alexander as well as French literary critic Gérard Genette.[6] By definition, a palimpsest is a type of writing material which is used more than once after earlier writing has been erased. As such, the palimpsest serves a type of documentary labor, bringing forth a new text elucidated and complicated by the writings that came before it.[7] A secondary definition points to the more metaphoric use of the term employed by Barnette via Hutcheon and Alexander: "something having usually diverse layers or aspects apparent beneath the surface."[8] Both definitions point to the semi-permanence of previous ideas, writings, and concepts. The more practical definition of the term puts a visual reference point on the idea; previous writings can never be fully erased or eradicated. The second definition, which focuses on the ideas of layers and multiple surfaces, suggests that a palimpsest is not marred by the presence of multiple writings; rather, its inherent meanings only deepen and diversify the object as a whole, presenting a fully layered type of physical history. Both definitions point to ideas of perception, and it is worth noting that "palimpsestuous pleasures" seem to move adaptation theory away from its more semiotic roots into a phenomenological lens, particularly given the experiential component of witnessing multiple writings and, by extension, multiple histories.

Alexander uses the term "palimpsestuous-ness" only once in his consideration of poet Ezra Pound, a term he defines as "the literary romance of the past carried to new depths of verbal resonance."[9] But his association of the palimpsest with a type of "literary romance of the past" helps us to understand the ways in which the palimpsest as a metaphor tends to maintain the genealogy of writing. While Alexander isn't interested in a thorough investigation of the employment of the term, his description of Pound as a "magician" with a "romance of the past" points to the possibilities of the term to be used as a framework for adaptation analysis, particularly given the association between the palimpsest and the idea of magic. Alexander's assertion, though narrowly defined to an explanation of Pound's word choices, suggests that the palimpsest could enter the world of metaphor, at least in terms of its application to other literary figures and schools of thought. By contrast, Genette refines the use of the word to discuss what he calls "a text in the second degree."[10] He goes on to broaden the term "palimpsest" as a means of understanding "second degree texts" as being "derived from another preexistent text."[11] He defines this relationship with the term "hypertextuality," a dynamic relationship between the preexisting text and the derivation.

Hutcheon married Michael's reference to the term "palimpsestuous-ness" with Genette's idea of intertextuality and arrived at the term "palimpsestuous pleasures" as a means of discussing the joy audiences feel when viewing an adaptation, particularly when they are familiar with the source material. This familiarity results in a type of "insider" mentality that encourages the idea that access to the material in its fullest palimpsestuous form leads to feelings of exclusivity.[12] Barnette and Hutcheon both use the idea of the "insider" to highlight the ways in which adaptation has taken on a commercial bent, particularly with the advent of Disney Theatricals and its reliance on previous knowledge of the film properties that they are adapting to the Broadway stage. This factor of Hutcheon's "palimpsestuous pleasures" actually complicates a discussion of LaChiusa as his choices of source material, excepting his musical adaptation of Euripides' *Medea* in the form of *Marie Christine*, would likely only be known to niche audiences. Despite this, there appears to be an awareness of unfamiliarity in LaChiusa's work, particularly given that his musicals tend to create palimpsests of their own that return as types of motif throughout the texts of his shows. The idea of the palimpsest, a material which allows for legibility of past texts through the derivative of the adaptation, becomes incredibly salient when considering the works of LaChiusa. In particular, the ways in which each of *Hello Again*'s ten scenes all create echoes that are heard in later encounters.

But other theories also help us to locate theoretical considerations in LaChiusa's oeuvre. Barnette bridges the practical and philosophical considerations of theatrical performance in her discussion of the geographies of adaptation.[13] In exploring the considerations of both literal and figurative theatrical space, Barnette suggests that the primary consideration for the adaptation dramaturg is the adaptation's reliance on the transformation of imaginary space into theatrical space.[14] In order to do this, Barnette sets up a carefully considered contrast between the terms "place" and "space." While conceding that scholars are still conflicted regarding the definitions of these two terms, Barnette designates the term "space" as more amorphous and general than the term "place." For theatrical purposes, she suggests that a "space is created by activating a place."[15] In other words, place is the location; space is the result of attaching meaning to the location. Space becomes both theoretical metaphor and practical place of performance, imbued with meaning. In terms of the theoretical, Barnette proposes the term "imaginary space" to designate "the space of ideas and cognition, usually driven by the director's concept but equally influenced by the spirit of adaptation."[16]

I borrow and extend the phrase "imaginary space" in order to understand the ways in which LaChiusa's works, particularly *See What I Wanna See*, begin life in a liminal imagined space that opens up the possibilities of place and, more importantly, space when relocating the setting of a source material. As will be discussed in more detail later, *See What I Wanna See* relocated Akutagawa's stories, many of which take place during Japan's medieval period, to twentieth- and twenty-first-century New York City, similarly to the resetting of time and place utilized in *Hello Again*. Barnette also discusses the more practical aspects that make considerations regarding space crucial for adaptation, particularly when writers are developing adaptations to play in a specified theatre, emphasizing the idea that "imaginary space" must eventually find a way to coexist and amalgamate with the practical space. Citing Marvin Carlson, Barnette emphasizes the importance of space in the theatrical formula, particularly exploring Carlson's emphasis on spatial configurations as a necessary for a consideration of how theatre works.[17] This becomes useful for understanding some of the structural constraints and challenges encountered by LaChiusa when adapting works.

As mentioned earlier, I will largely associate a single theoretical approach to each of the two musical titles discussed in the chapter. Yet, while Barnette presents these two frameworks as separate approaches to "adapturgy," I do bring them into conversation with each other. In particular, "palimpsestuous pleasures" and "geographies of adaptation" both involve ways to view the past in conjunction with adapted work. Additionally, the idea of geographies of adaptation introduces the principle of "imaginary space," a metaphoric place imbued with meaning that thrives on a lack of fixity. Because of this, it is nearly impossible for any discussion of LaChiusa and adaptation theory to only address one of these two approaches. For the sake of clarity, I have predominately associated the idea of "palimpsestuous pleasures" with *Hello Again* and geographies of adaptation with *See What I Wanna See*. These works, both adaptations of unlikely source materials, point to theoretical approaches that in of themselves resemble a palimpsest, occupy liminal "imaginary spaces," and look to the past and future simultaneously.

"The Bed Was Not My Own": Palimpsestuous Pleasures in *Hello Again*

If adaptations are palimpsests, containing remnants of the source material within their fabric, then it can be concluded that these echoes of the past function as contributors to the newly adapted work. With this idea in mind, the original author of the source material becomes a type of collaborator in the newly minted work. In order to identify Arthur Schnitlzer as a collaborator, a brief biography is in order. Schnitzler was born on May 15th, 1862 in Vienna, Austria. His father was a laryngologist and his mother was the daughter of a doctor as well. So, it isn't surprising that Schnitzler was trained as a medical doctor, earning his degree in 1885. While Schnitzler's parents assumed that he would follow in the steps of his father, he ended up favoring psychology, writing a thesis advocating for the use of hypnosis to combat neurosis.[18] He eventually gave up medicine to pursue writing and married Olga Gussmann, a young actress twenty years his junior, in 1903. Much of Schnitzler's work was controversial for both its depictions and critiques of anti-Semitic politics and its frank depictions of sex and sexuality. He was good friends with Sigmund Freud, who thought highly of Schnitzler's work, once stating in a letter, "I have gained the impression that you have learned through intuition—although actually as a result of sensitive introspection—everything that I have had to unearth by laborious work on other persons."[19] Additionally, Schnitlzer experimented a great deal with form. Four years before writing *Reigen*, he authored a fascinating play entitled *Anatol* that explored the exploits of a playboy over the course of seven vignettes. While *Anatol* is far more narrative than *Reigen*, it does provide a bit of foreshadowing, anticipating *Reigen*'s "ten dialogues" format.

Although the play is commonly known as *La Ronde* to most theatre scholars, the original German title for Arthur Schnitzler's dramatic piece was *Reigen*, which refers to either a roundelay, a circular dance, or a sequence, depending on the German dictionary consulted. The title *La Ronde* became popular in 1950 thanks to Max Ophüls' film version of the same name. Like its German counterpart, "La Ronde" refers to a circular-type of dance in French. For the sake of clarity, I will continue to use *La Ronde* throughout this chapter, though the title's change from German to French is worth noting, particularly given that Ophüls' French language film version helped to reignite curiosity over the original play. Schnitzler wrote *La Ronde* around 1896, but it wasn't performed until 1912 in an unauthorized production in Budapest, the same year that the play was published in French.[20] Despite the fact that it wasn't performed until over fifteen years after it was written, the text itself was banned in Germany in 1905.[21] Eventually, there was a German printing of the text around 1908. There is some disagreement over whether Schnitzler ever intended to have the play performed. Nicholas Rudall points out that the numerous scenic changes, which would have been improbable in the more realism-based theatres of the era, might suggest that Schnitzler did not intend for the play to be performed.[22] In the introduction to his adaptation of *La Ronde* entitled *The Blue Room*, David Hare firmly states that Schnitzler's play was not meant to be performed, citing Schnitzler as saying that the play was "completely unprintable" and was only intended to share with friends.[23] Despite the debate, it does seem that Schnitlzer must have wanted a production given that the play did officially premiere in Vienna in 1921 with his permission. That production was infamously shut down by the police and the play's Berlin premiere resulted in the production's cast standing trial for six days for obscenity charges.[24]

The play is composed of ten separate dialogues.[25] In each, the audience witnesses the prelude and postlude to a sexual encounter with one of the pair appearing in the following scene with a new partner. By the tenth dialogue, the play comes full circle with the first character introduced paired with the last. The first dialogue, between The Whore and The Soldier, takes place on the Augarten Bridge. The Soldier then pursues a parlor maid on a street outside an amusement park. The Parlor Maid has an illicit rendezvous with The Young Gentleman in his home where she is under the employ of his father and mother. In turn, The Young Gentleman welcomes The Young Wife into an untoward apartment that he keeps for sexual liaisons. The Young Wife and The Husband encounter each other in the master bedroom of their own home prior to The Husband's seduction of The Little Miss in a private dining room at a fashionable restaurant. The Poet then welcomes The Little Miss into his rented room before running off to a room in a country inn for an encounter with The Actress, who then meets with her lover, The Count, in her own bedroom. In the play's final scene, The Count encounters The Whore from the first dialogue in the play. Significantly, this scene doesn't follow the prelude/postlude structure of the rest of the piece. Instead, the scene begins with The Count waking up in The Whore's room fully dressed. It is uncertain whether the two characters ever engaged in sex and the circumstances of their meeting are kept ambiguous. Several analyses of *La Ronde* have engaged with the idea that the play was a commentary on the nature of sexually transmitted infections, syphilis in particular, though there is no evidence of Schnitzler confirming that theory. Film scholars, such as Elizabeth G. Ametsbichler, have pointed out the play's commentary on social class, particularly given that the vast majority of interactions happen across class barriers.[26] More importantly, there is debate about the tonal intention of *La Ronde*. From a contemporary perspective, the play can be read comedically, particularly the encounters between The Parlor Maid and The Young Gentleman as well as between The Husband and The Little Miss.

The debate over tone is also evident when considering the many other adaptations of *La Ronde*. In 1981, the original play fell out of its copyright, causing a great surge in the number of adaptations of the work across various media. There are at least eighteen film versions that are either based on *La Ronde* or inspired by it. The most noteworthy of those film adaptations is the previously mentioned 1950 film version by Max Opüls which takes a far darker look at the property. Philippe Boesmans wrote a German-language opera version in 1993, roughly around the same time as LaChiusa's adaptation. A few years later, playwright David Hare would write his own adaptation, entitled *The Blue Room*, which plays out a modern retelling of Schnitzler's ten dialogues using only two actors. This version, which met with some critical derision, would help place a new focus on Schnitzler's original work, given that it was a huge hit, thanks in no small part to the naked Broadway debut of Oscar-winning actress Nicole Kidman. Across these various versions, the resulting adapted work, the palimpsest, varies wildly in terms of tone, fidelity, and technique. Some versions, like Roger Vadim's 1964 French language version starring Jane Fonda, focused on the comedic elements in the original, lending an almost farcical tone to Schnitzler's work. Others, such as the 2011 film entitled *Love in the Time of Money*, take a decidedly darker approach, eliminating the comedic elements that are present in the source material. Some have remained faithful to Schnitzler's original characters; others have completely abandoned them, creating completely new characteristics for the ten actors. Several adaptations have utilized the two-actor casting model used by David Hare. All of these serve as an example for Hutcheon's "palimpsestuous pleasures," with some showing more of the residual writing of the source material than others. While it is impossible to know how many of the adaptations were known to LaChiusa, several, including Vadim's French language film and Ophüls German language film, are listed in the musical's dramaturgical protocol.[27]

While LaChiusa's version is somewhat faithful to the character conceits created by Schnitzler, his version, while occasionally comedic, reads far more meditatively. His version utilizes the ten characters originated by Schnitzler, albeit with some variations discussed below. Additionally, he relocates most of the action from *La Ronde* into an American idiom, with most of the scenes taking place in variations of New York City. The biggest change in LaChiusa's version, however, isn't related to character; it's related to time. Each of the scenes in LaChiusa's work takes place in a different decade of the twentieth century. These scenes are not presented in chronological order, though. For example, while the first scene takes place in the first decade of the twentieth century, the second scene jumps to the Second World War era. The third scene moves forward again in time to the Vietnam War era, while the fourth scene jumps back in time to the 1930s. Despite these movements in time, the characters do not age or grow younger based on the time period that they occupy. Instead, LaChiusa keeps the same character throughout the fluctuations of time and period. While remnants of the previous scene transition into the following scene, it could be argued that The Nurse in Scene 2 is not the same version of The Nurse that the audience meets in Scene 3, though the actress assaying the role is the same. Rather, the characters act as their own type of palimpsest, created new for their current moment, but containing figments and impressions from the scene before. I argue that, while *Hello Again* is certainly a palimpsest of Schnitzler's *La Ronde*, the play itself offers both a showcasing of the palimpsest and a commentary on the nature of reinvention.

One of the more noteworthy examples of "character as palimpsest" is seen in the character of The Nurse, a variation on Schnitzler's character The Parlor Maid. In Scene 2, her first scene with The Soldier, The Nurse is dancing with The Soldier at a USO Canteen. The Soldier is aggressively pursuing the possibility of sex with The Nurse, despite her hesitations. The Nurse is aware that she is potentially just a conquest. She mentions the fact that she was not the only woman who had caught The Soldier's eye. "You could've had that redhead in there," she sings in the middle of the song.[28] While the sex act is taking place, a quintet sings a beautiful close-harmony arrangement entitled "We Kiss," juxtaposing The Soldier's experience of sex with the more emotionally driven urges The Nurse is experiencing herself. After The Soldier climaxes, he says that he needs to go inside and get a beer. "You're gonna make for that redhead," The Nurse quips in his direction.[29] The Soldier concedes that this is likely a correct assumption. The Nurse says that she will wait in the rain until The Soldier is done so he can walk her home. He says fine and goes back in. While The Nurse that is introduced in Scene 3 is not necessarily the same as the one who was left in the rain in Scene 2, the emotional weight of her experience with The Soldier does inform her character in the third scene. Scene 3 takes place at the height of the Vietnam War in the 1960s. The College Boy, LaChiusa's adaptation of Schnitzler's The Young Gentleman, is sitting on a couch, sporting a twisted ankle that has likely already healed. He is milking the experience because he is attracted to the nurse that his parents hired to look after him. The meek, impressionable version of The Nurse that we met in Scene 2 has given way to a sexually voracious, aggressive version in Scene 3. The Nurse takes advantage of The College Boy's "injury" to engage in some elements of BDSM. Singing the high-belt rock anthem "In Some Other Life," The Nurse removes her panty hose and uses them to restrain The College Boy. She then mounts and rides him, eventually climaxing. During the song, The Nurse references elements of both her previous scene and the piece as a whole as she lists past sexual encounters.

A soldier I knew,
Then that redheaded teen;
The guy in the park
By the Pepsi machine
The first time an' last time
An' time in-between
Why couldn't I love you in some other life?[30]

The Nurse invokes the memory of The Soldier directly. Prior to naming him, she explains her views on the nature of men:

> Baby, there's a revolution goin' on
> And it's hard to keep my cool
> There's some things they didn't teach me back in
> Nursing school
> Like how men are gonna take and take and take and take
> And not give nothing back.[31]

While the structure of the musical doesn't lend itself to thinking of these characters as treading an "unbroken line" in the Stanislavskian sense from scene to scene, meaning that the characters are continuing within the same, uninterrupted narrative, elements of the previous scene do have an effect on the character in the following scene. Not only does The Nurse directly mention a soldier, the set-up to that reference explains that The Nurse had some type of encounter that took something from her that wasn't returned. She repeats that theme throughout the lyric to "In Some Other Life":

> Some little bit of me's gone.
> I'm gonna steal a little bit of you.[32]

There are multiple references throughout the musical that feature various characters acknowledging elements of their previous encounters. In Scene 5, The Young Wife mentions to her husband that her friend Marie is having an affair with a college boy. This palimpsest shows two elements of previous impressions. First, The Young Wife's friend shares the same name as the Nurse from Scenes 2 and 3. Second, while it is true that the Marie of the 1960s has a sexual encounter with The College Boy, The Young Wife also had an affair with The College Boy in the previous scene taking place in a 1930s movie house. Also, in Scene 5, which takes place in the 1950s, The Husband promises The Young Wife a gift from London when he returns. In Scene 6, The Husband informs The Young Thing, a queer adaptation of Schnitzler's The Little Miss, that the brooch he has is a gift for his wife. He tells The Young Thing that his wife's name is Marianne, then corrects himself when pushed, admitting that his wife's name is Emily.[33] Moving into Scene 7, The Young Thing mentions that he survived a shipwreck during the song "Safe," referencing the previous scene which took place on the *Titanic*.[34] The song is delivered in earnest to The Writer. Examples of this nature abound, particularly in the musical's final scene. When The Senator, LaChiusa's version of The Count, meets The Whore in Scene 10, he gives a recounting of all of the people he has been with in a dream during the haunting song, "The Bed Was Not My Own":

> A girlfriend I knew.
> My wife and my ex-
> My cousin Marie
> The thing in the park.
> The blond from the bar.
> The guy from the gym.
> Not really her.
> Not really him …[35]

While we cannot say for certain that this recounting makes direct reference to anyone in the musical, "Marie" and "The thing in the park" definitely bring to mind images of The Nurse and The Young Thing, respectively. In the final moments of the musical, the entire company begins singing an overlapping round of the show's central setting of the words "Hello again." While nothing in the musical literalizes the characters' various invocations of elements of past scenes, the fact that they are voiced at all lends weight to the theory that each separate scene serves as its own palimpsest, interwoven completely by the musical's final moments, displaying that each character remains a presence in the final product.

The musical also proves to be a palimpsest in more direct terms, particularly with LaChiusa's reinvention of certain characters. One of the concerns voiced by the dramaturg Christopher Burney in 1992 involves the problems presented by developing this piece in the wake of the AIDS crisis.[36] While AIDS doesn't make a direct impact on the musical, there is a theme, first iterated by The Whore in Scene 1, then echoed by The Senator in Scene 9, that baldly states, "We may die tomorrow."[37] Although the specter of the HIV/AIDS crisis had a definite impact on these tonal aspects, the queer characters in the piece aren't considered in the context of that moment given that their scenes don't take place in the 1980s or 1990s. The Husband, a closeted gay man, appears in the 1950s and the 1910s. The Young Thing, LaChiusa's queer take on Schnitzler's The Little Miss, shares the 1910s with The Husband, then appears with the bisexual character The Writer in the 1970s sequence. Although there is no physical evidence regarding the reasons for this decision, it may have been a strategic decision to avoid featuring queer characters post-1980s for fear that the musical may have been usurped by the theme of HIV/AIDS transmission, regardless of whether HIV/AIDS played a literal role in those depictions. That being said, despite the choices of time period, these characters retain many of the aspects of Schnitzler's definitions while allowing for a consideration of various queer male identities. The Husband's role is left largely intact from the source material to LaChiusa's version, excepting his penchant for young girls is now transferred to young boys. The move from The Poet to The Writer is also fairly faithful despite the fact that LaChiusa has set him up with both a male and female partner in Scenes 7 and 8, respectively.

The move from The Little Miss to The Young Thing is more noteworthy, particularly in terms of a tonal shift. Both of the scenes featuring The Little Miss have a comedic tone, playing on the character's naïveté and willing unawareness. While there are comedic moments throughout The Young Thing's journey, they are rooted in a self-aware way. In Scene 6, The Young Thing appears to be in control of the entire situation. He dictates the entire encounter with The Husband, even though The Husband is aggressively pursuing him. The Young Thing also makes a comment toward the end of the scene, prior to The Husband's revelation that the ship has struck an iceberg and the ship is sinking, that suggests the entire encounter was part of a hustle:

> … When we land in New York
> I suppose we'll be keeping in touch.
> Right?
> When I live in New York
> I suppose you will ask me to sup.
> Sir?
> 'Course to live in New York
> I'll be needing some help setting up …[38]

This dramaturgical decision forces a palimpsest as it changes the entire trajectory of Schnitzler's original. While some elements of The Little Miss are still present, they are faded markings on a newly developed character. Another change, in terms of gender, also presents a new perspective that is still rooted in the source material. Not only is The Young Thing generally cast with a cis-gender male, but the character is also described in the show's libretto as "androgynous."[39] The use of the term "androgyny" does not necessarily correlate with the way in which the role was originally cast and played. While the actor who played the role in the original off-Broadway run, John Cameron Mitchell, has a history of gender-bending performances, particularly the cult musical *Hedwig and the Angry Inch*, his performance in *Hello Again* reads as decidedly male.[40] I admit that my reading of the performance may not match the conception intended by LaChiusa and his chief collaborator, director-choreographer Graciela Daniele, but there is little evidence in the performance, costume choices, and writing to support the label of "androgynous" as the term would suggest in a contemporary context. Further, the performance of the role in the film version, featuring actor Tyler Blackburn, is decidedly masculine.[41] If the performance experimented with androgyny, it would find more of an imprint of The Little Miss in its employment in the musical, particularly given The Little Miss's age and gender stereotypically render her in a sort of in-between space in terms of gender roles. Instead, the role in performance reads as a more radical re-conception of the character in the source material. This, of course, largely relies on the audience's previous knowledge of either the source material or the libretto itself, though the gender/orientation presentation of the character still provides palimpsestuous pleasures for the audience when considering the ways the character's presentations of masculinity or androgyny are distinguished based on time periods, the 1910s and the 1970s, respectively.

Actors also appear in different scenes in order to fill out the smaller roles demanded by the adaptation. For example, The Senator appears in both Scenes 1 and 6 as a prospective "john" for The Whore and a steward on the Titanic, respectively. The Actress appears as a prima donna in both Scenes 5 and 6. And the entire company, except The Whore, appears in Scenes 6 and 7 as passengers on the *Titanic*, then partiers at the disco.[42] The most effective reintroduction of a character happens in Scene 5. During the song "Tom," The Young Wife, who sings what is perhaps LaChiusa's best known song, looks at herself in the mirror and sees The Whore. The Whore steps through the mirror and the two engage in a type of mirror dance, with The Young Wife mimicking the motions of The Whore.[43] The suggestion made by the juxtaposition of these two characters invites a plethora of readings, but the tone of the scene doesn't lend itself to any sort of reading of judgment. Instead, the audience sees The Young Wife, who is repressed and unhappy in her relationship with The Husband, exploring a type of sexuality that she has been made to see as forbidden. Conversely, The Whore is given the opportunity to provide a type of comment in movement, suggesting that the similarities between her desires and those of The Young Wife are not so different, hinting again at the class consciousness that pervades Schnitzler's original work.

It is remarkable that a film version of *Hello Again* was produced, particularly given that the audience for the film may have been limited, despite the casting of several prominent television, film, and theatre personalities. Despite that, the film version does present another example of a palimpsest and, as an adaptation of a lesser-known show, shows a myriad of palimpsestuous pleasures for those who viewed the film with previous knowledge of either the stage version of *Hello Again*, as well as other adaptations of *La Ronde* and, of course, the actual source material. The independently produced film version, released in 2017, incorporates a host of variations on LaChiusa's original stage work. Chief among them is the decision to change the gender of two characters. The Whore, noted with her character name Leocadia, was cast with a cis-gender male, and his first scene with the soldier was played in women's clothing. It is unclear whether the intention in this scene is to present the whore as cis-gender female, as some version of genderqueer or transgender, or whether the character is intended to be a cis-gender male in drag. The actor sings the role of The Whore in the original key in the octave that was intended for a cis-gender female playing the role, giving some weight to the possibility that The Whore is some variation on a cis-gender female identity. Conversely, Leocadia is presented as a cis-gender male in both the scene with The Senator, now named Ruth, and the two additional moments that bookend the film, an encounter between Ruth and Leocadia in a peepshow booth and the coda which features Ruth in Leocadia's bed. In some ways, the gender play with Leocadia's character fulfills the original musical's stated claim to play with the idea of androgyny, allowing The Young Thing to be read legibly as a gay cis-gender male. Additionally, the role of The Senator has been recast as female.

In her scene with The Actress, now named Sally, it is clear that Ruth is either lesbian or bisexual and is keeping the nature of her relationship with Sally closeted. This adds another new element to Schnitzler's original source material, which also featured a political bent to the nature of The Count's affair with The Actress. Additionally, LaChiusa authorized a new version of what is Scene 8 in the musical: the scene between The Writer and The Actress. In the licensed stage version, the scene is played as a faux-silent film, with The Actress eventually overpowering The Writer as a sexual conquest. LaChiusa was never satisfied with the scene and, in fact, wrote a short play about the development of the scene, which went through several iterations, as a joke.[44] For the film version, the action is moved from the 1920s to the early 2000s and The Actress is now a singer attempting to record a new pop hit. She engages in an argument with her ex, The Writer, who is now named Robert, that eventually leads to a sexual encounter intercut with the video for Sally's new song. The scene causes a disruption in the fabric created by the original musical, particularly given that it jumps out of the twentieth century and leaves the 1920s uncharted. This disruption, which is likely only perceptible to audience members familiar with the source materials, forces a reconsideration of the ways in which *Hello Again* performs its labor. This novelty is in itself a palimpsestuous pleasure, allowing audience's familiar with the material to experience something new.

The musical *Hello Again*, in its theatrical and cinematic forms, provides a feast of potential palimpsestuous pleasures for the viewer. Its structure alone causes each scene extending from Scene 1 to be a type of palimpsest, shaded with the "writings" of the scene before it. Additionally, the musical continues in a long line of palimpsestuous pleasures that are applicable to the many different adaptations of Schnitzler's original, controversial ten dialogues. Finally, the film version provides another level of palimpsestuous pleasures for the viewer who is already aware of the various versions that have come before it, including the musical. Since the idea of palimpsestuous pleasures involves elements of time represented in erased writing, *Hello Again*'s nontraditional, nonlinear structure brings the issue of time to the forefront of the audience's perception, allowing the musical to effect audience's in a variety of ways.

"All of Time Is Gone": *See What I Wanna See*

If *Hello Again*'s aim was to work closely with Arthur Schnitzler as a type of collaborator, then the collaboration between Ryūosuke Akutagawa and LaChiusa results in a far looser adaptation of the source material, as evidenced by the musical *See What I Wanna See*. In this musical, LaChiusa is far less reliant on his predecessor in terms of characters, location, and, in particular, conceptions of time and period. Despite that, Akutagawa and LaChiusa do approach their material from similar avenues. Akutagawa himself was adapting a folk-tale style that was more reminiscent of medieval Japanese stories.[45] This genealogical connection between the two writers may be a reason for LaChiusa's freer adaptation of the source material. In particular, LaChiusa manages to reorient concepts of space and time that bring Akutagawa's modernist short stories into a postmodern context. This relationship becomes clearer through Barnette's conception of "geographies of adaptation," which focuses on the physical transformation of adaptations as they move from the "imaginary into theatrical space."[46] While Barnette is mostly concerned with the practical application of this idea, namely the move from conceptual phase into production phase, I extend her definition to understand the ways in which space and, additionally, time function as an adaptable plane within the framework of adapted writing. My inclusion of "time" here may be a liberty taken too far, though I would argue that time has spatial configurations and geography that are similar to those associated with space. I take this stance while leaning on the work of Keumsoo Hong, who discusses the time-space relationship in discussing labor and power in the antebellum rural south.[47] Hong discusses how time, similarly to space, is "socially constructed," "invented," and "negotiated"; all three of these phrases bring to mind more geographic ideas that are usually associated with ordering and organizing space. By finding these common threads, Hong provides a framework for understanding both space and time in geographic terms. In order to move fluidly between conceptions of time and space, I also bring Barnette's work into conversation with more classical texts associated with phenomenology, in particular Maurice Merleau-Ponty's *Phenomenology of Perception*, in order to give a spatial argument about more thematic geographies.

To make this argument, it is helpful to briefly discuss the plots of the three short stories by Akutagawa that were adapted by LaChiusa. The first piece of source material is presented in the form of two complementary monologues. Though they are separate pieces, they are often referred to jointly as "Morito and Kesa." In the first monologue, Morito imparts the tale of his affair with Kesa and their plans to kill Kesa's husband, Wataru. In the second monologue, Kesa shares that she no longer wants to kill her husband and will have her lover Morito kill her instead. Both narratives offer a fascinating psychological profile, particularly given that both Kesa and Morito have become repulsed by each other. The second piece, "In a Bamboo Grove," became the basis for the famous 1950 film entitled *Rashomon*, directed by Akira Kurosawa.[48] In the story, a man's body is discovered by a woodcutter in an open field. The reader receives multiple reports of what happened from the woodcutter, a Buddhist priest, a bounty hunter, an old woman, and a thief and a woman that he raped, before hearing the final account of the ghost of the dead man through the guise of a medium.[49] The final story, entitled "The Dragon: The Old Potter's Tale," chronicles the practical joke of a monk named E'in, who posts a sign near a lake stating that a dragon will come up out of the water in three days. The sign attracts a host of visitors to the tiny town and, in the end, the dragon does appear, rendering E'in's joke moot. All three writings appear in print before and around the 1920s, toward the end of Akutagawa's brief life. Among the many themes that are present in all three stories, the idea of truth is most prominent. Additionally, these stories all present a universalizing effect, particularly the last two, that speaks to Akutagawa's larger geographical project—namely, the bringing together of Western culture and Japanese culture.

This facet of Akutagawa's work makes LaChiusa's interest in the project understandable. LaChiusa's methods of adaptation, which he labels as "mongrel," serve to further bring together Western and Eastern ideas, particularly in terms of the geography of each adaptation. Several "geographic adaptations" are evident in *See What I Wanna See*, particularly in terms of the settings employed for each story, the geography of the adaption itself, the geographies of time, and even the more theoretical geography of the concept of truth, a theme that is incredibly important in LaChiusa's adaptation of the piece. All of these geographies help make LaChiusa's adaptation of these stories, and his grouping of them together, more legible. In order to provide more context to Barnette's "geographies of adaptation," I utilize Merleau-Ponty's concept of "judgments" as a perception of the relationship between two objects.[50] This concept helps to explore the grouping of these stories, or "objects" in Merleau-Ponty's verbiage, as well as a framework for understanding each adaptation in relation to the short story that inspired it.

LaChiusa's musical opens with the sequence *Kesa and Morito (Kesa)*. Kesa enters, dressed in a kimono representative of the medieval Japanese roots that inspired Akutagawa's original writings. She is described by LaChiusa as being "a beautiful, sensual monster."[51] Also, her outfitting in a kimono helps to further sexualize the character while also exoticizing her, bringing to mind stereotypical images of the geisha. Over the course of the song, Morito appears and the audience learns that Kesa has decided to kill her lover tonight as her husband has "learned their secret."[52] At the end of the number, Kesa brandishes a knife as Morito moves his hands toward Kesa's throat. At the beginning of Act II, the number is repeated, this time from Morito's perspective. Morito also intends to kill Kesa now that her husband is aware of their indiscretions. Both versions of the song rest on the same melody, written in a modified version of AABA format. The lyrics are mostly the same with minor variations to allow for the differing perspectives of the characters in the scene. In both versions of the song, there is an invitation for the audience to consider conceptions of space and time, though in the case of both "Kesa" and "Morito," the focus is on leaving space and time, aspiring to a more liminal concept of each term. Before the song transitions from its second A section into its "B" section, both Kesa and Morito exclaim that as they give their lover a final kiss, "The room dissolves / Around me / I desert my body."[53] This lyric immediately brings to mind the idea of space and time occupied and, more to the point, departed. Both Kesa and Morito see their acts of passion and violence as a means of transporting them out of the location of their tryst and out of their corporeal prisons.

The next lyric similarly situates the characters as defying the bounds of corporeal and temporal geography:

> All of time is gone.
> Dusk is dawn
> Dawn is noon
> Late is now
> Now is soon
> This is what it's like to be God.[54]

This lyric performs a particular labor in setting up Kesa and Morito as transcending the boundaries of time, existing in a plane that allows them to experience the act of being God. This liminal space gives both Kesa and Morito the chance to view their actions apart from their corporeal geographies. "I watch myself outside myself … my God, it's hell to be God," they both exclaim, later commenting, "Watching from a distance, / I neither laugh nor cry."[55] Kesa and Morito both confirm that they have transcended the traditional bounds created by the geographies of space and time and this transcendence has given them the opportunity to look down on themselves.

In the production at The Anspacher Theatre, one of The Public Theater's smaller spaces, the director Ted Sperling kept the staging of both "Kesa" and "Morito" static, in some ways suggesting a counterposition to the transcendental quality of the lyrics.[56] It is more likely that the simple staging was intended to allow the lyrics to perform the labor of repositioning Kesa and Morito from their geographic boundaries into a plane where concepts of time and space are gone or, at least, are reconfigured. The pieces taken together produce a judgment regarding the nature of Kesa's transcendence separate from that of Morito. While Morito's version of the song presents a man who is making a difficult decision based in guilt and a need to reclaim honor, Kesa's version is almost animalistic. There is almost a pleasure in the task before her. The minor differences in the lyric help to elucidate this. A single word change between the two versions of the song aids the perception of Kesa's carnality and Morito's guilt. When describing what it is like to be God, Kesa comments that she is able to watch herself "Laugh and kiss and fuck and lie—…." In Morito's version, the word "fuck" is replaced with the less aggressive, arguably more polite word "screw." Additionally, while Kesa coldly concludes, "I'll end my lover's life," while brandishing a dagger, Morito gives us a description of how "She'll feel my hands about her, Tight around her throat." In Kesa's narrative, the appearance of the dagger gives us a visual manifestation of her intended violence. Conversely, Morito is reliant on the geographical bounds of words and his description almost suggests a sensuality regarding his chosen method of murder.

Two other conceptions of space and time merit mention. In the musical's world premiere in Williamstown, Massachusetts, and in the musical's New York City premiere, non-Asian actors were utilized for both "Kesa" and "Morito." In Williamstown, the roles were assayed by Audra McDonald and Michael C. Hall, respectively. At The Public Theater, they were performed by Idina Menzel and Marc Kudisch. There is an argument to be made that casting non-Asian actors in two scenes set in Medieval Japan, costumed in kimonos, participates in a type of "yellowface." While actors' faces were not painted in either production, the juxtaposition of non-Asian actors occupying the corporeal geography of Asian characters forces a consideration of racial casting politics. But it also points to one of Akutagawa's larger goals, namely to bring the East and the West together through a sense of universality in his stories. The casting particulars of both "Kesa" and "Morito" do inspire a type of phenomenological judgment regarding intentionality and legibility of identity politics. This conversation is further exacerbated by the fact that both of these actors must play other roles in the musical's other two storylines. This also lends weight to an argument regarding the porosity of casting dual roles, particularly in terms of weighing out the demands of one role in regard to another. The "borders" of these character geographies force a consideration of spatial occupation, a concept that could suggest either a radical rethinking of race in casting, as is discussed later in the chapter on *The Wild Party*, or an unintentional commentary reifying the effects of colonialism.

Finally, both the "Kesa" and "Morito" sequences upset the conceptions of time in the piece as a whole. While both versions of the lyric hold thematic relevance to both *R Shomon* and *Gloryday*, they are largely unintegrated into the rest of the piece. As such, they seem to reify McMillin's argument about the cohesion of differing elements in a musical.[57] But their inclusion in the musical as a whole also upsets the traditional conceptions of time that are inherent to a traditionally structured musical theatre piece. The distance in terms of time, given that both *R Shomon* and *Gloryday* take place in the twentieth and twenty-first century, respectively, provides both a literal and Brechtian distancing effect, forcing the audience to make the connections between a story of murder set in Medieval Japan with the other two acts of the musical. Further, the fact that "Kesa" and "Morito" are presented at a literal distance, with an entire act separating the two musical monologues, upsets generally held assumptions about the climax-driven nature of musicals. By reorienting the way that a musical relies on the geography of time, *See What I Wanna See* presents an alternative method of adapting work.

While "Kesa" and "Morito" inhabit a single literal space and a transcendental liminal space, *R. Shomon* utilizes multiple locations, though the majority of the story is told in an interrogation room. Largely in the spirit of Akutagawa's "In the Bamboo Grove," *R. Shomon* tells the story of a man murdered in Central Park in 1951 on the night of the American premiere of the film *Rashomon*. The act's title, missing the "a," refers to the marquee outside the theatre, which was missing the letter. Structurally, the musical moves back and forth between the interrogations of The Janitor, who discovers the body after finishing his shift at the movie theatre, The Thief, who confesses to raping the man's wife before killing him, The Wife, who confesses to killing her husband to relieve him of his shame before squelching on her promise to also kill herself, as well as the story told by The Husband himself, through the machination of The Medium. Each narrative is introduced in turn, though their interrogations weave in and out of each other. Extending from the geographical boundaries of the interrogation room, where the suspects' interlocutors are never visible or audible, the audience is eventually invited into a club near the movie theatre and, principally, in an area of Central Park where The Thief lures The Husband and The Wife with the promise of a hidden stash of cash. As scenes move fluidly in and out of the geography of the interrogation room—the act's principal setting—a type of porosity emerges from the various additional locales that appear in the musical. Each location exists simultaneously within the geography of the interrogation room and each witness is able to cross boundaries with ease.

The geography of time also becomes porous to an extent. Each character is forced to recount the same series of events from their perspective. Their stories don't align, signaling to the audience that someone in the story is lying. As time is rehearsed, the moment in question gains nuance while maintaining its ambiguity. This causes a type of breakdown in the traditional assumption regarding the way time generally works in a musical. Like *Hello Again* before it, *See What I Wanna See* aims to reorient audience expectations of the forward momentum that is commonly adhered to in musical theatre. Each reiteration of the story not only aids in the audience's disorientation, it complicates their relationships to each character, in particular The Wife, who is variously painted as victim, honorable murderer, and aggressive seductress. This reorientation not only remodels the geographies of time inherent to musical entertainment, it also alters the geography of the audience's relationship to the piece itself, forcing a reconsideration in the manner and methods of their spectatorship. Through the practical confines of the geographic configuration of the theatre, the audience understands their role to be entirely passive; they are taking in a play rather than engaging with it. *R Shomon* demands that the "place" that is the theatre become a "space" that is imbued with meaning as the result of the audience's modal transformation from "passive" to "active."

Barnette theorizes that one of the major distinctions between the terms "place" and "space" is that "place" refers to a location, while "space" is a "place" activated by meaning.[58] While a handful of locations appear throughout each witness's testimony, the primary location for each of the five characters is the clearing in Central Park: the location of the murder. This setting is imbued with meaning for all five of the characters in the act, particularly for The Janitor, who usually passed by the location of the murder when he went home from work in the early hours of the morning: "The truth is … I'll never be able to take my shortcut home through the park anymores—after what I saw, it's ruined for me. The city can be so beautiful and so mean …," he states toward the end of the act as his interlocutors demand that he recount the story once again.[59] Because Central Park becomes a place of trauma for all of these characters, it is activated as a space in which each character is forced to keep recounting the events of that night through their own perspectives. Their versions of "the truth" are deeply connected to the trauma that gives the space and their character arcs meaning.

Central Park is also activated with meaning in the narrative of Act II's *Gloryday*. The plot follows the basic framework of Akutagawa's "The Dragon," though the ending is dramatically different. A Catholic priest questions his faith in the wake of the 9/11 attacks and removes his clerical collar. He decides to play a practical joke by posting a sign in Central Park saying that a miracle will occur in three days. The sign draws significant attention and becomes a major media event, with celebrities swarming the park for the moment of the miracle. At the moment The Priest designated, a huge rainstorm engulfs Central Park, causing the onlookers to shield their heads and eyes. A miracle does occur, but The Priest is the only one who sees it. The event deepens The Priest's crisis of faith and, by the end of the act, he has put his clerical collar back on, though he still refrains from celebrating mass until he comes to some sort of conclusion. The act is framed as a confession from The Priest to the Monsignor. In the final moments of the act, The Priest pleads, "I created a lie that became the truth. The lie was for everyone. But the truth was only for myself. So what do I do with it? Monsignor? What do I do with the truth?"[60]

The word "truth" becomes the thematic conceit that ties all of the three short stories together in LaChiusa's adaptation. In "Kesa" and "Morito," both characters reflect that "A lie becomes the truth / And the truth becomes a lie."[61] Throughout *R Shomon*, each of the characters reiterates the phrase "I only told you the truth" throughout the entirety of the act, each challenging their interlocutors to challenge their version of events. This phrase forms the basis of the final musical sequence in the piece in which all five characters sing overlapping versions of the phrase.[62] In *Glorday*, The Priest must consider the very nature of truth. Throughout the evening, the geographies of truth have grown more and more complex. In "Kesa," truth is understood as something that is manipulated, as something that is reified when the same phrase is used by Morito at the beginning of Act II. *R Shomon* also encourages the thesis that truth is manipulatable, with the added complication that truth is never revealed to the audience with any degree of certainty.

While the geography of truth for The Priest in *Gloryday* is also a flexible boundary that he manipulates, he is challenged to consider that truth was never within his abilities to manipulate after all. In the final moment of the act and of the musical, in which the ensemble echoes The Priest's invocation of the word "truth," the audience is left to consider the ways in which truth as an organizing, geographic force is both within and outside human control.

The musical's structure as a whole, and its presentation of time, also becomes complicated by *Gloryday*'s location at the end of the show. While *R Shomon* works in a manner similar to *Hello Again* in regard to its geographic configuration of time, *Gloryday* is far more traditionally structured; the events fold out in a largely linear and causal manner coming out of said flashback. Traditional musical theatre tropes abound, including "I want" songs, a song in which a character clearly identifies their objectives, and even an 11 o'clock number, a large number full of emotion that usually begins the falling action of the musical's trajectory. The result is, again, disorienting by design, particularly given that *Kesa*, *R Shomon*, and *Morito* have all preceded *Gloryday*, signaling to the audience that nothing they are about to witness is traditionally structured. When *Gloryday* begins, the audience is now asked to follow a modified traditional structure, complete with inciting incident and climax. In terms of the geography of the piece, expectations and boundaries are realigned. The assumed geographies of time that were broken with the first three pieces are suddenly back in place, allowing the audience to consider a story in a presentation with which they are more comfortable. Despite that, it is arguable the change in narrative and organizational tactics produce a more distancing effect than expected, despite *Gloryday*'s bent toward traditional structure.

This extends outward into the show's choice of setting. While the phrase itself is never invoked, it becomes clear early in the text of *Gloryday* that the musical takes place roughly a year after the 9/11 attacks on the World Trade Center. In the opening moments of the act, The Priest references a "tragedy" that happened "last year." "What had constituted my calling disappeared, gradually—It wasn't kicked out of me—even though the tragedy that hit this city could have contributed, but I'm not going to blame that for it."[63] The Priest stumbles with words, trying to bring focus to his crisis of faith. Later, as he begins to sing, other phrases bring to mind the 9/11 moment:

> Last year.
> Last year.
> I saw the world exploding.
> I felt a weird foreboding
> Before I watched the city fall
> In silver clouds
> Consuming crowds
> Of unsuspecting souls.[64]

In addition, The Reporter references the event of the 9/11 attacks without directly naming it later in the act. When recounting to The Priest that they had met before, The Reporter states: "Last year. Last year, during the 'Tragedy'—you know, 'America's Tragedy.' Whatever we were calling it—I was downtown covering the fucking disaster—I remember bumping into you—you were running toward. I was running away."[65] For both the characters in the show, each of whom has encountered a variation of an existential crisis, and the audience, presumably American, the 9/11 moment becomes a type of space: a temporal place activated by meaning. The refusal to name the event is a fascinating tactic. In particular, the assumption of the audience's recognition of the event as well as the assumption of their response to its less-than-direct invocation, forces an emotional connection when the musical itself is perceived by the audience. LaChiusa wants his audience to question whether the above references are to the 9/11 attacks because it forces a more cerebral perception from the audience when considering the show, particularly given that the emotions that The Priest and other characters experience at the end are raw and vulnerable. This sense of detachment doesn't negate an emotional response to the material so much as it works in concert to allow the viewer to fully consider their reactions to the piece. Unlike *R Shomon*, which doesn't ask the audience to care for any of the characters, particularly since it is impossible to know which characters to trust, The Priest of *Gloryday* is all too human. His breakdown leading to the miracle is visceral as is the exits of The C.P.A and The Actress, both of whom came to the priest looking for hope and inspiration in connection to the announcement of the miracle. The geography of the piece, utilizing traditional frameworks, does allow for a sense of identification as well as a more cerebral consideration of the themes of the musical.

The three parts taken together, *See What I Wanna See* provides a fascinating consideration of Barnette's "geographies of adaptation." In each adapted work, spatial considerations become paramount, particularly in terms of places, both literal and imagined, that are activated by meaning. Barnette differentiates between the space of mimesis, what is happening on stage, and the space of the audience, what is being perceived by "the house."[66] It is my goal to see the adjacent spaces as inseparable, and I have endeavored to consider them both in tandem. Spatial and temporal considerations help define and manipulate the relationship between the inhabitants of the mimetic space and the audience space. When the three somewhat disparate elements of LaChiusa's musical work in tandem, they create a type of judgment between audience and performers in which the relationship is established through *Kesa*, cemented by *R Shomon* and "Morito," and then reconfigured and redefined through the more traditional structure of *Gloryday*. Place and space are concepts that are also defined in terms of habitus, particularly during *Kesa* and *Morito* in which the body is considered a place, activated into a space by meaning, that is both habitable and optional; both characters claim that they are able to desert their bodies during the act of sex. *R Shomon* also reifies the porosity of the geographical borders of the body by allowing The Husband to fully inhabit the body of The Medium. Finally, in *Gloryday*, The Priest also remarks that he feels that he is able to exit his body, making him feel like a deity in much the same way that Kesa and Morito express: "it's as though I am outside of my body and I see myself eating and breathing and sleeping and there is no sense of time. This is what it's like to be God, I realize. I only watch and I only listen," he muses as the rest of the company is engaged in prayer.[67]

While the geography of the body and its corporeal boundaries is largely theoretical, another type of geography is even more amorphous. Barnette defines the concept of "imaginary space," namely as a theoretical "space of ideas and cognition, usually driven by the director's concept but equally influenced by the spirit of adaptation."[68] Barnette suggests that imaginary space is a collaborative space between the director, writer, and adaptation dramaturg that works closely within the limitless geography of possibility. The trick, of course, is to merge the theoretical, the imagined, with the practical. I have employed this concept sparingly, largely because it is impossible to know what the imaginary space shared by LaChiusa and director Ted Sperling looked like. But the concept does help us in further bridging the relationship between the audience and the mimesis. The imaginary space in which LaChiusa and his collaborators conceived of *See What I Wanna See* is, eventually, bridged into the practical by concerns of playing space and, more importantly, by expectations of the audience response in "the house." While discussing *See What I Wanna See*, I have often assumed audience response by substituting my own responses to the work. While admitting this is important, it also complicates my analysis. Indeed, I have seen what I want to see.

"What Do I Do with the Truth?": Adaptation Theory and Musicals

Adaptation theory aids in the exploration of musical theatre writing processes, particularly given that the vast majority of musicals are adaptations of preexisting materials. The concept of "palimpsestuous pleasures" helps us to identify the recent tendency toward direct adaptations of popular films. In his review of *Pretty Woman*, Ben Brantley bemoans that the adaptation "lowers the already ground-scraping bar for literal-minded adaptations of film to stage."[69] Brantley's use of the term "literal-minded" seems an apt descriptor for the type of musical that attempts to place the entire screenplay of a film on stage with songs shoehorned in. Additionally, this emphasis on the "literal-minded" also defines a type of geography of adaptation. This geography is defined and, frankly, limited by the need to create a commercially successful product that will work on the audience's sense of nostalgia, allowing for little variation from the source material that came before it. Both theoretical concepts taken together help us to understand the ways in which the many musicals that populate what LaChiusa calls "The Great Gray Way" have created a type of formula for commercial success.

But it also helps in understanding the ways in which LaChiusa and his peers have tried to subvert those expectations. *Hello Again* and *See What I Wanna See* saw over a decade between their premieres in New York City. Yet, rather than succumbing to the theoretical positions that allowed the proliferation of the screen-to-stage craze, LaChiusa uses them in an entirely different manner, largely in an attempt to offer an alternative theatre to the more formula-driven film adaptations of the period. While *Marie Christine* and *The Wild Party* are notable efforts to subvert the commercial producing formula, they are discussed in great detail in other chapters. LaChiusa's adaptation of Federico García Lorca's *The House of Bernarda Alba*, simply entitled *Bernarda Alba*, deserves a mention, largely because it works against the grains of commercial expectations for musical entertainment while also remaining remarkably faithful to Lorca's play. The musical tells the story of Bernarda Alba, a stern woman who has just buried her second husband. She takes charge of her husband's house, which is also inhabited by Bernarda's five daughters and her senile mother. While she orders her daughters to maintain the ritual of mourning, things become complicated when a suitor meant for her eldest daughter Angustias is discovered to be having a secret affair with her youngest daughter, Adela. Bernarda shoots Pepe and leads Adela to believe that he is dead, though he survives. Adela, overcome with grief, hangs herself. In both the play and LaChiusa's musical, Bernarda insistently intones that her daughter died a virgin, despite the fact that the family is aware of Adela's affair with Pepe.[70]

LaChiusa's direct adaptation of Lorca's play serves to give audience's palimpsestuous pleasures, particularly those audience members who are familiar with Lorca's work. Further, the geography of LaChiusa's adaptive techniques would seem to more closely mirror those present in the screen-to-stage craze, particularly in light of the massive re-imaginings of *Hello Again*, *See What I Wanna See*, and other works by LaChiusa. This isn't to suggest that *Bernarda Alba* was an attempt at a commercially successful piece; those familiar with the Lorca play are likely aware of the play's darkness and lack of obvious music.

But *Bernarda Alba* may be an important tool in understanding the plurality that emerges in musical theatre entertainment, particularly in the 1990s and 2000s. Lundskaer-Nielsen discusses this type of plurality, in which the pieces that extend from the megamusical producing model can exist in tandem with more adventurous work, fostered by dramaturgical innovations more typically associated with nonmusical fare.[71] With the advent of the musical *Rent* in 1996, it appeared that Broadway may be able to support both commercially formulaic geographies of adaptation and more adventurous types of adaptations, namely Jonathan Larson's resetting of Puccini's *La Boheme* to New York City at the heart of the AIDS crisis. With Larson's death, a vacuum was created in which many critics looked to LaChiusa's work as a possible heir apparent. While Lundskaer-Nielsen is right to point out this plurality, it would be unwise to assume that it means these musicals were received on equal footing. Despite the massive success of *Rent*, more adventurous geographies of adaptation were the exception on Broadway through much of the 1990s and 2000s.

While the adventurous adaptation may not have found equal footing in the immediate wake of *Rent*, it can certainly be argued that Lundskaer-Nielsen's plurality has found more salience in the past ten years or so. Several musicals, developed in major nonprofit theatres by directors trained in more contemporary dramaturgical techniques, have found commercial viability in a market that once seemed hostile to such pursuits. In November of 2006, a musical adaptation of Wedekind's controversial play *Spring Awakening* settled in for a comfortable run of 859 performances at the Eugene O'Neill Theatre. In more recent years, unlikely adaptations have not only found critical success and Tony Awards, they've also become more commercially viable. New York City critics were shocked when The Public Theater-produced off-Broadway hit *Fun Home*, with music by Jeanine Tesori and book and lyrics by Lisa Kron, announced it would transfer in a new arena-style staging to Broadway's Circle in the Square Theatre. Yet, the Broadway production managed to turn a profit in its over-a-year run on Broadway as well as winning the Tony Award for Best Musical over crowd pleasers *Something Rotten* and *An American in Paris* prior to launching a national tour. The musical, based on the graphic novel and memoir by Alison Bechdel, tells the story of the cartoonist and her complicated relationship with her closeted father. More recently, a musical adaptation of the 2007 independent film *The Band's Visit* managed to recoup its entire capitalization over a year-and-a-half run at the Ethel Barrymore Theatre after having an initial run with the Atlantic Theatre Company. The musical, with music and lyrics by David Yazbek and book by Itamar Moses, follows an Egyptian police band who find themselves stranded in the Israeli town of Bet Hatikva. While the runs of these shows were modest, the largest hit of recent Broadway memory, Lin Manuel Miranda's *Hamilton*, was also an unlikely adaptation, namely a hip-hop/rap-inflected retelling of Ron Chernow's biography *Alexander Hamilton*. The musical has not only swept the Tony Awards, it has also won the Pulitzer Prize for Drama, launched numerous tours and sit-down productions, and has inspired a pop culture phenomenon not seen on Broadway since the initial reception to *Rent*.

While recent changes in what is considered commercially viable on Broadway are a positive sign for fans of "The New Musical Drama," it would be presumptuous to assume the developments of the past ten years have instituted a trend. Regardless of the future of "The New Musical Drama" on Broadway, it does seem that the form is likely to stick around as long as nonprofits are willing to develop them. It is unsurprising, then, that LaChiusa has found a steady home in New York City's major nonprofits: Playwrights' Horizons, The Public Theater, and Lincoln Center. The geographies of production may be changing and LaChiusa's work, which has constantly challenged the geographic boundaries of adaptation, may have played a pivotal role in breaking down some of those formula-dependent borders.

CHAPTER 5
"TO LIVE IN LIGHT": HISTORICAL CONVERSATIONS IN *THE WILD PARTY*

Issues of race and casting have been prevalent throughout the history of the Broadway musical. Many examples throughout the history of the American musical point to the occasionally uncomfortable relationship between musical theatre and "nontraditional casting."

Angela C. Pao defines nontraditional casting as extending from "a larger social mission of inclusion and stimulated by the interpretative possibilities opened up when the bodies, minds, and experiences of a new set of actors are brought together …."[1] Pao then goes on to discuss examples of revivals of canonical musicals that have engaged in nontraditional casting to varying degrees of success. Among them, she includes all-Black Broadway revivals of *Hello Dolly!* and *Guys and Dolls* as well as an all-Asian off-Broadway production of the Jewish musical *Falsettos*. Pao argues that the "highly composite" nature of the musical makes it a fertile ground for considerations of the impact of nontraditional casting. Pao's work helps us to understand the issues with casting in Michael John LaChiusa and George C. Wolfe's musical *The Wild Party* particularly in terms of the recasting of an actress of color with a white actress. This change in casting plays on what Pao calls the "borderlands of fantasy" that are endemic to the American musical by a white body in a role originally conceived for an actress of color, a move that forces the central role of "Queenie" and the other guests of *The Wild Party* into a historical conversation with histories of vaudeville in particular and musical entertainment in general.[2]

On April 9th, 1997, The Public Theatre, under the artistic leadership of George C. Wolfe, gave Michael John LaChiusa a blind commission to develop a musical of his choosing.[3] This offer in many ways continued The Public Theatre's association with LaChiusa as the theatre had produced *First Lady Suite* in 1993 and *The Petrified Prince* in 1994. By April 27th, LaChiusa had presented three songs for a property based on John Moncure March's 1928 poem *The Wild Party* to Wiley Hausam, who would become the musical's dramaturg.[4] A reading of the musical followed in October of the same year, after which Wolfe decided to come on board as director. The process of developing the musical went slowly and the casting net was thrown wide. Stars as big as Madonna took meetings with Wolfe about the possibility of staring in the musical as "Queenie." In July of 1998, the shape of the musical took another turn as Wolfe decided to take on an additional role as book writer of the musical. As the musical came closer to a production timetable, The Public Theatre was able to bring on board Tony Award–winning actor Mandy Patinkin for the role of "Burrs" and internationally acclaimed singer and actress Eartha Kitt in the role of Dolores in the early months of 1999.

On February 2nd of that year, it was announced that African American actress-singer Vanessa Williams would play the role of "Queenie" on Broadway in the spring, foregoing initial plans to open the musical downtown at The Public Theatre's home space. Rumors had been swirling for months that the well-known singer and actress would be involved in the Broadway premiere of the musical, LaChiusa's second entry into the 1999–2000 season. These rumors were fueled by LaChiusa himself who leaked the possibility of Williams casting in an article to theatre columnist Michael Riedel on January 8th, a month before the casting was official.[5] A two-week workshop was scheduled in which the role of "Queenie" was tailored to Williams, who is African American, adding an additional racialized subtext given the character is defined as a "blonde" whose "face was a tinted mask of snow" in March's poem.[6]

In September of 1999, Williams shared with the producers that she was pregnant and would not be able to commit to an opening for the next season. Wolfe and The Public Theatre made attempts to adjust the schedule, but Patinkin's other commitments problematized that effort and Williams had to withdraw from the production. Producers felt the need to keep the show on track, scheduling wise, particularly when Manhattan Theatre Club announced that they would produce another musical based on "The Wild Party" poem, this one with book, music, and lyrics by Andrew Lippa, in February of 2000, meaning LaChiusa's version would open about a month later than the Lippa version. Less than two weeks after Williams' decision to withdraw, Wolfe and LaChiusa met with white actress Toni Collette and immediately agreed that she was the fit they needed. A month later, producers announced that Williams would be replaced by Collette while much of the cast from the developmental workshop in February 1999 would remain the same.[7]

LaChiusa was excited by the racialized narrative of Williams, an African American woman passing in "white face" in contrast to her lover Burrs, a white man performing in "black face." The casting change is significant, particularly given that little of the show's textual references, particularly those explicitly discussing the concept of "masks," were eliminated or rewritten. The linguistic motif of Queenie's "mask of snow" remains prominent in the shows final text, particularly in the show's final scene when Queenie, symbolically and quite literally, smears off the white make-up that is hiding her face in order to finally "live in light." As a result, Collette's performance, lauded by most critics, becomes trapped in a kind of dissonance with a theatrical concept that her white body cannot support. This creates a disruption and intervenes in the musical's racialized narrative. Relying heavily on Brenda Dixon Gottschild's work on the historical relationship of white appropriation of black culture in racialized performance, I argue that the move from casting an actress of color to a white actress participates in a historicized conversation regarding the role and place of black and white bodies in the vaudeville-style performances indicative of early Broadway musicals.[8] This conversation extends from early twentieth-century New York-based vaudeville, where the story of *The Wild Party* is set, into considerations of race and casting in contemporary musical theatre.

African American music, dance, and performance have a long history of appropriation by white performers, choreographers, and other theatre artists. But it is important to understand that, while the above statement is true, a type of binarism emerges when thinking of "black performance" and "white performance" as separate genealogies. Brenda Dixon Gottschild's proposition that the study of "black dance" must assume and posit the existence and possible cultural prevalence of "white dance" suggest a binary that forces these casting decisions into a conversation with each other. Particularly, Gottschild is interested in the ways in which white culture fetishizes black culture while also showing disdain for the creators of black culture.[9] Because the text of the musical, which allowed for a black actress to perform in whiteface, remains largely unchanged, the white Queenie in "whiteface" suggests an appropriation of black situations, norms, and cultural expressions.

Dialogue and song lyrics are, therefore, understood in two ways. First, Queenie's text, the words and music she is asked to perform and the performance vocabulary that emerges as a result, is understood within its original context and casting concept, namely the casting of Williams. Second, Queenie's appropriation of the words and lyrics is understood as participating in a long-form history of appropriation, here focusing on the recasting of Collette and participating in what Allen Woll suggests as the long-form history of interaction between Afro-American issues and the musical theatre.[10] Within this concept, the symbol of face paint, white for Queenie, black for Burrs, becomes both a theatrical symbol and a theoretical hallmark, calling into mind the long-form history of racial and ethnic "masks" that are prevalent throughout the American musical theatre.[11] Harvey Young has helped to link the concept of historical conversation and theatre in *Embodying Black Experience*, particularly in his discussion of plays depicting sexual violence on black female bodies.[12] Young's concept aids in understanding both the text and the production of *The Wild Party* as a participant, intentional or otherwise, in a narrative of historical memory. Pao also comments on the nature of nontraditional casting as an upset to the need for verisimilitude expressed by audiences that are intent on resting comfortably in the realm of realism, despite the form's active rejection of realism.[13] Taken together, Gottschild, Young, and Pao assist in identifying *The Wild Party*, and musical theatre in general, as subjects fit for the realm of Critical Race Studies.

To establish this argument, I begin with a close reading of the written text of LaChiusa and Wolfe's *The Wild* Party as well as the *performed text* of the piece, noting how different staging concepts, performance choices, and performance contexts contribute to a more nuanced understanding of the musical's narrative. I also briefly look at the reviews of the original production as a means for understanding the musical's initial reception. Next, I explore three different strands that bring the racialized casting of *The Wild Party* into conversation with its historic antecedents. First, I explore the ways in which *The Wild* Party was already participating in a historical conversation based on its framing of several of the characters in the musical, particularly roles that are based on or inspired by historical figures as well as the historical role of blackface in vaudeville and early twentieth-century popular culture at large. Second, the role of "Queenie" is situated between both casting concepts, explicating the ways in which the casting change not only resituated the musical's narrative but made a firm comment on the role of racial appropriation and reappropriation for white vaudeville performers. Finally, calling specifically on the work of Pao, the text of *The Wild Party* is analyzed in order to establish the ways in which the writers intentionally and unintentionally set their musical in conversation with historical circumstances which frame the strictures between white and black vaudevillian performers.

It is worth noting that both LaChiusa and Wolfe contest the idea that Queenie must be played by an African American actress. Shortly after the announcement of Collette, Wolfe made a comment in *Variety* that none of the roles in *The Wild Party* was racially specific, contending the only thing that was important was that "Queenie be a blonde."[14] LaChiusa is less willing to dismiss the fact that Williams' race afforded the writing team an opportunity to further explore the idea of "masks." Responding to an interview question about *The Wild Party* and race, he notes:

> It was originally written for Vanessa Williams. She got pregnant, so we decided to go with the remarkable Toni Collette. I don't think of it as something that was lost in the piece, but would have been fascinating to see how an audience responded to a black Queenie. The show is all about the masks that we wear culturally, and the removal of those masks over the course of the party. So it's all there ….[15]

LaChiusa's framing of "masks" in *The Wild Party* is directly referenced in the show's dramaturgical protocol packet. The document, compiled by Hausam, includes many quotes from Claude Levi-Strauss theorizing on the nature of masks from an anthropological standpoint. In particular, he notes, "A mask is chiefly not what it represents but what it transforms, that is, what it chooses NOT to represent."[16] As such, the essential narrative of *The Wild Party*'s casting change speaks volumes about the ongoing color-blind casting issues. Further, the monumental success of *Hamilton*, discussed in more detail in this chapter's conclusion, has produced a new logic for reading bodies of color on stage, particularly in terms of upsetting the insistence on verisimilitude voiced by Pao.[17]

The Wild Party on Broadway[18]

The Wild Party began preview performances at the Virginia Theatre on March 10th, 2000, and officially opened on April 13, 2000. As previously mentioned, the musical featured score and lyrics by LaChiusa and a book by LaChiusa and George C. Wolfe. Wolfe also directed with choreography by Joey McKneely. In addition to The Public Theatre, Scott Rudin and Paramount Pictures were billed as coproducers. The costume designer was Toni-Leslie James; the lighting design was done by Jules Fischer and

Peggy Eisenhower and the scenic design was by Robin Wagner. Wagner's work in transforming the Virginia Theatre into a 1920s vaudeville house was immediately evident. As the audience filed into the theatre, a grand red curtain, accented in golden yellow fringe, caressed the stage floor. Above the curtain, a false proscenium, reminiscent of Ziegfeld-era vaudeville, framed the stage. At stage left, an easel showcased a placard that read "Opening Act."

In the book for the musical, the following section is labeled as "The Vaudeville." As a dissonant chord blares from the audience, the curtain parts at center, revealing an empty stage. Slowly, the male members of the cast file into the space, some smoking. Marc Kudisch, in the role of Jackie, begins the brassy anthem "Queenie Wazza Blonde," a theme that is quickly picked up by the other men. While the men wander the space aimlessly, the women enter in a chorus line. Among the chorus line stands Queenie. Immediately, the character, as embodied by Collette, presents her body as an eroticized space. "Queenie was sexually ambitious," sings a male member of the ensemble, echoing March's original poem.[19] Slowly, the other men take up the refrain, echoing into a growing chant. Each of the men reaches out and fondles Queenie's body. Eventually, the women join them. The entire ensemble makes physical contact with Queenie's sexualized body, furthering the idea that, while Queenie may maintain and control her sexual identity, her actual body is not her own. The final chorus of the song climaxes as Queenie, surrounded by the entire ensemble, removes her top, exposing her bare breasts to the audience.

There is a gunshot and the company scatter across the stage as a spotlight surveys the playing area. The placard on the easel is changed; the new placard reads "Burrs the Clown." And Burrs, played by Mandy Patinkin, enters. "He was comical as sin, he was comical as hell," the female chorines sing.[20] Burrs is in blackface and wearing a felt hairpiece. He begins to sing a vaudeville tune, "Marie Is Tricky," which is interspersed with short comic lines delivered directly to the audience. Burrs' number is brief and soon a painted drop is lowered, revealing Burrs and Queenie's apartment. The placard on the easel now reads "Comic Interludes." Queenie and Burrs engage in a fight after she asks him to pour her a cup of coffee. The exchange quickly becomes violent, with Burrs aggressively lowering Queenie to the bed and kissing her. Queenie slaps him and breaks free. He advances on her and Queenie takes a knife and, lunging at Burrs, cries, "You touch me—I'll kill you, you filthy bastard!"[21] The music and the action stop. While everything prior to this moment was played with a presentational style, evoking the feel of vaudeville, Queenie's action of grabbing the knife breaks the artifice of that style. Collette reads the above line with a heavy dose of psychological realism. Her previous physical manner—loose, open, permissive—becomes rigid, scared, and almost animalistic. Her vocal timbre loses its airy quality and becomes piercing, direct, and focused. It is this moment that Wolfe's concept for the production becomes clear; Queenie will spend the rest of the evening combatting two worlds. The first, the world of vaudeville, positions her body as a commodity. The second, her real life, is a terrifying place of nakedness and internal truth. This break from the vaudevillian tone of the show is brief, however, as Burrs recommends that they throw "a wild party …" that evening. Both Queenie and Burrs sing a duet ("Wild Party") describing the possibilities of throwing a party.

At the end of the number, a colorful scrim drops from the fly space as Burrs and Queenie exit. The next section of the musical is labeled as the "Promenade of Guests." One by one, the audience is introduced to most of the denizens that will attend the wild party. As they enter, they sing the song "Dry," a number that humorously details the dangers of being sober. The first is Jackie, a rich playboy who describes himself as "ambisextrous."[22] As he exits, he changes the placard on the easel to a new card reading "Olio-Promenade of Guests." Next is Madelaine True, a former stripper, and her date Sally. Next is Eddie, a black ex-boxer, and his white wife Mae and her little sister Nadine, a young girl of fourteen. The Brothers D'Armano enter next, Phil and Oscar, a vaudeville brother act that the text of the musical describes as "the epitome of 'continental colored.'"[23] The final guest to enter during the promenade is Dolores Montoya, described as "an ageless, eternal, ferocious performer of vaguely Latin origins."[24] Dolores was played by the late Eartha Kitt, whose own storied career added a layer of nostalgia and legitimacy to the role. Burrs, wearing a smoking jacket, enters to greet his guests in a series of short scenes reminiscent of quick vaudeville interactions. As such, the delivery of these moments is consistent with the vaudeville tone with actors delivering lines straight out for the benefit of the audience.

As the number ends, the scrim flies out to reveal Burrs and Queenie's apartment, this time a realized, four-room apartment sitting on a turntable at center, supplanting the painted backdrop that represented the apartment in the scene before. Queenie enters and Oscar and Phil D'Armano take to the piano to sing "My Beautiful Blonde" to introduce Queenie. The number directly segues into the jazzy "Welcome to My Party," in which Queenie overtakes the room. Queenie reminds the audience of the central conceit of Wolfe's staging—the battle between truth and illusion, light and dark—in the song's lyric: "The creatures of the night / Have come here to play. We don't like the light / And we don't need the day." The song delivers a big finish and segues into the next number. For the rest of the "Olio" section, guests of the party sing individual numbers, introducing themselves to the audience while remaining in context of the party. Madelaine True sings to Burrs about her date in "Like Sally," a humorous number that describes Sally in expressive ways, comedically juxtaposed with the nearly catatonic performance of Sally Murphy as Sally. Next, Jackie regales Queenie, Mae, and Nadine with the story of his life as "the proverbial black sheep" during "Breezin' Through Another Day."[25]

Moving back to the piano, the Brothers D'Armano sing a duet, "Uptown," which bemoans how uptown is beginning to resemble the more bohemian, liberal downtown area of Manhattan. During the number, two producers, Goldoff (who has changed his name to just "Gold") and Goldberg, join the party at the invitation of Burrs, who hopes to hitch himself and Queenie to the producers' move to an uptown theatre. The Brothers scat and dance and are eventually joined by Burrs, who, likely in an attempt to impress his producer guests, also scats, forcibly juxtaposing the blackface performer between two African American performers. "Eddie and Mae" allows both of the song's title characters to explain their new lives as Eddie has become a novelty act in his retirement. Gold and Goldberg then sing a number titled "Gold and Goldberg" about their need to move a hit act into an uptown theatre. This number is immediately followed by a solo moment for Dolores, who, having heard about Gold and Goldberg's plans, attempts to seduce the men to take her with them as they are "Moving Uptown."

The "Promenade of Guests" ends as Queenie fakes a fainting spell in order to refocus attention back on her. When asked what's wrong, Queenie says that she needs to dance the Black Bottom, leading the rest of the company to break out in laughter. The dance begins the next part of the show, simply entitled "The Party." Queenie begins a type of chant as she and the Brothers D'Armano lead the company in dancing "The Black Bottom," an African American vernacular dance craze that became popular with white dancers and audiences in the 1920s.[26] During the course of the number, Queenie once again drops the vaudevillian artifice and reveals her fears of reality and truth. While she begins the number with a reckless abandon, she is vacant and left behind by the number's end. She is rescued, however, by the entrance of the party's final two guests, Queenie's best friend Kate and Kate's date. Kate, who also used to dance in vaudeville, has scored a degree of celebrity, a fact that is confirmed by the reaction of other guests to her entrance.

She and Queenie engage in a bit of competitive insulting, each ribbing the other in turn, before celebrating their antagonistic friendship in the song "My Best Friend." During the number, Kate introduces Queenie to her new beau, Black. The attraction between Queenie and Black is instantly palpable. Burrs pulls Kate aside, suspecting she is up to something as the Brothers D'Armano perform the number "A Little M-m-m." During the number, a series of vignettes are played. During one of these short scenes, Kate tells Black that she senses he wants to "go play." She gives her permission, but not before curtly reminding him, "No matter what, we leave together."[27] She then kisses him, in essence marking her territory.

The party continues and Black eventually gets Queenie alone. Black confesses that he is a "moocher," using his good looks and charisma to survive as a kept man. Queenie asks to see Black's "mooch" and he obliges, performing the number "Takin' Care of the Ladies." The two dance and Burrs, clearly agitated, confronts Kate. Kate needles him, and Burrs explodes, performing a very tongue-in-cheek retort in "Wouldn't It Be Nice?" Black pulls Queenie aside to ask how she and Burrs ended up together. Queenie performs the stunning solo "Lowdown Down" where she speaks, largely in metaphors, insinuating that she lives with Burrs because she deserves nothing better. Collette's performance of this number is fascinatingly nuanced. While she begins the number in a very presentational manner, her focus out to the audience, she also takes some moments of the number directly to Black, showing the ongoing fight between her presentational persona and her need to share honestly with another human being. By the end of the number, Queenie backs away from both Black and the audience and has a very insular, intimate moment, lost in a vulnerable thought: "Small town girl, she comes to town / Tin of rouge and backless gown. Dies a lot before she gets to die."

The intimate moment is interrupted again by an explosive Burrs, who, seeing the connection between Black and Queenie, decides to attempt to ramp up the party. He leads the bombastic, defiant number "Gin/Wild" as the guests become more and more intoxicated. This number is also frequently interrupted with a series of vignettes, during which more of Burrs' violent behavior directed at Queenie is displayed. Additionally, small pieces of Burrs' history with domestic violence are revealed by Dolores and Kate. As the number reaches a frenzied, drunken climax, Black leads off a distraught Queenie, who is suddenly horrified by the ruckus. The action then moves to the bedroom of the apartment, where Burrs and Kate begin to engage in foreplay. Kate sings about her relationship with Black, a relationship built on lies and artifice, in the bluesy number "Black Is a Moocher." Behind the headboard of the bed, the rest of the company can be seen dancing with each other, groping each other. As the song climaxes, the guests at the party form a group at center. The catatonic Sally is hoisted in the air, her body suddenly writhing, her breasts exposed. The group seemingly melts into the stage picture as the wild party suddenly transitions into a wild orgy.

As the lights dim on the bacchanalia, a balcony unit appears downstage left, revealing Queenie and Black. Again, Queenie articulates the musical's ongoing theme with light and dark: "I was that girl. I'm all of them. Trapped in a room full of shadows and not enough light. And soon we will fade away, into the walls, into nothingness. The end." Queenie and Black join together in a song where they both question where people like them belong in the world. The number "People Like Us" is a significant departure from the rest of the score. The vaudeville and jazz idioms that tie most of the score are largely abandoned for a more pop feel, relying on a verse-chorus structure. Additionally, this is the first time Queenie drops her "persona" for the length of an entire number. Black gently kisses her as the number fades out.

As the lights fade on Black and Queenie on the balcony, they fade up dimly on the apartment unit. The next section of the show is called "After Midnight Dies." This is also the title of the first song sung in this section. It is performed by Sally as she observes the aftermath of the orgy. The lyric to the song is only four lines and succinctly foreshadows the forthcoming section of the show:

Down goes the wall, down goes the guard.
After midnight dies, it ain't so hard.
To see the truth, no need for lies.
What we are is all we are after midnight dies.[28]

Several short numbers are presented without break, wallowing in the literal and figurative darkness of the late hour. Eddie sings the plaintive "Golden Boy," in which he expresses remorse over his faded career and the tensions of being a black man in the spotlight, particularly a black man with a white wife. Oscar and Phil, who had previously fought over Jackie's sexual overtures toward Phil, reconnect through a reprise of the song "A Little M-m-m." Gold and Goldberg, sitting stunned in the kitchen, recount the sordid night via "The Movin' Uptown Blues." This reversion back to the structure of the "olio" sequence is interrupted by a longer scene between the young Nadine and playboy Jackie in the apartment bedroom. Jackie offers Nadine her first line of cocaine, sending the young girl into a spirited reprise of her theme "The Lights of Broadway." At the end of the number, Nadine requests more cocaine. Jackie fixates on the word "more," which leads him into a song of the same name in which he articulates his constant need for more. At the song's end, he forces himself on top of Nadine and attempts to rape her. Nadine's screams are overheard in the other room, and Eddie rushes in, pulls Jackie off of Nadine, and punches him in the face. The incident breaks up the party.

Kate finds Black and chastises him. While Black protests that it was Kate who told him to play, Kate retorts saying, "Play, yes. Not fall in love."[29] Kate kicks off a series of overlapping numbers with "Love Ain't Nothin / Welcome to Her Party." The later theme is picked up by Burrs, who, after threatening Queenie physically, warns Black not to touch Queenie's painted face. Queenie responds, claiming the "only thing that'll wash me clean … is seeing you dead."[30] Black pulls her into the bedroom to calm her down while Burrs blames Kate for bringing Black as a means to pull apart his relationship with Queenie. Kate informs Burrs that he only has himself to blame as Burrs launches into the intense number "How Many Women in the World?," in which he bemoans his love for Queenie. During the number, Burrs overhears Gold and Goldberg fighting over which one of them should inform Burrs that he won't be moving uptown with their show. From this point, Burrs loses himself and begins slipping into a reprise of "Marie Is Tricky." At the end of the song, Burrs begins to "black up" as he ominously begins to intone, "How many, many, many, many, many, many, many women? / Her. Her. Her."[31]

The final moment in the "After Midnight Dies" sequence belongs to Dolores, who is seen wondering around the party in the dark, unaware that everyone has left. Dolores muses on the relationship between light and dark. While she used to enjoy being shrouded in darkness, her feelings have changed. "But now I want the light stark and unforgiving, the kind of light that reveals all and spares none." She then launches into the 11 o'clock number "When It Ends," during which she asserts that no "party's gonna last forever" and that "you better hope … that you got the right stuff when it ends."[32]

The final section of the show, appropriately entitled "Finale," begins with a single spotlight on Queenie in the bedroom. Only the bed and the Victrola are left on the turntable. Black is sleeping in bed. As the lights of dawn seep into the bedroom, Queenie sings "This Is What It Is," in which she resists the urge to remain in the dark and considers the possibility of living in the day, in the light. Black wakes up and kisses her, then takes his hand to her face to remove her makeup. Queenie is initially resistant, then allows him to proceed. There is a quiet moment, followed by the offstage sound of a Victrola recording of Burrs singing "Marie Is Tricky." The easel, which was abandoned over an hour ago, returns with the placard "Closing Act" placed on its lip. Burrs takes over the vocals live, storming into the bedroom in full blackface, echoing his first appearance in the show. He pulls a gun on Queenie as the entire turntable unit begins to slowly revolve. Burrs goes to fire on Queenie as Black rushes in on him. The two men struggle stage right of the bed, and then a gunshot is heard. The action goes into slow motion as Queenie screams. Burrs falls onto the bed, dead. Then, cacophony. The company rushes the stage singing a reprise of "Queenie Was a Blonde" as the bed melts away. The company surrounds Queenie in an arc formation. As they finish singing, a crying Queenie attempts to keep the song going: "Queenie was a blonde in a vaudeville show / And she hid what she was with a mask of snow."[33] She then begins to sing a reprise of "This Is What It Is," which is echoed by the company. While singing, Queenie finishes removing her make-up. The final image of the show is Queenie, staring forward, her face lit with a strong, bald light. She is still crying, but she is attempting to smile as the lights fade.

Critical Reception

New York critics were largely dismissive of the Broadway production of *The Wild Party*. Some critics were torn between the show's goals and its execution. In a mixed-to-positive review, Charles Isherwood praises the show's ambitions but concedes that the production was "uneven" and that it lacked "the emotional punch it could carry."[34] Other critics were far less forgiving. In a decidedly negative review, *New York Times* chief critic Ben Brantley highlights the initial excitement of a collaboration between Wolfe and LaChiusa, whom he mentions as being heralded "one of the freshest new talents in musical songwriting." He lumps the LaChiusa version of *The Wild Party* with Andrew Lippa's, claiming that both musicals "are equally effective at guaranteeing that a good time is had by no one."[35] While reserving some praise for both Collette's and Pinkins' performances, most of the elements of the Broadway production, including choreography and design, are given harsh treatment in Brantley's summation. The little scholarship written on the production was just as conflicted. In a performance review discussing both the LaChiusa and Lippa versions, Shane Vogel concedes that The Public Theatre production was more adherent to the poem's historical context but also points out the lack of narrative cohesion of Burrs' identity as a blackface performer, particularly when the character "blacks up" at the end of the musical before attempting to kill Queenie.[36]

Not all critics were dismissive. In a largely positive review, John Heilpern writes in the *New York Observer* that *The Wild Party* is "wonderful, messy, and dangerous …" and that Collette in particular is "a major triumph from start to finish."[37] Historians writing about the musical in retrospect have been far kinder to the show. In his consideration of recent Broadway musicals, Ethan Mordden includes the LaChiusa-Wolfe version of *The Wild Party* among his "five special shows" that flew under the radar. While he concedes that the final moments of the musical "were intellectual rather than dramatic …" he also praises most of the performances, particularly Patinkin and Collette, as well as Wolfe's staging. As for LaChiusa's work, his praise was effusive: "LaChiusa's musical hocus-pocus and his dazzling mixture of art and fuck in a musical are probably a generation ahead of most theatregoers."[38] Also writing on the state of contemporary musical theatre, Barry Singer decries the vitriolic response of critics to LaChiusa's work in the 1999–2000 season, particularly in terms of *The Wild Party*. Singer praises LaChiusa's score and claims "Under George Wolfe's direction *The Wild Party* cooked. Obviously, the characters were a creepy crew … But LaChiusa and Wolfe pulled it off, abetted by a frighteningly intense performance from Patinkin, predictably lusty work from Kitt and an unexpectedly luminous turn from Collette."[39]

Critical reception aside, *The Wild Party*'s brief run qualifies it as an unquestionable flop. The musical closed on June 11th, 2000, after coming up empty-handed at the fifty-fourth annual Tony Awards, where the show had received seven nominations, including Best Musical. The musical ran in the red most weeks, only managing a gross of $339,247 in its final week of performances, that is, only 50 percent of the theatre's potential gross.[40] The show would close without paying back any of its $5 million capitalization.

The Promenade of Guests: *The Wild Party* as a Participant in Historical Conversation

Allen Woll challenges the notion that musical theatre is simply "frivolous entertainment" by asserting the prominence of musical entertainment in Afro-American history, particularly in making a space for black performers.[41] As such, he suggests that musical theatre as a whole is in conversation with a historical narrative, particularly African American history. Additionally, scholar John Bush Jones asserts that many musicals, particularly titles he distinguishes as "socially relevant" as opposed to "diversionary" are also a reflection of the tenor of the times and the conversations happening contemporaneously. In particular, he notes that musicals are often "theatrical vehicles that intend to transform, not just report, the tenor of the times."[42] Taking these ideas in mind, it makes sense to understand *The Wild Party*, despite its brief run of thirty-six previews and sixty-eight regular performances, as participating in a conversation that had been going on since the turn of the nineteenth century into the twentieth century. Further, it is important to acknowledge that this conversation, particularly in terms of race and ethnicity in American vaudeville, is rooted in the time of the musical's writing. In terms of historicizing *The Wild Party*, Wolfe acknowledged this conversation frequently in interviews, often mentioning that Historian Ann Douglas' book *Terrible Honesty: Mongrel Manhattan in the 1920s* was a key text when developing the musical.[43] While the focus in this chapter surrounds the casting of the central role of Queenie, the narratives created by the adaptation of characters from March's poem into LaChiusa and Wolfe's musical help to reify the musical's historical aims while also establishing the important role that race plays not only in the writing of *The Wild Party*, but in the show's original casting and staging.

While March's poem provides the template for most of the guests that populate LaChiusa and Wolfe's *Wild Party*, some are codified with additional layers of historical reference, either in being fashioned as an actual historical figure or by some sort of associating quality. Not all historical associations are limited to the 1920s. Queenie's look in the musical, embodied by Collette, brings to mind Marilyn Monroe, an association that is noted in Brantley's review of the musical.[44] Additionally, Brantley also notices that Madelaine, described in the poem as "heavy-lidded," "obscene," and identified as both a stripper and a lesbian, seems to be referencing a latter-day Gypsy Rose Lee, who would not even emerge in burlesque until the late 1920s.[45] Some of the characters in the musical have direct correlations to historical figures. Pugilist Eddie is described in the poem as "short," "squat," "gorilla-like," and "hirsute."[46] The poem goes on to describe Eddie's tendency to drink and its unwanted effect on his boxing career. The text of the poem does not define Eddie in terms of race or ethnicity. This description serves as a foundation for the musical's take on Eddie, who is clearly modeled after boxing great Jack

Johnson. His complications resulting from affairs with white women have forced him to resort to public appearances. Scholar Harvey Young details Jack Johnson's demise, highlighting his dependence on public appearances, specifically an appearance at the 1933 World's Fair, in order to survive.[47] He attends the party with his wife, Mae, who is white and Mae's younger sister Nadine, both of whom are more directly adapted from March's descriptions in the poem.

While it is very likely that the narrative of Jack Johnson was an inspiration in the development of the character "Eddie," other characters have less direct inspiration, though still historically connected. The Brothers D'Armano are defined broadly in the poem with several references to their possible homosexuality, such as "They must have worn / Pink silk underwear."[48] Again, no explicit reference to their race or ethnicity is present in the poem. The book of the musical, however, does identify them as "continental colored."[49] While the Brothers D'Armano may not have a historical antecedent, their identity as a black performing team does bring to mind black vaudevillian duos such as the Nicholas Brothers. Unlike the Nicholas Brothers, who were actually related and, by all accounts, heterosexual, the Brothers D'Armano use their association as black brothers to conceal their homosexual relationship.

March describes Queenie's best friend Kate as "red-headed" and "about as healthy as a cobra's bite."[50] Like Eddie and the Brothers D'Armano, the casting of Tonya Pinkins, an African American woman, brings an embodied history onto the stage that gives a type of dual narrative. Harvey Young, building on the work of Hortense Spillers, argues that "the black body exists as a theoretical construct that both represents and creates the experiences of multiple, individuated bodies within specific contexts."[51] Using Young as a starting point for organizing the logic of casting decisions in *The Wild Party*, the casting of African American performers in the roles of Eddie, the Brothers D'Armano, and Kate provides an additional layer of narrative to the given circumstances present in the text of the libretto. These characters, by virtue of their black and brown bodies, bring a racialized reading of the text to the forefront. As such, it is difficult not to associate Kate, who has found great fortune and fame by relying on her racialized sexuality to rise as a vaudeville star, with the story of Josephine Baker. While I am not arguing that Kate is modeled on Baker, Baker's history is made potentially legible to the audience through the casting of Pinkins as her African American identity presents an embodied history of other African American identities. The association is made even more apparent in the musical's text when Oscar D'Armano jokingly exclaims, "Move over, Josephine!" after revealing to the other party guests that Kate's show is going to Paris.[52]

The casting of Eartha Kitt as Dolores Montoya furthers Young's idea of multiple narratives embodied in an African American identity. March's description of Dolores (the last name "Montoya" is an invention of the writers of the musical) reads "Dark, Tall / Slim / Wrapped in a Spanish shawl," and "A singer / Without a Voice."[53] Other comments are made in the text about Dolores' made-up connection to the "Spanish aristocracy." The libretto to the musical also makes note of Dolores' Spanish heritage in the character description, claiming that the character is of "vaguely Latin origins."[54] This Spanish ethnic identification is suggested to be a disguise, however, in both the poem and the libretto. In the poem, March mentions in parentheses "(As a matter of fact, / If one only knew, / She was somewhat Negro / And a great deal Jew)."[55] Burrs repeats an approximation of this quote near the end of the musical: "Dolores, I've got secrets. Well, so do you. I hear you're somewhat Negro and a great deal Jew."[56] Despite both the reference in the poem and the libretto to Dolores' feigned Spanish heritage, very little in the text of the musical hints that Dolores is perpetuating this charade. Kitt's body is legible on stage as an African American body.

This issue of Dolores' mixed heritage is not broached until the very end of the show. This problem is, perhaps, exacerbated by the more directly embodied history that Eartha Kitt herself brings to the stage. Kitt's status as an international star helps to exoticize her African American identity. She began her career by touring as a member of Katharine Dunham's dance company, eventually becoming one of the troupe's solo dancers as the company moved through the United States, Mexico, South America, and Europe. Soon after, she would star in two French films and play Helen of Troy in Orson Welles' production of *Faust* while also cementing her reputation as both a cabaret and Broadway star.[57] Kitt also helped to further her international image by often singing in other languages, including Tagalog, French, Japanese, and Yiddish.[58] With this in mind, it is possible that Kitt's own exoticized identity as a performer and celebrity acts as a type of guise that obscures the secret "negro" identity of the character of Dolores. This possibility adds many layers of potential narrative not only for the character of Dolores but for the legendary actress playing the role. While it would be wrong to assume that Kitt herself used her international status to "hide" her own African-Americanness, her exoticized image is inseparable from her presence on stage. Additionally, Kitt's line readings, movement, and vocal performance are all clearly indicative of her persona. In short, Kitt wasn't playing Dolores; she was playing Eartha Kitt, making her own embodied history even more legible as it intermingles with the narrative of the musical and, by extension, the historical conversations in which the musical is a participant.

While the character of Dolores and the actress playing the role may have combined to add additional layers to the musical's narrative, particularly in terms of racialized identities and "masks," the two leading characters of *The Wild Party* engage with this idea more directly. The development of the character Burrs, Queenie's live-in lover and fellow vaudeville performer, merits special attention. Burrs is referenced as a "clown of renown" in March's poem, a title that could have applied to several specialty style acts popular within the revue format of American Vaudeville.[59] LaChiusa and his collaborators chose to develop Burrs as a minstrel performer, and both his first and final scenes in the musical are performed in blackface. It is impossible to behold the image of Mandy Patinkin in full "blackface" make-up, felt hairpiece, and suit without referencing legendary minstrel performer Al Jolson. In fact, Burrs is associated with Jolson directly in a stage direction in the musical.[60] Mandy Patinkin clearly channels Jolson's vocals in the theatre and on the original cast recording, relying on his silky tenor voice to create a sort of seamlessness, bringing the lyric tenor quality even into the chest register. The association with the Jewish Al Jolson vis-à-vis blackface performance, and the added association of Jewish Mandy Patinkin *channeling* Al Jolson, brings to mind a sort of essentialized embodied history that problematically associates the plight of Jewish immigrants in America with the struggles of African Americans. David Walsh and Len Platt comment on the association of black and Jewish culture in their consideration of the emergence of the American musical, suggesting that "the structural position that Jews came to occupy on Broadway was made possible by Jewish history and popular culture and that [position] allowed [them] to successfully broker a relationship between black and white culture."[61] This is a problematic, ethnocentric argument, but it does speak to the cultural association of these groups, and its inherent hierarchy, particularly in the world of show business in the early twentieth century. It is important to note, however, that many Jewish persons, particularly in the realm of show business, harbored antagonistic feelings toward African American performers in particular.[62] Irving Berlin, among others, was quick to deny the African American roots in his own appropriation of jazz. That aside, Jolson did have a history of championing black rights to a degree, often advocating for black performers, despite the fact that he gained popularity during the 1910s, the often called "years of exile" for black musical theatre.[63] The marriage of Jolson and Patinkin's Jewish identity with the act of blackface performance makes this association and pecking order legible within the text and staging of *The Wild Party*.

There are further connections between Jolson and the fictional Burrs. Jolson's offstage and offscreen persona was often erratic, insulting, and violent. One of his favorite jokes was to urinate on unsuspecting persons and he would often pull out wads of money from his pockets when in public.[64] Jolson has been well studied by scholars who suggest his racial "mask" as a covering for his own Jewish ancestry. Others have posed a more masculinist bent in the performance of blackface, with noted scholar Eric Lott stating:

> For the white minstrel man to put on the cultural forms of "blackness" was to engage in a complex affair of manly mimicry …. To wear or even enjoy blackface was literally, for a time, to become black, to inherit the cool, virility, humility, abandon, or *gaité de coeur* that were the prime components of white ideologies of black manhood.[65]

Whatever the reason for Jolson's participation in blackface performance, the idea of "blackface-as-mask" haunts the proceedings at LaChiusa and Wolfe's *Wild Party*. LaChiusa and Wolfe are specific in the libretto that Burrs is modeled on vaudeville singer and blackface performer Al Jolson. The positioning of Burrs as a minstrel performer not only invites this association with Jolson, it also helps to understand Queenie's racialized presentation as inherently about passing. With the casting of Williams, the white Burrs puts on blackface as his means of economic sustenance and provides a stark, sharply defined contrast to his lover Queenie, who performs in the same vaudeville troupe and, presumably, must keep a white identity to continue this type of work. With the casting of Collette, the audience comes to understand both Queenie and Burrs as performers relying on racialized narratives in order to make a living. With either casting decision, Burrs performs a particular labor in putting the musical *The Wild Party*, and the racial presentation of Queenie, into a historical conversation.

"Queenie Was a Blonde" … or Was She?

The first chord of the score is piercing, immediately bringing a sense of jazz energy and tension to the stage. The opening number, "Queenie Wazza

Blonde," helps to establish the aural vocabulary that will be prominent throughout the musical's proceedings. It also firmly places the emphasis of the musical on the character of Queenie. The first sections of the song's lyric are a direct quote from the first five lines of March's poem:

> Queenie was a blonde and her age stood still
> And she danced twice a day in the vaudeville.
> Grey Eyes.
> Lips like coals aglow.
> Her face was a tinted mask of snow.[66]

The final phrase, referring to Queenie's face as a tinted mask of snow, is taken as an invitation by LaChiusa and his collaborators to explore Queenie's racial identification. Much like Eddie, Kate, and the Brothers D'Armano, there is nothing in March's poem that would lead us to understand Queenie's race at all. In fact, the mention of the "tinted mask of snow" brings about a pervading image of whiteness, though the words "tinted" and "mask" certainly invite a reading of artifice, of concealment. The casting of Williams and her participation in the development of the musical help to situate the piece as a racialized exploration of Queenie as a black body performing whiteness. LaChiusa confirmed that the role was written for Williams and that her race was, initially, a site of exploration for the project in terms of the masks we wear "culturally."[67]

LaChiusa's mentioning of "masks" that we "wear culturally" immediately brings to mind the work of Frantz Fanon, who famously argued that bodies with embodied history of colonization adopt white masks in their efforts toward upward mobility and relevance within the colonizers' world. The adoption of these masks often comes in the pursuit of proving to white persons "the wealth of the black man's intellect and equal intelligence."[68] Utilizing Fanon as a starting point, it becomes clear that the casting of Williams, and her hypothetical performance, would have added a layer of embodied history to the performance, particularly in the literal painting of a "mask" upon an African American woman's face. In order to fully excavate the myriad ways in which the language and use of painted "masks" communicate various histories within the text of *The Wild Party*, it is imperative to understand the musical's embodied narratives in two ways. First, it is important to explore a reading of the text of the musical *The Wild Party* as if the casting of Williams did not change. How does the text read with a light-skinned African American actress in the role? In what ways would Williams' own embodied history have interacted with the text of the musical to create multiple meanings, particularly the sensationalized events surrounding her abdicating her crown as Miss America in the 1980s. Second, the text is re-explored to understand the shifts that occur when the body inhabiting Queenie, in this case, the body of Australian actress Toni Collette, is clearly white while *still performing in whiteface.* What logics and narratives emerge when a white actress in whiteface becomes the focal point of the musical's story? What were the artists collaborating on this musical trying to achieve in utilizing a white body with white make-up? This dual reading leads to the chapter's final section of analysis that argues the musical *The Wild Party* is participating in an unintentional historical conversation with racial tensions in the world of vaudeville.

Williams as Queenie

The character of Queenie is introduced to the audience under the auspices of a vaudeville number. When the audience first sees her, her face is painted powder-white. This painting of the face remains throughout the duration of the musical's two-hour playing time. If the body inhabiting the role of Queenie is black, and if the face behind "*the tinted mask of snow*" is in fact African American, a new logic becomes apparent in many of the musical's references leading up to and including the show's final moments. Throughout Wolfe's staging of the musical, Queenie is constantly checking her visage in the mirror to be sure her face is completely covered. Additionally, Queenie's lover Burrs makes noted references to Queenie's need to keep her makeup perfect. During the frenzied full-company number *Gin/Wild* halfway through the musical, Burrs finds Queenie reapplying white powder to her face. "Missed a spot …," he warns, almost tauntingly, before accusing her of flirting with Black.[69] Queenie hurriedly and anxiously corrects the flaw in her painted face. After a violent exchange, Burrs "kisses her hard—a desperate, angry kiss"—then pats her on the cheek. Burrs identifies Queenie's mask as essential, even taunting her by pointing out a missed spot in the powder. Additionally, his violent kiss and pat on the cheek do literal physical violence to Queenie's painted visage.

Burrs mentions Queenie's makeup again very close to the musical's climax. After the party has ended with the attempted rape of the young Nadine by Jackie, Burrs confronts Black, who has fallen in love with Queenie, slowly slipping into his minstrel "coon" inflection as the series of lines progress:

And Blackie, my boy, since you're planning on throwin' a torpedo into the S.S. Queenie, I better warn you—don't touch the face … Cuz nuthin' gets da little lady so-o-o riled up as getting' caught wit' her face minus all of dat paint … 'Cause like the cheap whore she is, everything's got to be all perfumed and painted so's you don't smell the stink that's just a festerin' underneath.[70]

In this example, Burrs bluntly spells out Queenie's dependence on her painted face and, in a sense, demonizes what is hidden underneath it. With Williams in the role, this vilification of Queenie that exists under the mask becomes instantly racialized. The "stink that's just-a festerin' underneath" becomes an attack on Queenie's concealed racialized visage. Burrs becomes an indicator and a reminder of Queenie's need to conceal her true identity. Her fixation on her white makeup, and her refusal to appear without it, helps to shroud her racialized identity in mystery. Immediately after the altercation with Burrs, Queenie sings to Black:

I don't want the night
I don't want the dark, The "Wazza-Wazza Blonde,"
The gin-and-screw-it eyes
The tinted mask of snow and lies[71]

Queenie articulates a desire to remove the mask that conceals who she is. In the confines of the party, her mask is a survival tactic, but alone with Burrs, she craves revelation. She articulates this more directly a few minutes later, singing the song "This Is What It Is" after she has made love to Black. The craving for "darkness" that once consumed Queenie has been replaced by a tentative need to "live in light." She gets her chance as Black tries to wipe the makeup off of her face. She tries to stop him but eventually relents. Black is unable to finish "revealing" Queenie, however, because the scene is interrupted by Burrs, in blackface, who has come to kill Queenie. After a struggle for the gun, Burrs shoots himself and Queenie breaks down, symbolized by a haunting reprise of her initial vaudeville number introduction. The number ends with Queenie sobbing and wiping the makeup from her face. The musical's final image is a lone spotlight, focusing on Queenie, without her white mask, both smiling and scared.

These references to the hiding of the face, the whitening of a character's visage, mark the musical as an inherently racialized project. Queenie's story becomes one of a light-skinned African American woman attempting to pass, similar in many respects to the Nella Larsen novella *Passing*, which centers on the trials and tribulations of a society woman attempting to pass in the 1920s.[72] Whereas Larsen's heroine must maintain her white identity to remain a member of the New York elite, Queenie must maintain her allure of whiteness to continue to navigate within the racialized contours of vaudeville performance.

Continuing a hypothetical exploration of Williams' performance, it is revealed that Queenie's racialized identity is further complicated by the identities of others within the musical. Her relationship with Burrs, a blackface performer, places the two characters in an awkwardly inverse relationship. Both must paint their faces in order to sustain themselves, Burrs by employing his legible Jewish identity to, in some ways, justify his blackface performance and Queenie literalizing Fanon's "white mask" as a way of maintaining her own methods of survival. Queenie's association with other black vaudeville performers and celebrities such as the Brothers D'Armano and boxing champ Eddie maintains an additional tension. Eddie, Oscar, and Phil have all managed to incorporate their black identities into their branding while Queenie conceals her identity in order to "perform" as a white woman. The duality expressed between Queenie and the more successful Kate all serve to reify Queenie's racialized narrative. Like the men mentioned above, Kate has utilized her race as well as stereotypical assumptions about black female sexuality, assumptions that date back to the "Jezebel" stock character in minstrel shows, in order to create an exalted place for herself within the hierarchy of vaudeville performance. Queenie, by contrast, has concealed her racial identity in order to continue dancing as one of the vaudeville chorines.

These racialized relationships help to mark and nuance the black Queenie's character arc while also adding a healthy dose of irony. Other characters in the play have found varying levels of success in performance while allowing the public to associate them as African American. For Queenie, understood as black-passing-as-white, these levels of success are insufficient and unsatisfactory. In the final moments of the musical, Queenie, emotionally broken, sings a short reprise of "Queenie Wazza Blonde" a cappella through tears with a revised lyric: "Queenie was a blonde in a vaudeville show/ And she hid what she was with a mask of snow."[73] This lyric is telling, particularly in the hypothetical performance of Williams. It can be understood as dually rooted in her racialized social situation as well as reifying Queenie's understanding of the limits of her race. All of the other performers are billed as subjects of their racialized bodies. Eddie is understood as the black boxer who dared to sleep with white women. The Brothers D'Armano are understood as a black duo act who employ acts of femininity to aid in their novelty. And Kate has depended on a racialized sexuality that marks her as "black" first and "woman" second, typical of the black sexualization that the white gaze uses to organize black and brown bodies.[74] For Queenie, being understood as a white performer, and therefore a majority performer, is, at the beginning of the show, more important, and while that trajectory helps to minoritize the various narratives of the black characters around her, it also confines her in a liminal space between two worlds, neither of which seems accessible to her until, perhaps, the show's end.

Collette as Queenie

After Williams informed the producers of *The Wild Party* about her pregnancy, there was an effort to move up the musical's opening so that Williams could open the show while she was still physically able, but Patinkin's concert schedule made that impossible. Once it was clear that *The Wild Party* would have to open without Williams' involvement, a long list was drafted of potential actresses to take on the role of Queenie. This list of forty-five names features prominent Broadway performers, music stars, and film stars, ranging from superstars like Madonna and Paula Abdul to established theatre actresses like Carolee Carmello and Bebe Neuwirth.[75] The actresses on this list comprise a variety of different racial and ethnic backgrounds, though a significant number of the names belonged to white performers. While Collette's name was on this list, she was unknown to Wolfe and LaChiusa until producer Scott Rudin arranged an introduction while Collette was in New York City doing press for the film *The Sixth Sense*, a film that would bring the actress an Academy Award nomination. Wolfe was immediately impressed:

> We instantly got along; she went into a room with Michael John and the music director, learned an entire song in one minute (mind you, she had never taken singing lessons in her life), and we were all thrilled because we had our Queenie again.[76]

With Collette engaged for the role of Queenie, rehearsals began in January of 2000. Wolfe recounts a problematic process that was exacerbated by infighting among the show's producers, tensions between the cast and director, and fights between Patinkin and the rest of company, particularly

Collette. It is perhaps due to this chaotic process that the script's reference to Collette's painted mask remained unchanged. Once a white actress assumed the role, Queenie's narrative moved from a telos of passing to a trajectory of appropriation. The score still relies heavily on racialized idioms and musical syncopation that originated among African American musicians. Queenie still uses this music as if it were her own, dancing the famous "Black Bottom" as if she were performing in Harlem nightclubs.

Queenie's rivalry with her best friend Kate suddenly becomes more petty and more nuanced. While nothing in the text suggests that race plays any part in Kate and Queenie's playful antagonism, Kate has achieved a level of success as a black woman that has been denied the white Queenie. While Queenie is still dancing with the other chorines down in "the Bowery," Kate has become a star and is taking her show to Paris. Kate's role in the piece is full of fascinating contradictions, particularly given that she brings Black to the party with the intention of luring Queenie away from Burrs. While Kate does sexually engage with Burrs, it is unclear whether this assignation was the purpose for her meddling. Burrs accuses Kate of trying to break up his relationship with Queenie, stating that Kate doesn't understand the relationship because she doesn't "know a goddamn thing about love."[77] Kate doesn't necessarily refute the claim that she was intending to break up Burrs' relationship with Queenie, though she does implicate Burrs' role in the ordeal. While Kate's function may be antagonistic, her relationship to Queenie throughout the show is protective. More than once, she raises concerns about Burrs' violent nature. It could be read that Kate is acting out of care for Queenie, trying to end a relationship that could end violently for her friend. With Queenie's racialized narrative removed, Queenie's neuroses regarding her life and relationship become pitiable and it is possible that Kate's scheme is trying to rectify that situation. Additionally, the tension between Kate's success and confidence as a black woman and Queenie's fragility as a white woman painted white brings an entirely new racialized telos to their relationship as opposed to the hypothetical Williams casting.

Because the musical's text and Wolfe's staging still makes a great deal out of Queenie's obsession with her "painted mask of snow," a new logic must be presented in order to make Queenie's given circumstances legible. Throughout her beautifully nuanced performance in *The Wild Party*, Collette frequently employs moments where she "drops" her vaudeville/performer persona. These moments include the first fight in her apartment with Burrs, the moment when she is physically and emotionally overwhelmed after dancing "The Black Bottom," and in most of her scenes alone with

Black. The first instance of this dissonance, when she threatens Burrs with a knife, is animalistic, desperate, and vulnerable. This choice stands in stark contrast to the presentational, smiling, knowing quality of the performance that preceded it. While dancing "The Black Bottom" with Oscar, Phil, and the rest of the company, Queenie's face melts. She looks as if she has seen a ghost. She grabs at her throat and pulls away from the group, seemingly tired and scared. She sings, "I'm dry / Burrsie, I'm dry / Dry …"[78] The moment, in which it looks as if Queenie may be on the verge of breaking down, is interrupted by the entrance of Kate. During the scenes with Black, Queenie is constantly struggling between maintaining her cool, alluring, performative persona and allowing herself to be emotionally naked and vulnerable. Physical poses always tend to break. Queenie's attention veers from squarely on the audience to squarely on Black.

Queenie's psychological positioning wouldn't seem to merit a reading of body dysmorphia. So why, when the musical changed the racial identity of its leading lady, did it continue to paint her in white face? Whether intentional or not, Queenie's obsession with whitening her already white appearance, in connection to Burrs' "blacking up," would seem to reify her need for cover, to wear a racialized mask that hides her from the world she is so scared of confronting. In the hands of Toni Collette, Queenie's journey reflects a fight between the mask that presents the created persona of "Queenie" and the vulnerable, scared internal identity that the mask protects. Regardless of Collette's identity as a white woman, the musical's emphasis on masks, painted literally on her face, participates in a struggle for identity politics that maintains a racialized component. Suddenly, her anthem "This Is What It Is" expresses a desire not to upend the politics of passing but rather to reorient the racialized world that places whiteness and purity into a privileged position. Further, Queenie utilizes and appropriates black culture as a means of sustenance, given the method and manner of her vaudeville performances. White vaudeville was becoming increasingly dependent on black culture to maintain relevancy, a factor which brings *The Wild Party's* historical conversation into focus.

"Black Folks Are Sounding More Like White Folks Who Are Sounding More Like Black Folks"

During the number "Uptown," the Brothers D'Armano remark that "Black Folks / Are Sounding More Like / White Folks / Who Are Sounding More

Like / Black Folks / In Every Way!" During the era in which *The Wild Party* takes place, black culture was becoming increasingly prevalent in various ways in white culture. With the emergence of "Tin Pan Alley" songwriters, a group of mostly Jewish men, tensions began to grow as Jewish male composers began to divorce themselves from the African American musical roots that informed their compositional styles.[79] Additionally, black vernacular dance was making its way into white vaudeville and musical revues, particularly "The Charleston" and "The Black Bottom" by way of ballrooms, such as The Grand Central Palace in New York, which began to increase in popularity starting in 1911.[80]

On Broadway, all-black musical entertainment was beginning to disappear. During the 1910s, often referred to as the "term of exile" by James Weldon Johnson, the all-black musical entertainments that had been so prevalent at the turn of the century began to die out, largely because the major stars of the movement had passed on, begun to pursue other careers, or, in the case of Bert Williams, had found a home in predominately white forms of entertainment such as the *Ziegfeld Follies*.[81] Interestingly, blackface entertainment was on the wane throughout the 1920s largely due to controversy over its overt racism, though some major starts like Williams, Jolson, and Ma Rainey would continue utilizing blackface in their acts throughout the decade.[82] This factor alone helps to situate *The Wild Party*, and Burrs and Queenie's painted visages, into a consideration of history. Further, the complex nature of black-and-white performance, its thorny reliance on each other for survival, and its relevance to the history of musical entertainment at large forces a historical consideration of the original production of *The Wild Party*. In particular, understanding the white casting of "Queenie" forces the emergence of a narrative that comments on and participates in the cyclical relationship between black-and-white performance common to the 1920s and, arguably, still present in popular music and stage works.

In order to fully explore the conversation Collette's performance as "Queenie" engages in, it is important to establish the historical world of vaudeville that informs and defines the lives of the fictional Queenie and her party guests. As white vaudeville began to decline in the wake of other entertainment forms, such as "talkie" pictures, musical revues, and the emerging "book" musical, it turned to dances, music, and cultural expressions from black vaudeville to gain any level of relevance. In establishing the "connection" of this conversation, I briefly look at the relational world of black and white vaudeville performers as vaudeville faced its greatest crisis moment before drawing real-life parallels that give further weight to *The Wild Party*'s historical conversation.

Even as black vaudevillians, such as Josephine Baker, began to find success and some wealth, they were marred in a system of show business that was run by white men. Although black vaudeville shows found some mainstream success, black vaudevillians usually were subject to white managers, white dancer directors, and white booking agents.[83] While "Jim Crow laws" in the Southern states kept black and white performers from sharing the same space, black performers did perform in vaudeville nationwide, often for largely black audiences. The Theater Owners Booking Agency (TOBA) was a white-owned vaudeville circuit, often referred to as the "chitlin' circuit" which focused on black vaudeville entertainment for white audiences below the Mason-Dixon line.[84] Working conditions with TOBA were less than ideal and often unsafe to such a degree that many African American performers referred to the TOBA as "Tough on Black Asses."[85] Despite this, predominately white vaudeville troupes did recognize the monetary value of including black specialty acts, thereby allowing for a mixing of racialized entertainment on the same stage, though this cultural mixing was often limited to the confines of performance. In many ways, Bert Williams paved the way for this cultural intermingling when he accepted an offer from Florenz Ziegfeld to join his Follies in 1910. Many of the white performers in the *Follies* threatened to quit, but Ziegfeld called their bluff.[86] Williams was a star within the *Follies* until he departed in 1920, though his offstage relationship with his white costars was nothing short of tense. Despite Williams' pioneering decision, black performers were almost always paid less than white performers, and in the rare event when a white specialty act was booked into a black vaudeville show, the performers would rarely interact backstage.[87] Regardless, African American performers, and their performance styles, were largely commodified by white producers and management, reinforcing the idea of race hegemony as a "societal tool of power."[88]

Although Queenie's "wild party" is a mixed-race event, it is unlikely, though not impossible, that many of the black characters that are guests at Queenie's party would have been performing with Queenie in the same vaudeville troupe, particularly her best friend and rival Kate. This disparity of socializing, namely that separate races would come together at a social event, but not necessarily socialize at work, is consistent with the trends of the 1920s, when so-called "rent parties" would often involve a mélange of racial identities and celebrity appearances.[89] While Burrs and Queenie aren't asking an admission to their party in the tradition of "rent parties," the diversity of their guest list does provide a similar queer space, a type of Foucauldian "heterotopia," that would have been endemic of 1920s rent parties that were often hosted by single, often widowed women as a means of economic sustenance.

Knowingly or not, LaChiusa and Wolfe relied heavily on the historical narrative of "rent parties" to offer their version of March's poem to Broadway. The almost radical depiction of inter-race relationships onstage at the Virginia Theatre called to mind the illicit, secretive, permissive atmosphere that became central to the idea of downtown "rent parties." In engaging directly with Ann Douglas' detailed history in the 1920s, *Terrible Honesty*, both writers were able to infuse several of the characters within the musical's narrative with cultural history. Additionally, the writing and directing teams' adoption of a vaudeville format, which appears, disappears, and reappears throughout the staging, clearly signals an engagement with a performance medium of the 1920s that was in flux and, by the end of the decade, fighting for survival amid the emergence of "talkie" pictures as well as the fallout from the Crash of 1929.

LaChiusa and Wolfe's musical also engages with the racial intermingling, tension, and appropriation that were related to live performance and representative of racialized relations in the culture at large in the 1920s. Recalling the way Gottschild frames the cyclical nature of the black cultural fetish by white appropriators, Queenie becomes guilty of relying on racialized cultural idioms not only as a performer but as the host of the party.[90] In order to keep white vaudeville salient in a changing commercial entertainment industry, white performers would often appropriate and reconceive black music and dance trends. Both the "Charleston" and the "Black Bottom" are examples of dance crazes that originated in the dance halls and cabarets of Harlem, then transmuted into white culture through the efforts of upper-class "slummers" who would visit these late-night spots and through dance teachers and directors who would learn the combinations, "sweeten" them for white consumption, and teach them to performers.[91]

Queenie's grooming choice, namely her painting of her face, is also emblematic in trends that emerge from the culture of appropriation, in this case, black appropriation of a white image. With the original casting concept of Vanessa Williams, the choice for Queenie to keep her face concealed with white makeup called to mind a very specific moment of black vaudeville history. Margot Webb, part of the dance duo of Norton and Webb, relied heavily on her light-skin pigment in order to pass, or at least, to give the impression of passing. Because Norton and Webb were a ballet-trained adagio team, working mostly in white European dance vocabulary and idioms, their racial identity often proved problematic for white audiences. This led Webb to often wear a type of "disguise" to style her features as white-indicating as possible, complete with a "natural white mask."[92] Webb would often model herself on Hollywood stars of the era, leading her to be dubbed "the Marlene Dietrich of Harlem."[93] In fact, the act of painting the face white became a vogue for many African American performers, a vogue that was eventually adopted and appropriated by white vaudeville performers. Although much of the text regarding Queenie's "mask of snow" retains its racialized tenor, Queenie's "whitening up" could seem to suggest another appropriation of black culture, this time appropriating a racialized mask that was, in its original form, meant to provide a racialized mask.

Queenie's use of the white mask also suggests a sort of emotional appropriation that communicates with the historicized conversation of vaudeville race relations. With the initial casting of Williams, during the musical's final moments, Queenie decides to remove her makeup in order to "live in light" as a sort of "coming out" about her concealed racial identity. In the casting of Collette, the moment is instantly problematized. Yet, it would seem that "white" Queenie's inability to show herself as well as her need to remain concealed becomes a type of appropriation of the emotional language of "passing." Queenie's insecurities, as played by Collette, seem to signal a sort of emotional vacancy that denies her the ability to live without concealment, a sort of physical shyness that requires makeup and dim light in order to maintain an illusion of confidence. With the unchanged text of *The Wild Party*, Queenie understands her own journey toward "living" in light with the same emotionally nuanced language as if the character were still African American passing for white. Queenie appropriates the emotional concept of "passing" to perform the labor of verbalizing her own struggles with emotional nakedness. To this end, Queenie uses the logics of black racial "masks" to explore her own insecurities and to organize her own struggles with a very different type of physical identity. In this way, the musical reaches across time to reorient a white body in conversation with the racialized language of a black body.

The Wild Party and Race in Contemporary Musicals

The substitution of a white body in the role of "Queenie" for a presumed black body helps to frame *The Wild Party* in a historical conversation with racialized idioms of vaudeville past. Although the musical, through its invocation of racialized figures from vaudeville's past, is already participating in a historical conversation, this concept is fully realized as the role of Queenie is read in both its workshop casting concept and the second revised concept that utilizes a white actress with a racialized text and narrative. In analyzing the role of a white Queenie in whiteface, a specific historical conversation emerges that calls on the nature of race relations in vaudeville circuits, the nature of appropriation of black music and dance, and a reliance on the aesthetics of racial presentation in order to express nonracialized emotional distress. The goal here is not to characterize the casting of Collette as a mistake or opportunistic but to understand how decision-making processes, intentional or not, participate in a historical conversation that provides comment and context for cultural understanding at large. In explicating the problematized racialization of *The Wild Party*, a larger conversation begins to emerge about another long-form narrative surrounding race and commercial theatre.

Nontraditional casting has been an issue that has plagued commercial theatre, particularly musical theatre, since the inception of the form. Todd Decker mentions the casting of Juanita Hall, a light-skinned African American actress, in two Asian roles in two different Rodgers and Hammerstein musicals during her lifetime.[94] Much is often made regarding the casting of the Puerto Rican characters in *West Side Story*. In April of 2018, actress-singer Sierra Boggess, who is white, withdrew from a concert production of the musical because she saw her casting as the Puerto Rican Maria problematic.[95] Over twenty years ago, playwright David Henry Hwang led a campaign of outrage over the casting of Jonathan Pryce in the musical *Miss Saigon*. Casting scandals have plagued regional productions of the Gilbert and Sullivan operetta *The Mikado* and Katori Hall's play *The Mountaintop*. Within the confines of the American theatre, racialized casting decisions will continue to problematize the effect of theatre as a force of popular culture. With the postmodern racial casting concept of the blockbuster musical *Hamilton*, new questions emerge regarding the role casting plays in interacting with historical narratives. If an African American man can play Aaron Burrs, can a white actor play Martin Luther King, Jr. in *The Mountaintop*? Does the role of historical conversation render such a decision unthinkable, or does the theatre risk its postmodern project by placing a set of restrictions and rules on casting?

Subsequent productions of LaChiusa's *The Wild Party* have been infrequent at best. In two notable productions, one in California and one recently in Canada, the role of Queenie has been cast with an actress of color, re-establishing the racialized narratives of passing that were inherent in the original workshops of the musical.[96] The production garnered acclaim with many critics feeling that the musical had been "fixed." As of this writing, the Encores! series at New York City Center is planning a production of *The Wild Party* in the 2026 season. As such, *The Wild Party* continues to participate in a historical conversation that positions the role of black and brown bodies within the confusing confines of American vaudeville.

CONCLUSION: "WHEN IT ENDS": THE NEW MUSICAL DRAMA MEETS COMMERCIAL SUCCESS

When LaChiusa drew his metaphorical line in the sand with his essay "The Great Gray Way," he created a kind of manifesto that gave life to a movement that was already under way. His work in particular became a type of vanguard for the movement, especially in terms of LaChiusa's continued association with major nonprofit theatres. While LaChiusa's story is far from being finished, his output to date helps us to define the ways in which musical theatre was challenging, or perhaps trying to coexist with the more commercially oriented theatre typical of Broadway entertainment. While LaChiusa has three Broadway credits, his work in the nonprofit theatres of New York City and throughout the country have, in many ways, helped to define nonprofits as possible alternatives for the development of musical theatre. While The Public Theatre did develop some works in the 1960s (*Hair*) and the 1970s (*Two Gentlemen of Verona, A Chorus Line*), nonprofits began to take up the cause of musical theatre development in earnest in the 1980s, particularly at Playwrights Horizons, which would help develop both one-acts that would eventually form *Falsettos* as well as Stephen Sondheim and James Lapine's Pulitzer Prize–winning musical *Sunday in the Park with George*. While LaChiusa came into a system that was already in place, his continued association with nonprofits helped to cement the association between experiments in musical theatre form with the nonprofit sector. This is an important designation, particularly given that many of the other composers in his unofficial cohort have played on both sides of the commercial fence. Jason Robert Brown, arguably the best known of "The New Musical Drama" class, has worked with nonprofits and regionals, but has also worked on more traditional Broadway fare following a more commercial path, such as the musicals *13* and *Urban Cowboy*. Jeanine Tesori, arguably the most successful of LaChiusa and his colleagues, has also managed to maintain ties in both commercial and nonprofit sectors, with

Thoroughly Modern Millie and *Shrek* following different models than her *Violet, Caroline, or Change,* and *Fun Home.*

What's more, LaChiusa's work continues to push conceptions of form and storytelling outside of the normative constraints of commercial musical theatre, particularly in terms of source material, musical sophistication, and utilization of nontraditional storytelling devices. Although it is impossible to determine whether the storytelling techniques taken up by LaChiusa are completely his own, it does seem likely that his work is a type of watershed, mixing experiments with the musical theatre form that took place in the past. Certainly, the myriad of book writers who worked with Stephen Sondheim in the 1970s and 1980s brought about experiments in form that had a heavy influence on LaChiusa. His interest in playing with linearity and time finds roots in George Furth's books to *Company* and *Merrily We Roll Along.* His interests in approaching musical theatre as a historian may have roots in John Weidman's book to the musical *Pacific Overtures,* which historicizes the Westernization of Japan. Also, his tendency to play with already established forms, such as vaudeville, finds echoes of James Goldman's book for the musical *Follies* as well as Hugh Wheeler's manipulation of melodrama in *Sweeney Todd: The Demon Barber of Fleet Street.* Going further back in musical theatre history, the musical *Allegro,* written by Richard Rodgers and Oscar Hammerstein II, played with form and expectations in a way that inspired Sondheim, who worked as an assistant on the production, who, in turn, likely inspired LaChiusa. Although LaChiusa certainly owes a debt to the past, it is a debt that has, in some ways, been paid off by LaChiusa's possible influences on the contemporary Broadway market.

Successes of "The New Musical Drama"

While the Broadway of 1999 and 2000 seemed inhospitable to the types of experiments LaChiusa was attempting, things seemed to have changed over the last twenty years. The nonprofit producing model has continued to thrive and produce a number of musicals, several of which have found a comfortable, profitable home on Broadway. This trend reaches back to the success of Adam Geuttel and Alfred Uhry's musical *The Light in the Piazza,* which was produced by Lincoln Center in the same space where *Marie Christine* had premiered almost six years earlier. While *Marie Christine* was marred by the debate over its genre classification, *The Light in the Piazza* took delight in its mixing of musical theatre and opera conventions.

What's more, critics seemed to embrace the interplay to an extent. While Ben Brantley's review of the original production was mixed, he did praise the music composed for the central character, Margaret Johnson, which includes several Euro-centric-style arias, including the final show-stopping number "Fable."[1] The musical's score deals solidly with musical ideas that bring about associations of Leonard Bernstein as well as Sondheim, but none of this intermingling of forms seemed to impact the show's modest success, playing just over a year, sending out a national tour, and winning six Tony Awards.

Lightning struck again over a year later when the Atlantic Theatre Company's production of the musical *Spring Awakening* by composer Duncan Sheik and lyricist-librettist Steven Sater began performances on Broadway in December of 2006. Very much in the tradition of *Hello Again*, Sheik and Sater took a provocative turn-of-the-century German play dealing frankly with sex and developed it into a musical production. Yet, while there were no whisperings of a transfer for the original production of *Hello Again*, the euphoric praise for *Spring Awakening* seemed to ensure that the musical would move to a commercial Broadway run, despite the controversies over its content which feature school-age teenagers dealing with issues like abortion, masturbation, same-sex attraction, and suicide in a world in which their parents are ill-equipped to offer guidance in such matters. Sex has always held an uncomfortable place in the American musical, which has necessarily attempted to favor family-friendly entertainment. Charles Isherwood points to this fact in his review of the Broadway opening of the musical when he points out that *Spring Awakening* may break from that tradition of discomfort by presenting a musical that is "pure sex."[2] While LaChiusa's "ballet with words" approach in *Hello Again* also generated its share of positive notices, it would have been unthinkable to conceive of its chances of a commercial Broadway run in 1994, particularly with the HIV/AIDS crisis continuing to loom heavily over New York City. Yet, while it seems unlikely that LaChiusa's work provided inspiration to Sheik, who comes from the singer-songwriter tradition, and Sater, whose background was largely as an English Literature scholar, there is a conversation created by the juxtaposition of these two pieces, particularly in terms of dealing with discussions of frank sexuality within the confines of the musical. While *Spring Awakening*'s was only a modest success, particularly in relation to the nature of its critical reception, it did manage to play for just over two years while also sending out a successful tour. The show was revived on Broadway in September 2015 by the nonprofit theatre Deaf West, which specializes in producing musicals that mix hearing, hard-of-hearing, and deaf actors in casting.

In 2008, the musical *Next to Normal* opened on Broadway at the Booth Theatre after two developmental productions at two nonprofits: Second Stage Theatre in New York City and Arena Theatre in Washington, D.C., after having been initially shepherded by The New York Musical Theatre Festival. *Next to Normal* continues LaChiusa's traditions of translating unlikely topics to the musical stage, although *Next to Normal* is one of the few to do it with a completely original story dealing with bipolar depression as its primary topic. The musical is built around Diana, a mother of two who suffers from bipolar depression and, as is revealed roughly one-quarter through the musical's playing time, delusions. The show opened to strong reviews on Broadway and would go on to win three Tony Awards. In addition, the musical managed to win the Pulitzer Prize for Drama in 2010 despite not being nominated by the jury.[3] *Next to Normal* played a successful run for nearly two years before sending out a national tour.

After the modest success of *Next to Normal*, few shows falling under the label "The New Musical Drama" found commercial viability on Broadway for the next five years. One musical, an adaptation of the film *Once*, developed by American Repertory Theatre and New York Theatre Workshop, took a unique perspective in translating its source material to the stage, although the fact that its score wasn't explicitly written for the musical somewhat disqualifies it from consideration as a "New Musical Drama." Regardless, the musical, which certainly satisfies Miranda Lundskaer-Nielsen's definition of "musical drama" if not mine, ran a respectable run of almost three years on Broadway beginning in 2012 before launching a national tour. Beginning in 2015, examples of "The New Musical Drama" found significant success on Broadway as four Tony Award winners for Best Musical were all experimental pieces that began their life in the nonprofit sector.

Fun Home seemed an especially unlikely candidate for a Broadway run, despite its laudatory reviews. The production premiered at The Public Theatre in a proscenium staging. When the show transferred to the Circle in the Square Theatre, director Sam Gold reconceived his staging to arena style, resulting in a completely different take on the show. The musical is based on a 2006 graphic memoir of the same name written and illustrated by Alison Bechdel. The story charts the journey of Alison through three different phases of her life with a different actress assaying the roles of "Small Alison," "Medium Alison," and "Alison." Alison's journey toward accepting her sexual orientation is contrasted with that of her father, a high school teacher, funeral home director, and antiques aficionado whose own same-sex desires were closeted, often resulting in trouble for his family. Alison explores memories with her father in an attempt to understand his apparent suicide while she was in college. Throughout the musical, Alison asks herself if her father's decision to take his own life was in any way connected to her own process of coming out. Given the complicated dimensions of the story, composer Jeanine Tesori and lyric and book writer Lisa Kron, both of whom won Tonys for their work, decided to take a nonlinear approach in telling Alison's story, with each of the three Alison's experiences intersecting with the others. The result was critical gold with Ben Brantley exclaiming that the musical "pumps oxygenating fresh air into the cultural recycling center that is Broadway."[4] Tesori and Kron's decision to play with the geographies of time and their unlikely source material immediately suggest the work of LaChiusa. Although LaChiusa hasn't expressed his opinions on *Fun Home* in public, its rich score, fully human characters, and experiments with form would all seem to suggest that, in many ways, the project of which LaChiusa was a part had found a new home on Broadway. The musical managed to return its investment, spend almost a year and a half on Broadway, and win five Tony Awards.

While *Fun Home* made its way uptown to Broadway, another "New Musical Drama" was finishing its development at The Public Theatre. Initially entitled *Hamilton Mixtape*, the musical *Hamilton* from composer, lyricist, and librettist Lin-Manuel Miranda was preparing to begin its off-Broadway premiere in the winter of 2015. The musical charts the biography of Alexander Hamilton, the nation's first Secretary of Treasury, utilizing a series of Brechtian devices, such as direct address, and employing a score largely consisting of R&B, Hip-hop, and rap. The musical's reviews were ecstatic and the question of when to transfer the musical to Broadway was only a matter of timing. It did open at the Richard Rodgers theatre that following summer and would go on to win eleven Tony Awards, including Best Musical, as well as spawning multiple national tours as well as productions in Chicago and London. In his review of the Broadway transfer, Brantley mused:

I am loath to tell people to mortgage their houses and lease their children to acquire tickets to a hit Broadway show. But "Hamilton," directed by Thomas Kail and starring Mr. Miranda, might just about be worth it—at least to anyone who wants proof that the American musical is not only surviving but also evolving in ways that should allow it to thrive and transmogrify in years to come.[5]

Shockingly, the strength of *Hamilton*'s reviews as well as its obsessive word-of-mouth managed to put musical theatre back into popular consciousness, with the musical being featured on talk shows, the Grammy Awards, and with Miranda being selected to host the television program *Saturday Night Live*. *Hamilton* was even supported by the Oval Office, with President Barack Obama speaking in favor of the musical on several occasions, even giving an early draft of the title song an audience at the White House. The degree of *Hamilton*'s success cannot be overstated, but there are also a number of parallels to the work of LaChiusa that go beyond *Hamilton*'s employment of nontraditional music and its development in the nonprofit sector. In particular, Miranda's adaptation of a historical biography places his work on the musical within the lens of dramatist-historian, bringing to mind LaChiusa's invocation of the ideas of historical imagination. *Hamilton* may take fewer liberties with its source material than LaChiusa's *Suites*, but there is still a degree of historical creativity in deciding what moments are accessible for dramatization. Further, Miranda's positioning of Eliza Hamilton as protagonist of the story in the musical's final moments and the racialized utopia achieved by the musical's casting all seem to suggest that Miranda exercises historical imagination in much the same way as LaChiusa.

There is less commonality between LaChiusa's works and the musical *Dear Evan Hansen*, but it is worth mentioning that the musical continued the streak of wins for "The New Musical Drama" on Broadway. Similar to *Next to Normal* before it, *Dear Evan Hansen* also developed at the Washington, D.C.-based Arena Stage prior to opening off-Broadway at the nonprofit Second Stage Theatre. The musical also shares the same pop-rock sensibility that informs much of the score to *Next to Normal* while also dealing with social stigmas and possible mental illness. The musical follows Evan Hansen, who mistakenly gets caught up in stories about a classmate's suicide. The musical, which positions Evan as a type of antihero, brings in incredibly relevant themes from the current social climate, particularly the ubiquitous nature of social media and the nature of school bullying. While none of these are themes that are incredibly relevant to the work of LaChiusa, the musical, which was an original, nonadapted story, does continue in the tradition of unlikely narrative and nonprofit association that is so central to "The New Musical Drama." *Dear Evan Hansen* won six Tony Awards, including Best Musical, and recently launched a national tour.

The most startling example of "The New Musical Drama" on Broadway, and the title that has the most relevance to LaChiusa's project, is the musical

The Band's Visit. With music and lyrics by David Yazbek and book by Itamar Moses, the musical was developed by Atlantic Theatre Company. The musical, which tells the story of an Egyptian police band who mistakenly end up in a small town in Israel, seemed a very unlikely bet for transfer to a commercial run. Based on a 2007 independent film, the musical utilizes Middle Eastern musical motifs in the employment of its story. The use of musical vocabulary not endemic to the Broadway stage brings the musical into conversation with the work of LaChiusa, whose "mongrel" approach celebrates the use of eclectic musical motifs in the musical. More importantly, its structural concept is firmly in line with many of the experiments with structure that are found in the work of LaChiusa. *The Band's Visit* is an attempt to make a naturalistic musical. This is aided by the fact that several of the songs in the musical are diegetic. Yet, even the more traditional "book numbers" tend to come directly out of speech in much the way Richard Rodgers and Oscar Hammerstein II intended. That being said, the musical's plot is not in any way traditionally structured, even though it is told linearly. The musical has no traditional climax and its structure is loose. A type of romance between Tewfiq, the band's leader, and Dina, a woman in the town, gives the musical some through line, but even this seems incidental to the more nuanced attempt to replicate the movie's use of *cinéma vérité* by eschewing the normative assumptions of inciting incident and climax that figure into much of standard musical theatre repertoire. While none of LaChiusa's output can be said to be naturalistic, there is a kinship between *The Band's Visit* and LaChiusa's oeuvre in terms of the project of dismantling the structural assumptions of musical entertainment. Although *The Band's Visit* closed in April of 2019, it still managed to win ten Tony Awards while also returning its initial capitalization.

Taken together, the past twenty years have seen an uneven trajectory of increasing relevance of "The New Musical Drama" to the Broadway stage, particularly if Tony Awards can be seen as any sort of barometer for success. The fact that all of the titles mentioned in this section also managed to make a profit, albeit a modest one in some cases, further proves that, while "The New Musical Drama" may not be the norm in Broadway entertainment, it at least has a place at the table.

LaChiusa and the Future of "The New Musical Drama"

The work of LaChiusa and, by extension, "The New Musical Drama" both seem to have a future. For the purposes of this study, I have ended my consideration with the 2015 opening of *First Daughter Suite*. It was necessary to delimit LaChiusa's work because he is extremely prolific. Since the opening of *First Daughter Suite*, LaChiusa has had several other projects either continue in development or premiere in full production. Most notably, the musical *Rain*, based on the 1921 short story "Rain" by Somerset Maugham, premiered at the Old Globe Theatre in San Diego in 2016. The short story has been adapted several times to both stage and screen and the root of the story—a young missionary attempts to bring the prostitute Sadie Thompson to Jesus, but finds himself overwhelmed by his own sexual desire for her—remains the central through line of the musical. *Rain* received positive notices in San Diego, but there is still no word on whether the show will eventually be produced in New York or if it will become available for licensing. LaChiusa has several other titles in various stages of development, including a musical about the life of Graciela Daniele and another musical about the Gabor sisters and their mother. Recently, it was announced that LaChiusa received a commission from Williamstown Theatre Festival, where *R Shomon*, the earlier version of *See What I Wanna See*, had its world premiere, to adapt the recent Pulitzer Prize–winning play *Cost of Living* into a musical.[6] The play, which also had its world premiere at Williamstown Theatre Festival, concerns four characters and the relationships between disabled and able-bodied people. While there is currently no timeline for production, the idea for the musical does signal that LaChiusa and his project are far from over.

APPENDIX

The following licensing houses provided printed copies and perusals of the scripts and scores references in this book. Licensing information for the titles referenced in this book follows:

First Lady Suite, Hello Again, Little Fish, Lucky Nurse, and *See What I Wanna See* are all licensed through Dramatists Play Services.

Giant, First Daughter Suite, Marie Christine, Queen of the Mist, and *The Wild Party* are all licensed through Concord Theatricals.

Lyrics reprinted here with kind permission from Michael John LaChiusa.

NOTES

Introduction

1. Michael John Lachiusa, "The Great Gray Way." *Opera News* 70, no. 2 (2005): 30.

2. Ibid., 33.

3. Ibid., 32.

4. Ibid.

5. Miranda Lundskaer-Nielsen, *Directors and the New Musical Drama: British and American Musical Theatre in the 1980s and 90s* (NYC: Palgrave Macmillan, 2008), 7.

6. Ibid., 6.

7. LaChiusa, "The Great Gray Way," 33.

8. Rebecca Paller, "High Scorers: Michael John LaChiusa." *Opera News* 64, no. 5 (November 1999): 52.

9. Ibid.

10. Nelson Pressley, "At Long Last, All Systems Are Gogh for 'Yellow': Composer LaChiusa's Difficult Musical Shapes Up," *The Washington Post,* October 31st, 2004, N01.

11. Bud Coleman, "New Horizons: The Musical at the Dawn of the Twenty-First Century," in *The Cambridge Companion to the Musical; Second Edition*, eds. William A. Everett and Paul R. Laird (NYC: Cambridge University Press, 2008), 291.

12. Ben Brantley, "Both a Sendup and an Embrace, Based on Bergman Again," *The New York Times*, December 19, 1994.

13. Lawrence Van Gelder, "On the Eve of a New Life, an Untimely Death," *The New York Times*, December 13, 1996.

14. Lundskaer-Nielsen, *Directors and the New Musical Drama*, 6.

15. Ibid., 80–1.

16. Bruce Kirle, *Unfinished Show Business: Broadway Musicals as Works-in-Process* (Carbondale, IL: Southern Illinois University Press, 2005), 6.

17. Ibid., 7–8.

18. Ibid.

Chapter 1

1. Ben Brantley, "Crossing Fingers, Broadway Sings a Hopeful Tune," *The New York Times*, Sunday, September 12, 1999.

2. Michael John LaChiusa, "I Sing of America's Mongrel Culture," *The New York Times*, November 14, 1999.

3. Ibid.

4. Online Etymology Dictionary. "Listing for 'Mongrel'," *The Sciolist*. https://www.etymonline.com/word/mongrel. (Accessed November 14, 2018.)

5. "Mongrel," Merriam-Webster.com. (Accessed November 14, 2018.) https://www.merriam-webster.com/dictionary/mongrelization.

6. LaChiusa, "I Sing of America's Mongrel Culture."

7. Ibid.

8. It is important to note that there was a great deal of discussion at Lincoln Center about whether to refer to the piece as a musical or an opera. While Ira Weitzman, producer of Musical Theatre at Lincoln Center, wanted to refer to the piece as an opera, he was eventually overruled.

9. LaChiusa, "I Sing of America's Mongrel Culture."

10. This reading of Daniele's staging of *Marie Christine* is compiled from my own memories of the original production as well as two separate viewings of the archival video of the production housed at the Lincoln Center Library for the Performing Arts. The video documents the January 6, 2000, performance. The most recent viewing was on August 18th, 2018.

11. Michael John LaChiusa, *Marie Christine* (New York: Rodgers and Hammerstein Theatricals, 1999), I-2A.

12. Ibid., I-4.

13. Ibid., I-10.

14. Ibid., I-21.

15. Ibid., I-32.

16. Ibid., II-53.

17. Ibid., II-60.

18. Ibid., II-65.

19. Ben Brantley, "The Promises of an Enchantress," *The New York Times*, December 3, 1999.

20. Ibid.

21. Ibid.

22. Terry Teachout, "A 'Musical' That's Really an Opera," *The New York Times*, January 2, 2000.

23. Ibid.

24. Ibid.

25. kalamu ya salaam, "A Rambling Response to the Play *Marie Christine*," *Lincoln Center Theatre Review* 9, no. 13 (Fall 1999): 17–20.

26. Ibid., 17.

27. Ibid.

28. Letter from Michael John LaChiusa to Lincoln Center Theatre, September 21, 1999, T-MSS 2017-017; Electronic Record 14, Lincoln Center Library for the Performing Arts, Special Collections.

29. LaChiusa, Letter from Michael John LaChiusa to Lincoln Center Theatre.

30. salaam, "A Rambling Response to the Play *Marie Christine*," 17–20.

31. LaChiusa, Letter from Michael John LaChiusa to Lincoln Center Theatre.

32. Ray Allen and George P. Cunningham, "Cultural Uplift and Double-Consciousness: African American Responses to the 1935 Opera '*Porgy and Bess*'." *The Musical Quarterly* 88, no. 3 (2005): 342. http://www.jstor.org/stable/4123229

33. Ray Allen, "An American Folk Opera? Triangulating Folkness, Blackness, and Americaness in Gershwin and Heyward's '*Porgy and Bess*'." *The Journal of American Folklore* 117, no. 465 (2004): 243. http://www.jstor.org/stable/4137739

34. Arts Beat Blog, "Stephen Sondheim Takes Issue with Plan for Revamped *Porgy and Bess*," *The New York Times*, August 10, 2011.

35. Ibid.

36. Adam Hetrick, "Tony Award Nominee Diane Paulus Responds to *Porgy and Bess* Criticism," playbill.com, August 11, 2011. (Accessed February 13, 2019.) http://www.playbill.com/article/tony-award-nominee-diane-paulus-responds-to-porgy-and-bess-criticism-com-181715.

37. Brantley, "The Promises of an Enchantress."

38. Anthony Tommasini, "Critic's Notebook: 'Once in Love with Carmen?!' Nope!" *The New York Times*, January 24th, 2000.

39. Paller, "High Scorers: Michael John LaChiusa."

40. Ibid., 50.

41. Teachout, "A 'Musical' That's Really an Opera."

42. Brantley, "The Promises of an Enchantress."

43. Sherry Boone played the role of Marie Christine on Wednesday and Saturday matinees.

44. John Bush Jones, *Our Musicals, Ourselves: A Social History of the American Musical Theatre* (Boston, MA: Brandeis University Press, 2004), 353. Please note that Jones misidentifies LaChiusa as "John LaChiusa" as opposed to "Michael John LaChiusa."

45. Ibid., 1.

46. Ibid., 353.

47. Ibid., 354.

48. Statement from Michael John LaChiusa to the National Endowment of the Arts, March 30, 1999, T-MSS 2017-017; Box 27, Folder 27.14, Lincoln Center Library for the Performing Arts, Special Collections.

49. Geoffrey Block, "Integration," in *The Oxford Handbook of the American Musical*, eds. Raymond Knapp, Mitchell Morris, and Stacy Wolf (New York: Oxford Press, 2011), 98–9.

50. Lehman Engel, *The American Musical Theatre* (New York: Macmillan, 1975), 76.

51. Scott McMillin, *The Musical as Drama: A Study of the Principles and Conventions Behind Musical Shows from Kern to Sondheim* (Princeton, NJ: Princeton University Press, 2006), 2.

52. Ibid., 7.

53. Ibid., 5.

54. LaChiusa, *Marie Christine*, I-2A.

55. Ibid., II-53.

56. The term "through-composed" generally applies to songs that are nonstrophic, meaning that musicals sequences aren't necessarily repeated on rhythmically similar lyrics.

57. "Charles Strouse in Conversation with Michael John LaChiusa," *The Legacy Project*, The Dramatist Guild Fund, dir. Jeremy Levine and Landon Van Soest, 2011.

58. Kirle, *Unfinished Show Business; Broadway Musicals as Works-in-Process.*

59. Ibid., 1.

60. LaChiusa, *Marie Christine*, I-32.

61. Ibid., I-33.

62. Ibid.

63. Ibid., I-33.

64. Mervyn Rothstein, "A Life in the Theatre: Director-Choreographer Graciela Daniele," *playbill.com*, June 15, 2006. https://web.archive.org/web/20060723191117/http://www.playbill.com/features/article/100342.html. (Accessed March 29, 2024.)

65. LaChiusa, *Marie Christine*, II-53.

66. Ibid.

67. Ibid.

68. Ibid.

69. Ibid.

70. Ibid., II-54.

71. LaChiusa, "I Sing of America's Mongrel Culture."

72. McMillin, *The Musical as Drama*, 3.

73. Anthony Tommasini, "Opera? Musical? Please Respect the Difference," *The New York Times*, July 7, 2011.

74. Ibid.

75. LaChiusa, "I Sing of America's Mongrel Culture."

76. Letter from Michael John LaChiusa to Lincoln Center Theatre, entitled "Fuckers" ca. 1999. T-Mss 2015-017; ER13. Lincoln Center Library for the Performing Arts, Special Collections.

Chapter 2

1. Barry Singer, *Ever After: The Last Years of Musical Theatre and Beyond* (New York: Applause Books, 2004), 87.

2. Ibid.

3. Shoshana Greenberg, "For Michael John LaChiusa, When It Rains, It Pours," *American Theatre Online*, March 16, 2016. https://www.americantheatre. org/2016/03/16/for-michael-john-lachiusa-when-it-rains-it-pours/. (Accessed February 14, 2019.)

4. Singer, *Ever After: The Last Years of Musical Theatre and Beyond*, 87.

5. Courtney Marie, Interview: Michael John LaChiusa on Spotlighting History's Mothers and Daughters in "First Daughter Suite," *StageBuddy: The Insider's Guide to Theatre*, March 29, 2016. https://stagebuddy.com/theater/theater-feature/interview-michael-john-lachiusa-spotlighting-historys-mothers-daughters-first-daughter-suite. (Accessed May 24, 2024.)

6. While the opening number of *First Lady Suite* does mention the idea of flight, it wasn't initially presented during the musical's premiere. The number was written later and is now included in the licensed version of the show.

7. R. G. Collingwood, *The Idea of History* (Oxford: Clarendon Press, 1948; Kindle Edition, 2018), 4511, 4522.

8. Ibid., 4679.

9. Ibid.

10. Ibid. 4701.

11. George Chauncey, *Gay New York: Gender, Urban Culture, and the Making of the Gay Male World, 1890–1940* (New York: Basic Books, 1994), 284.

12. Lynn Speer Lemisko, "The Historical Imagination: Collingwood in the Classroom," *Canadian Social Studies* 38, no. 2 (Winter 2004): 1–8.

13. For more on Collingwood in general, see William H. Dray's *History as Re-enactment: R. G. Collingwood's Idea of History* (Oxford: Carendon Press, 1995).

14. Ibid., 3.

15. Collingwood, *The Idea of History*, 5419.

16. Michael John LaChiusa, *First Lady Suite* (New York: Dramatists Play Service, 1995), 10.

17. Michael John LaChiusa, *First Daughter Suite* (New York: Rodgers and Hammerstein Theatricals, 2015), I-2-5.

18. Ibid., I-1-1.

19. Ibid., 9–10.

20. Ibid., 19–20.

21. Ibid., 21.

22. Ibid., 24.

23. Ibid., I-2-7.

24. Ibid., I-2-25.

25. Mary Brennan, "The Nixon Administration, 1969–1974: Patricia Ryan Nixon," in *First Ladies: Presidential Historians on the Lives of 45 Iconic American Women*, ed. Susan Swain and C-Span (New York: Perseus Book Group, 2015), 364.

26. Mary Barelli Gallagher, *My Life with Jacqueline Kennedy* (New York: David McKay, 1969), 312–13.

27. LaChiusa, *First Lady Suite*, 10.

28. Ibid., 13.

29. Ibid., 13–14.

30. Collingwood, *The Idea of History*, 2018, 756.

31. LaChiusa, *First Daughter Suite*, I-2-21.

32. Brennan and Naftali, "The Nixon Administration, 1969–1974: Patricia Ryan Nixon," in *First Ladies: Presidential Historians on the Lives of 45 Iconic American Women*, 357–8.

33. LaChiusa, *First Lady Suite*, 20.

34. Ibid., 21.

35. Ibid.

36. Ibid., 19.

37. This reading of the performance comes from both a live viewing of the original production while it was still in previews and the video of the original

production of *First Daughter Suite* available at the Lincoln Center Library for the Performing Arts, Theatre on Film and Tape division. The most recent viewing of this footage occurred on August 11th, 2018.

38. LaChiusa, *First Daughter Suite*, I-2-7.

39. Ibid.

40. Ibid.

41. Ibid., I-2-13.

42. Ibid., I-2-14-15.

43. Ibid., I-2-19.

44. Ibid., I-2-22.

45. Ibid., I-2-23.

46. Ibid., I-2-24-25.

47. Michael Beschloss and Barbara Perry, "The Kennedy Administration, 1961–1963: Jacqueline Bouvier Kennedy," in *First Ladies: Presidential Historians on the Lives of 45 Iconic American Women*, ed. Susan Swain and C-Span (New York: Perseus Book Group, 2015), 330–1.

48. Ibid., 333.

49. Naftali, "The Nixon Administration, 1969–1974: Patricia Ryan Nixon," in *First Ladies: Presidential Historians on the Lives of 45 Iconic American Women*, 357.

50. Brennan and Naftali, "The Nixon Administration, 1969–1974: Patricia Ryan Nixon," in *First Ladies: Presidential Historians on the Lives of 45 Iconic American Women*, 364.

51. Collingwood, *The Idea of History*, 4556.

52. LaChiusa, *First Lady Suite*, 31.

53. Ibid., 33.

54. LaChiusa, *First Daughter Suite*, I-3-31.

55. Ibid., I-3-52.

56. Ibid., I-3-55.

57. Marilyn Irvin Holt, "The Eisenhower Administration, 1953–1961: Mamie Doud Eisenhower," in *First Ladies: Presidential Historians on the Lives of 45 Iconic American Women*, ed. Susan Swain and C-Span (New York: Perseus Book Group, 2015), 324.

58. Ibid.

59. Ibid., 317.

60. Edith Mayo, "The Eisenhower Administration, 1953–1961: Mamie Doud Eisenhower," in *First Ladies: Presidential Historians on the Lives of 45 Iconic American Women*, ed. Susan Swain and C-Span (New York: Perseus Book Group, 2015), 322.

61. LaChiusa, *First Lady Suite*, 36.

62. Ibid., 37.

63. LaChiusa, *First Daughter Suite*, I-3-31-32.

64. Ibid., I-3-29.

65. Ibid., I-3-27-29.

66. Grace Hale, "The Carter Administration, 1977–1981: Rosalynn Smith Carter," in *First Ladies: Presidential Historians on the Lives of 45 Iconic American Women*, ed. Susan Swain and C-Span (New York: Perseus Book Group, 2015), 380.

67. LaChiusa, *First Daughter Suite*, I-3-31-29 and I-3-31-32.

68. Hale, "The Carter Administration, 1977–1981: Rosalynn Smith Carter," in *First Ladies: Presidential Historians on the Lives of 45 Iconic American Women*, 386.

69. LaChiusa, *First Daughter Suite*, I-3-31-33.

70. LaChiusa, *First Lady Suite*, 42.

71. Ibid.

72. LaChiusa, *First Daughter Suite*, I-3-34.

73. Ibid., I-3-37.

74. LaChiusa, *First Lady Suite*, 41.

75. Ibid., 32–3.

76. LaChiusa, *First Daughter Suite*, I-3-49-50.

77. Ibid., I-3-32.

78. Collingwood, *The Idea of History*, 4742.

79. Lemisko, "The Historical Imagination: Collingwood in the Classroom," 5.

80. Patti Davis, *The Way I See It* (New York: G.P. Putnam's Sons, 1992), 92–3.

81. LaChiusa, *First Daughter Suite*, II-1-62.

82. Ibid., II-1-61, II-1-67, II-1-73.

83. Ibid., II-1-75.

84. Ibid., II-1-76.

85. Ibid., II-1-69.

86. Ibid., II-1-73.

87. Ibid., II-1-66.

88. Ibid., II-1-67.

89. Ibid., II-1-69.

90. Ibid., II-1-75.

91. Ibid., II-1-78.

92. Ibid., II-1-74.

93. McMillin, *The Musical as Drama*, 7.

94. LaChiusa, *First Daughter Suite*, II-1-70.

95. Ibid.

96. Ibid., II-1-72.

97. Ibid., II-1-62. Underlined words are in the original text.

98. Curtis M. Wong, "A Musical Look at the Women of the White House as You've Never Seen Them," *Huffington Post*, November 17, 2015. https://www.huffingtonpost.com/entry/michael-john-lachiusa-first-daughter-suite_us_5644eefee4b06037734843a1. (Accessed May 24, 2024.)

99. Ibid.

100. Greenberg, "For Michael John LaChiusa, When It Rains, It Pours."

101. Ben Brantley, "Review: In *First Daughter Suite:* Unelected but Still Under a Microscope," *The New York Times*, October 21, 2015.

Chapter 3

1. Interview with Michael John LaChiusa; June 25, 2024.

2. Jesse Green, "So Many Musicals to Write, So Little Time," *The New York Times*, March 5, 2006.

3. Lehman Engel and Howard Kissel, *Words with Music: Creating the Broadway Musical Libretto,* Applause Books; Updated Edition; January 1, 2006.

4. Jennifer Hochschild, *Facing Up to the American Dream: Race, Class, and the Soul of the Nation* (Princeton, NJ: Princeton University Press, 1995), 15.

5. Ibid., 18.

6. Michael Schudson, "American Dreams." *American Literary History* 16, no. 3 (Autumn 2004): 566.

7. Ibid.

8. Rebecca Applin Warner, *The Musical Theatre Composer as Dramatist: A Handbook for Collaboration* (London: Methuen Drama, 2023), 4.

9. Les Spindle, "INTERVIEW: Michael John LaChiusa Is a Giant Talent," theatermania.com, May 19, 2012.

10. Michael John LaChiusa and Sybille Pearson, *Giant* (New York: Rodgers and Hammerstein Theatricals, 2012), I-1.

11. Ibid., I-16.

12. Ibid., I-24.

13. Ibid., I-30.

14. Ibid., I-33.

15. Ibid., I-36.

16. Ibid., II-68.

17. Ibid., II-79.

18. Ibid., II-88.

19. Ben Brantley, "Theater Review: A Texas Tale Too Big for a Lone Star," *The New York Times*, November 15, 2012.

20. Terry Teachout, "A Texas Sized Achievement," *The Wall Street Journal*, November 16, 2012.

21. Steven Suskin, "Theater Review: *Giant*," *Variety*.

22. Peter Marks, "Daring to Do a Texas-Sized Task, Create a *Giant* of Note," *The Washington Post*, May 10th, 2009.

23. Mark Lubbock, "American Musical Theatre: An Introduction," in *The Complete Book of Light Opera*, ed. Mark Lubbock (New York: Appleton-Century-Crofts, 1962), 753–6.

24. Stacy Wolf, *Changed for Good* (New York: Oxford University Press, 2011), 8.

25. LaChiusa and Pearson, *Giant*, I-8.

26. Ibid., I-34.

27. Ibid., I-35.

28. Ibid., I-36.

29. Ibid., II-109.

30. Ibid., I-48.

31. Ibid., II-81.

32. Ibid.

33. Terrence McNally, Stephen Flaherty, and Lynn Ahrens, *Ragtime* (New York: Musical Theatre International, 2000), 51.

34. Michael John LaChiusa, *Queen of the Mist* (New York: Rodgers and Hammerstein Theatricals, 2011), I-2.

35. Steven Suskin, "*Heartbreak Country*: Lincoln Center's American Songbook Presents Works of Michael John LaChiusa," *playbill.com*, February 3, 2014. https://playbill.com/article/heartbreak-country-lincoln-centers-american-songbook-presents-works-of-michael-john-lachiusa-com-214470. (Accessed September 29, 2024.)

Chapter 4

1. Jane Barnette, *Adapturgy: The Dramaturg's Art and Theatrical Adaptation* (Carbondale, IL: Southern Illinois University Press, 2019), 1.

2. Linda Hutcheon, *A Theory of Adaptation: Second Edition* (New York: Routledge Press, 2012), 5.

3. Barnette, *Adapturgy: The Dramaturg's Art and Theatrical Adaptation*., 53.

Notes

4. Ibid., 91.

5. Jonathan Frank, "Interview with Michael John LaChiusa," TalkinBroadway Website, 2000. https://www.talkinbroadway.com/cabaret/lachiusa.html. (Accessed January 31st, 2019.)

6. Hutcheon, *A Theory of Adaptation: Second Edition*, 6.

7. These definitions were cited from the Merriam-Webster Dictionary website. https://www.merriam-webster.com/dictionary/palimpsest. (Accessed January 31, 2019.)

8. Ibid.

9. Michael Alexander, *The Poetic Achievement of Ezra Pound* (Edinburgh: Edinburgh University Press, 1978), 144.

10. Gerard Genette, *Palimpsests: Literature in the Second Degree* (Nebraska, NE: University of Nebraska, 1997), 5.

11. Ibid.

12. Barnette, *Adapturgy: The Dramaturg's Art and Theatrical Adaptation*, 53.

13. Ibid., 89.

14. Ibid.

15. Ibid., 90.

16. Ibid., 98.

17. Marvin Carlson, *Places of Performance: The Semiotics of Theatre Architecture* (Ithaca, NY: Cornell University Press, 1993), 128.

18. Nicholas Rudall, "Introduction," in *La Ronde in a New Translation by Nicholas Rudall* (Chicago, IL: Ivan R. Dee, 2010), 5.

19. A letter from Sigmund Freud to Arthur Schnitzler. "Schnitzler's Hidden Manuscripts Explored," April 1, 2007. https://www.cam.ac.uk/research/news/schnitzler's-hidden-manuscripts-explored.

20. Carl R. Muller, "Introduction," in *Arthur Schnitzler: Four Major Plays*, ed. Carl R. Mueller (Los Angeles, CA: University of California, 1999), ix.

21. Maria P Alter, "From 'Der Reigen' to 'La Ronde' Transposition of a Stageplay to the Cinema." *Literature/Film Quarterly* 24, no. 1 (1996): 53. http://www.jstor.org/stable/43796698.

22. Rudall, "Introduction," in *La Ronde in a New Translation by Nicholas Rudall*, 7.

23. David Hare, "Introduction," in *The Blue Room* (London: Faber and Faber, 1998), vii.

24. Ibid.

25. While I consulted several translations of the text for *La Ronde* throughout the course of this project, I am largely relying on Eric Bentley's 1954 translation, which is the version that was primarily utilized by LaChiusa and the creative team.

26. Elizabeth G. Ametsbichler, "'Der Reiz Des Reigens': 'Reigen' Works by Arthur Schnitzler and Werner Schwab." *Modern Austrian Literature* 31, no. 3/4 (1998): 292. http://www.jstor.org/stable/24648834

27. Dramaturgical protocol for the original development of *Hello Again* prepared by Chris Burney, December 1, 1992. T-MSS 2017-017; Box 16, Folder 16.7, Lincoln Center Library for the Performing Arts, Special Collections.

28. Michael John LaChiusa. *Hello Again* (New York: Dramatists Play Service, 1995), 14.

29. Ibid., 18.

30. Ibid., 24.

31. Ibid.

32. Ibid.

33. Ibid., 47.

34. Ibid., 56.

35. Ibid., 72.

36. Dramaturgical protocol for the original development of *Hello Again* prepared by Chris Burney, December 1, 1992. T-MSS 2017-017; Box 16, Folder 16.7, Lincoln Center Library for the Performing Arts, Special Collections.

37. LaChiusa. *Hello Again*, 9, 66.

38. Ibid., 51.

39. Ibid., 45.

40. This reading of the performance comes from two viewings of the original production of *Hello Again* available at the Lincoln Center Library for the Performing Arts, Theatre on Film and Tape division. The most recent viewing of this footage occurred on October 15, 2018.

41. For the film version, characters were given names as opposed to their "labels" in the stage version, so the role of "The Young Thing" is noted simply as "Jack."

42. LaChiusa. *Hello Again*, 5.

43. Ibid., 43.

44. Short one-act play written by LaChiusa regarding the rewrites of Scene 8 in *Hello Again*, Undated, T-MSS 2017-017; Electronic Record 8, Lincoln Center Library for the Performing Arts, Special Collections.

45. Haruki Muramkami, "Introduction—Akutagawa Ryūnosuke: Downfall of the Chosen," in *Rashomon and 17 Other Stories*, trans. Jay Rubin (New York: Penguin Group, 2006), xxviii.

46. Barnette, *Adapturgy: The Dramaturg's Art and Theatrical Adaptation*, 89.

47. Keumsoo Hong. "The Geography of Time and Labor in the Late Antebellum American Rural South: Fin-de-Servitude Time Consciousness, Contested Labor, and Plantation Capitalism." *International Review of Social History* 46, no. 1 (2001): 1–27. http://www.jstor.org/stable/44582612

48. This is a bit confusing given that Akutagawa also wrote a short story entitled *Rashōmon*. This story does not provide the source material for the film, however, nor is it the story on which LaChiusa based his first act, called "R Shomon."

49. Ryūnosuke Akutagawa, "In a Bamboo Grove," in *Rashomon and 17 Other Stories*, trans. Jay Rubin (New York: Penguin Group, 2006), 10–19.

50. Maurice Merleau-Ponty. *Phenomenology of Perception* (New York: Routledge, 2012), 36.

51. Michael John LaChiusa, *See What I Wanna See* (New York: Dramatists Play Service, Inc., 2007), 11.

52. Ibid.

53. Ibid., 11, 36.

54. Ibid.

55. Ibid., 12, 37.

56. This reading of the performance comes from two viewings of the original NYC production of *See What I Wanna See* available at the Lincoln Center Library for the Performing Arts, Theatre on Film and Tape division. The most recent viewing of this footage occurred on August 18, 2018. Please note that, while this production marked the 2005 NYC premiere, the musical's world premiere occurred in 2004 at the Williamstown Theatre Festival in Williamstown, Massachusetts.

57. McMillin, *The Musical as Drama*, 2.

58. Barnette, *Adapturgy: The Dramaturg's Art and Theatrical Adaptation*, 90.

59. LaChiusa. *See What I Wanna See*, 11.

60. Ibid., 62.

61. Ibid., 12, 37.

62. Ibid., 33–5.

63. Ibid., 38.

64. Ibid.

65. Ibid., 54.

66. Barnette, *Adapturgy: The Dramaturg's Art and Theatrical Adaptation*, 90.

67. LaChiusa, *See What I Wanna See*, 55.

68. Barnette, *Adapturgy: The Dramaturg's Art and Theatrical Adaptation*, 98.

69. Ben Brantley, "Chasing Shopworn Dreams in *Pretty Woman: The Musical*," *The New York Times*, August 16, 2018.

70. Michael John LaChiusa, *Bernarda Alba* (New York: Rodgers and Hammerstein Theatricals, 2007), 59–60.

71. Lundskaer-Nielsen, *Directors and the New Musical Drama*, 6.

Chapter 5

1. Angela C. Pao, *No Safe Spaces: Re-Casting Race, Ethnicity, and Nationality in American Theatre* (Ann Arbor, MI: University of Michigan Press, 2010), 2.

2. Ibid.

3. Program for The Public Theatre Season, 1999–2000, Box 51, Folder 51.1, Michael John LaChiusa Papers, 1970s–2015, New York Public Library for the Performing Arts, Billy Rose Theatre Division.

4. Ibid.

5. Michael Riedel, "Rough Sledding Ahead," *The New York Post*, January 8, 1999.

6. Joseph Moncure March, *The Wild Party* (New York: Pascal, Covici, Publisher, Inc, 1928), 10.

7. Kenneth Jones, "Collette, of *Muriel's Wedding,* to Throw Broadway *Wild Party.*" playbill.com October 14, 1999. http://www.playbill.com/news/article/collette-of-muriels-wedding-to-throw-bway-wild-party-patinkin-kitt-also-in-84812. (Accessed April 18, 2016.)

8. Brenda Dixon Gottschild, *The Black Dancing Body: A Geography from Coon to Cool* (New York: Palgrave Macmillan, 2003), 5.

9. Ibid.

10. Allen Woll, *Black Musical Theatre: From Coontown to Dreamgirls* (Baton Rouge, LA: Louisiana State University Press, 1989), xiv.

11. Todd Decker, "Race, Ethnicity, Performance," in *The Oxford Handbook of Musical Theatre*, eds. Raymond Knapp, Mitchell Morris, and Stacy Wolf (New York: Oxford Press, 2011), 198.

12. Harvey Young, *Embodying Black Experience: Stillness, Critical Memory and the Black Body* (Ann Arbor, MI: University of Michigan Press, 2010), 158.

13. Pao, *No Safe Spaces*, 176.

14. Robert Hoffler, "B'Way 'Party' Cast Set," *Variety*, October 15, 1999.

15. Jonathan Frank, "Interview with Michael John LaChiusa," TalkinBroadway Website https://www.talkinbroadway.com/cabaret/lachiusa.html. (Accessed October 5, 2018.)

16. Notes and Research packet for *The Wild Party* Compiled by Wiley Hausam, Box 51, Folder 51.4, Michael John LaChiusa Papers, 1970s–2015, New York Public Library for the Performing Arts, Billy Rose Theatre Division.

17. Pao, *No Safe Spaces*, 176.

18. This close reading of Wolfe's staging of *The Wild Party* is compiled from my own memories of the original production as well as two separate viewings of the archival video of the production housed at the Lincoln Center Library for the Performing Arts. The video documents the May 18, 2000, performance. The most recent viewing was on August 17, 2018.

19. March, *The Wild Party*, 10.

20. Michael John LaChiusa and George C. Wolfe, *The Wild Party* (New York: Rodgers and Hammerstein Theatricals, 2001), 4.

21. Ibid., 6.

22. Ibid., 18.

23. Ibid., 8.

24. Ibid., 9.

25. Ibid., 18.

26. Brenda Dixon Gottschild, *Waltzing in the Dark: African-American Vaudeville and Race Politics in the Swing Era* (New York: St. Martin's Press, 2000), 18.

27. LaChiusa and Wolfe, *The Wild Party*, 40.

28. Ibid., 65.

29. Ibid., 73.

30. Ibid., 75.

31. Ibid., 77.

32. Ibid., 78.

33. Ibid., 81.

34. Charles Isherwood, "The Wild Party," *Variety*, April 14, 2000.

35. Ben Brantley, "Having Fun Yet, Jazz Babies?" *The New York Times*, April 14, 2000.

36. Shane Vogel, "Performance Review," *Theatre Journal* 53, no. 1 (March 2001): 145–8.

37. John Heilpern, "Welcome to *The Wild Party!* Dangerous, Seedy … Fantastic," *The New York Observer*, April 24, 2000.

38. Ethan Mordden, *The Happiest Corpse I've Ever Seen: The Last Twenty-Five Years of the Broadway Musical* (New York: Palgrave Macmillan, 2004), 212.

39. Singer, *Ever After: The Last Years of Musical Theatre and Beyond*, 193.

40. Accessed from the Internet Broadway Database, September 24, 2018.

41. Woll, *Black Musical Theatre: From Coontown to Dreamgirls*, xiv.

42. Jones, *Our Musicals, Ourselves: A Social History of the American Musical Theatre*, 1.

43. Ed. Jackson R. Bryer and Richard A. Davison, *The Art of the American Musical: Conversations with the Creators* (New Brunswick, NJ: Rutgers University Press, 2005), 295.

44. Brantley, "Having Fun Yet, Jazz Babies?"

45. Ibid.

46. March, *The Wild Party*, 33.

47. Young, *Embodying Black Experience*, 100.

48. March, *The Wild Party*, 35.

49. LaChiusa and Wolfe, *The Wild Party*, 8.

50. March, *The Wild Party*, 40.

51. Young, *Embodying Black Experience*, 10.

52. LaChiusa and Wolfe, *The Wild Party*, 34.

53. March, *The Wild Party*, 35.

54. LaChiusa and Wolfe, *The Wild Party*, 34.

55. March, *The Wild Party*, 35.

56. LaChiusa and Wolfe, *The Wild Party*, 34.

57. Ed. Darlene Clark Hine, *Black Women in America; Second Edition* (New York: Oxford University Press, 2005), 207.

58. Ibid., 208.

59. Ibid., 10.

60. LaChiusa and Wolfe, *The Wild Party*, 4.

61. David Walsh and Len Platt, *Musical Theater and American Culture* (Westport, CT: Praeger Publishers, 2003), 67.

62. Ann Douglas, *Terrible Honesty: Mongrel Manhattan in the 1920s* (New York: Noonday Press, 1995), 359.

63. Ibid., 362.

64. Ibid., 363.

65. Eric Lott, *Love and Theft: Blackface Minstrelsy and the American Working Class* (New York: Oxford University Press, 1993), 52.

66. March, *The Wild Party*, 9.

67. Frank, "Interview with Michael John LaChiusa."

68. Frantz Fanon, *Black Skin, White Masks* (New York: Grove Atlantic, 2008), xiv.

69. LaChiusa and Wolfe, *The Wild Party*, 54.

70. Ibid., 74.

71. Ibid., 75.

72. Nella Larsen, *Passing* (New York: Penguin Classics, 2003), 5.

73. LaChiusa and Wolfe, *The Wild Party*, 81.

74. Gottschild. *The Black Dancing Body*, 41.

75. List of potential replacements for Vanessa Williams, Box 50, Folder 50.16, Michael John LaChiusa Papers, 1970s–2015, New York Public Library for the Performing Arts, Billy Rose Theatre Division.

76. Ed. Bryer and Davison, *The Art of the American Musical*, 296.

Notes

77. LaChiusa and Wolfe, *The Wild Party*, 76.

78. Ibid., 33.

79. Douglas, *Terrible Honesty*, 356–9.

80. Kathy J. Ogren, *The Jazz Revolution: Twenties America and the Meaning of Jazz* (New York: Oxford University Press, 1989), 79–80.

81. Woll, *Black Musical Theatre: From Coontwon to Dreamgirls*, 50.

82. Douglas, *Terrible Honesty*, 77.

83. Gottschild, *Waltzing in the Dark*, 28.

84. John Kenrick, *Musical Theatre: A History; Second Edition* (New York: Bloomsbury Methuen Drama, 2017), 86.

85. Ibid.

86. Woll, *Black Musical Theatre: From Coontown to Dreamgirls*, 48.

87. Gottschild, *Waltzing in the Dark*, 25.

88. Ibid., 28.

89. Ogren, *The Jazz Revolution*, 82–3.

90. Gottschild, *Waltzing in the Dark*, 8.

91. Danielle Robinson, "Oh You Black Bottom! Appropriation, Authenticity, and Opportunity in the Jazz Dance Teaching of 1920s New York." *Dance Research Journal* 38, no. 1 & 2 (Summer/Winter 2006), 19.

92. Gottschild, *Waltzing in the Dark*, 7.

93. Ibid.

94. Decker, "Race, Ethnicity, Performance," 205.

95. "Sierra Boggess Pulls Out of BBC *West Side Story* Prom over 'Whitewashing,'" BBC.com, April 25, 2018. https://www.bbc.com/news/entertainment-arts-43891939. (Accessed October 19th, 2018.)

96. K. Kelly Nestruck, "*The Wild Party* Explores the Troubled Tradition of Blackface in Surprising New Ways," *The Globe and Mail*. Friday, February 27th, 2015. http://www.theglobeandmail.com/arts/theatre-and-performance/the-wild-party-and-different-shades-of-blackface/article23227865/. (Accessed October 19, 2018.)

Conclusion

1. Ben Brantley, "A Wise Autumnal American in Florence," *The New York Times*, April 19, 2005.

2. Charles Isherwood, "Sex and Rock? What Would the Kaiser Think?" *The New York Times*, December 11, 2006.

3.   Adam Hetrick, "Pulitzer Drama Juror David Rooney Weighs in on *Next to Normal* Win," playbill.com, April 13, 2010. (Accessed March 3rd, 2019.)

4.   Ben Brantley, "*Fun Home* at the Circle in the Square Theater," *The New York Times,* April 19, 2015.

5.   Ben Brantley, "Review: *Hamilton,* Young Rebels Changing History and Theatre," *The New York Times,* August 6, 2015.

6.   Olivia Clement, "Pulitzer Prize-Winning *Cost of Living* to Be Adapted into a Musical," playbill.com, July 12, 2018. (Accessed March 4, 2019.)

BIBLIOGRAPHY

Akutagawa, Ryūnosuke. *Rashomon and 17 Other Stories*, New York: Penguin Group, 2006.

Alexander, Michael. *The Poetic Achievement of Ezra Pound*, Edinburgh: Edinburgh University Press, 1978.

Allen, Ray. "An American Folk Opera? Triangulating Folkness, Blackness, and Americaness in Gershwin and Heyward's *Porgy and Bess.*" *The Journal of American Folklore* 117, no. 465, 2004: 243–261.

Allen, Ray and George P. Cunningham. "Cultural Uplift and Double-Consciousness: African American Responses to the 1935 Opera '*Porgy and Bess*'." *The Musical Quarterly* 88, no. 3, 2005: 342–69.

Alter, Maria P. "From 'Der Reigen' to 'La Ronde' Transposition of a Stageplay to the Cinema." *Literature/Film Quarterly* 24, no. 1, 1996: 52–6.

Ametsbichler, Elizabeth G. "'Der Reiz Des Reigens': 'Reigen' Works by Arthur Schnitzler and Werner Schwab." *Modern Austrian Literature* 31, no. 3/4, 1998: 288–300.

Barnette, Jane. *Adapturgy: The Dramaturg's Art and Theatrical Adaptation*, Carbondale, IL: Southern Illinois University Press, 2019.

Block, Geoffrey. "Integration," in *The Oxford Handbook of the American Musical*, eds. Raymond Knapp, Mitchell Morris, and Stacy Wolf, New York: Oxford Press, 2011, pp. 98–9.

Brantley, Ben. "Both a Sendup and an Embrace, Based on Bergman Again," *The New York Times*, December 19, 1994.

Brantley, Ben. "Chasing Shopworn Dreams in *Pretty Woman: The Musical*," *The New York Times*, August 16, 2018.

Brantley, Ben. "Crossing Fingers, Broadway Sings a Hopeful Tune," *The New York Times*, Sunday, September 12, 1999.

Brantley, Ben. "*Fun Home* at the Circle in the Square Theater," *The New York Times*, April 19, 2015.

Brantley, Ben. "Having Fun Yet, Jazz Babies?" *The New York Times*, April 14, 2000.

Brantley, Ben. "The Promises of an Enchantress," *The New York Times*, December 3, 1999.

Brantley, Ben. "Review: *Hamilton*, Young Rebels Changing History and Theatre," *The New York Times*, August 6, 2015.

Brantley, Ben. "Review: In *First Daughter Suite*: Unelected but Still under a Microscope," *The New York Times*, October 21, 2015.

Brantley, Ben. "Theater Review: A Texas Tale Too Big For a Lone Star," *The New York Times*, November 15, 2012.

Brantley, Ben. "A Wise Autumnal American in Florence," *The New York Times*, April 19, 2005.

Bryer, Jackson R. and Richard A. Davison. *The Art of the American Musical: Conversations with the Creators*, New Brunswick, NJ: Rutgers University Press, 2005.

Carlson, Marvin. *Places of Performance: The Semiotics of Theatre Architecture*, Ithaca, NY: Cornell University Press, 1993.

Carter, Rosalynn. *First Lady from Plains*, Boston, MA: Houghton Mifflin, 1984.

Chauncey, George. *Gay New York: Gender, Urban Culture, and the Making of the Gay Male World, 1890–1940*, New York: Basic Books, 1994.

Clement, Olivia. "Pulitzer Prize-Winning *Cost of Living* to Be Adapted into a Musical," playbill.com, July 12, 2018. (Accessed March 4, 2019.)

Coleman, Bud. "New Horizons: The Musical at the Dawn of the Twenty-First Century," in *The Cambridge Companion to the Musical; Second Edition*, eds. William A. Everett and Paul R. Laird, New York: Cambridge University Press, 2008.

Collingwood, R. G. *The Idea of History*, Oxford: Clarendon Press, 1948; Kindle Edition, 2018.

Davis, Patti. *The Way I See It*, New York: G.P. Putnam's Sons, 1992.

Decker, Todd. "Race, Ethnicity, Performance," in *The Oxford Handbook of Musical Theatre*, eds. Raymond Knapp, Mitchell Morris, and Stacy Wolf, New York: Oxford Press, 2011, pp. 197–205.

Douglas, Ann. *Terrible Honesty: Mongrel Manhattan in the 1920s*, New York: Noonday Press, 1995.

Edens, John A. *Eleanor Roosevelt: A Comprehensive Bibliography*, Westport, CT: Greenwood Press, 1994.

Eisenberg, Deborah. *The Collected Stories of Deborah Eisenberg*. 1st Picador ed., New York: Picador/Farrar, Straus and Giroux, 2010.

Eisenhower, Julie Nixon. *Pat Nixon: The Untold Story*, New York: Simon and Schuester, 1986.

Engel, Lehman. *The American Musical Theatre*, New York: Macmillan, 1975.

Engel, Lehman and Howard Kissel, *Words with Music: Creating the Broadway Musical Libretto*, Applause Books; Updated Edition; January 1, 2006.

Fanon, Frantz. *Black Skin, White Masks*, New York: Grove Atlantic, 2008.

Frank, Jonathan. "Interview with Michael John LaChiusa," TalkinBroadway Website, , 2000. https://www.talkinbroadway.com/cabaret/lachiusa.html. (Accessed January 31st, 2019.)

Freud, Sigmund. A letter from Sigmund Freud to Arthur Schnitzler, "Schnitzler's Hidden Manuscripts Explored," April 1st, 2007. https://www.cam.ac.uk/research/news/schnitzler's-hidden-manuscripts-explored. (Accessed January 29th, 2019.)

Gallagher, Mary Barelli. *My Life with Jacqueline Kennedy*, New York: David McKay, 1969.

Genette, Gerard. *Palimpsests: Literature in the Second Degree*, Nebraska, NE: University of Nebraska, 1997.

Gottschild, Brenda Dixon. *The Black Dancing Body: A Geography from Coon to Cool*, New York: Nebraska, 1997.

Gottschild, Brenda Dixon. *Waltzing in the Dark: African-American Vaudeville and Race Politics in the Swing Era*, New York: St. Martin's Press, 2000.

Green, Jesse. "So Many Musicals to Write, So Little Time," *The New York Times*, March 5, 2006.

Greenberg, Shoshana. "For Michael John LaChiusa, When It Rains, It Pours," *American Theatre Online*, March 16, 2016. https://www.americantheatre.org/2016/03/16/for-michael-john-lachiusa-when-it-rains-it-pours/. (Accessed February 14th, 2019.)

Hare, David. *The Blue Room*, London: Faber and Faber, 1998.

Heilpern, John. "Welcome to *The Wild Party!* Dangerous, Seedy … Fantastic," *The New York Observer*, April 24, 2000.

Hetrick, Adam. "Pulitzer Drama Juror David Rooney Weighs in on *Next to Normal* Win," playbill.com, April 13, 2010. (Accessed March 3, 2019.)

Hetrick, Adam. "Tony Award Nominee Diane Paulus Responds to *Porgy and Bess* Criticism," playbill.com, August 11, 2011. (Accessed February 13, 2019.)

Hine, Darlene Clark. *Black Women in America; Second Edition*, New York: Oxford University Press, 2005.

Hochschild, Jennifer. *Facing Up to the American Dream: Race, Class, and the Soul of the Nation*, Princeton, NJ: Princeton University Press, 1995.

Hoffler, Robert. "B'Way 'Party' Cast Set," *Variety*, October 15, 1999.

Hoffman, Warren. *The Great White Way: Race and the Broadway Musical*, New Brunswick, NJ: Rutgers University Press, 2014.

Hong, Keumsoo. "The Geography of Time and Labor in the Late Antebellum American Rural South: Fin-de-Servitude Time Consciousness, Contested Labor, and Plantation Capitalism." *International Review of Social History* 46, no. 1, 2001: 1–27.

Hurston, Zora Neale. "The Back Room." *Amerikastudieren/American Studies* 55, no. 4, 2010: 557–60.

Hutcheon, Linda. *A Theory of Adaptation; Second Edition*, New York: Routledge Press, 2012.

Isherwood, Charles. "Sex and Rock? What Would the Kaiser Think?" *The New York Times*, December 11, 2006.

Isherwood, Charles. "The Wild Party," *Variety*, April 14, 2000.

Jones, John Bush. *Our Musicals, Ourselves; A Social History of the American Musical Theatre*, Boston, MA: Brandeis University Press, 2004.

Jones, Kenneth. "Collette, of *Muriel's Wedding*, to Throw Broadway *Wild Party*," playbill.com, October 14, 1999. http://www.playbill.com/news/article/collette-of-muriels-wedding-to-throw-bway-wild-party-patinkin-kitt-also-in-84812. (Accessed April 18th, 2016.)

Kenrick, John. *Musical Theatre: A History; Second Edition*, New York: Bloomsbury Methuen Drama, 2017.

Kirle, Bruce. *Unfinished Show Business; Broadway Musicals as Works-in-Process*, Carbondale, IL: Southern Illinois University Press, 2005.

Knapp, Raymond. *The American Musical and the Performance of Personal Identity*, Princeton, NJ: Princeton University Press, 2006.

LaChiusa, Michael John. *Bernarda Alba*, New York: Rodgers and Hammerstein Theatricals, 2007.

LaChiusa, Michael John. *First Daughter Suite*, New York: Rodgers and Hammerstein Theatricals, 2015.

LaChiusa, Michael John. *First Lady Suite*, New York: Dramatists Play Service, 1995.

LaChiusa, Michael John. *Giant*, New York: Rodgers and Hammerstein Theatricals, 2012.

LaChiusa, Michael John. "The Great Gray Way." *Opera News* 70, no. 2, 2005.

LaChiusa, Michael John. *Hello Again*, New York: Dramatists Play Service, 1995.

LaChiusa, Michael John. "I Sing of America's Mongrel Culture," *The New York Times*, November 14, 1999.

LaChiusa, Michael John. *Little Fish*, New York: Dramatists Play Service, 2003.

LaChiusa, Michael John. *Marie Christine*, New York: Rodgers and Hammerstein Theatricals, 1999.

LaChiusa, Michael John. *Queen of the Mist*, New York: Rodgers and Hammerstein Theatricals, 2011.

LaChiusa, Michael John. *See What I Wanna See*, New York: Dramatists Play Service, 2007.

LaChiusa, Michael John and George C. Wolfe. *The Wild Party*, New York: Rodgers and Hammerstein Theatricals, 2001.

Larsen, Nella. *Passing*, New York: Penguin Classics, 2003.

Lee, Ashley and David Rooney, "Broadway's *The Great Comet* to Close after Casting Controversy," *Variety*, August 8, 2017.

Lemisko, Lynn Speer. "The Historical Imagination: Collingwood in the Classroom," *Canadian Social Studies* 38, no. 2, Winter 2004.

Lott, Eric. *Love and Theft: Blackface Minstrelsy and the American Working Class*, New York: Oxford University Press, 1993.

Lubbock, Mark. "American Musical Theatre: An Introduction," in *The Complete Book of Light Opera*, New York: Appleton-Century-Crofts, 1962, pp. 753–6.

Lundskaer-Nielsen, Miranda. *Directors and the New Musical Drama: British and American Musical Theatre in the 1980s and 90s*, New York: Palgrave Macmillan, 2008.

March, Joseph Moncure. *The Wild Party*, New York: Pascal, Covici, Publisher, Inc, 1928.

Marie, Courtney. Interview: Michael John LaChiusa on Spotlighting History's Mothers and Daughters in "First Daughter Suite," *StageBuddy: The Insider's Guide to Theatre*, March 29, 2016. https://stagebuddy.com/theater/theater-feature/interview-michael-john-lachiusa-spotlighting-historys-mothers-daughters-first-daughter-suite. (Accessed May 24, 2024.)

Marks, Peter. "Daring to Do a Texas -Sized Task, Create a *Giant* of Note," *The Washington Post*, May 10, 2009.

McCubbin, Lisa and Susan Ford. *Betty Ford: First Lady, Women's Advocate, Survivor, Trailblazer /. First Gallery Books hardcover edition*, New York: Gallery Books, an Imprint of Simon & Schuster, 2018.

McMillin, Scott. *The Musical as Drama: A Study of the Principles and Conventions Behind Musical Shows from Kern to Sondheim*, Princeton, NJ: Princeton University Press, 2006.

Bibliography

McNally, Terrence, Stephen Flaherty, and Lynn Ahrens. *Ragtime*, New York: Musical Theatre International, 2000.

Merleau-Ponty, Maurice. *Phenomenology of Perception*, New York: Routledge, 2012.

Merriam-Webster Dictionary, "Listing for Mongrel," Merriam-Webster. https://www.merriam-webster.com/dictionary/mongrelization. (Accessed November 14th, 2018.)

Michael John LaChiusa Papers. 1970s–2015. Special Collections, Billy Rose Division of Theatre. New York: New York Library for the Performing Arts.

Mordden, Ethan. *The Happiest Corpse I've Ever Seen: The Last Twenty-Five Years of the Broadway Musical*, New York: Palgrave Macmillan, 2004.

Most, Andrea. *Making Americans: Jews and the Broadway Musical*, Cambridge, MA: Harvard University Press, 2004.

Muller, Carl R. "Introduction," in *Arthur Schnitzler: Four Major Plays*, trans. Carl R. Muller, Los Angeles, CA: University of California, 1999, pp. viii–xii.

Muramkami, Haruki. "Introduction- Akutagawa Ryūnosuke: Downfall of the Chosen," in *Rashomon and 17 Other Stories*, trans. Haruki Muramkami, New York: Penguin Group, 2006, pp. xiv–xxxviii.

Nelson Pressley. "At Long Last, All Systems Are Gogh for 'Yellow': Composer LaChiusa's Difficult Musical Shapes Up," *The Washington Post*, October 31, 2004.

The New York Times, Arts Beat Blog, "Stephen Sondheim Takes Issue with Plan for Revamped *Porgy and Bess*," August 10, 2011.

Ogren, Kathy J. *The Jazz Revolution: Twenties America and the Meaning of Jazz*, New York: Oxford University Press, 1989.

Online Etymology Dictionary. "Listing for 'Mongrel'," *The Sciolist*. https://www.etymonline.com/word/mongrel. (Accessed November 14, 2018.)

Paller, Rebecca. "High Scorers: Michael John LaChiusa," *Opera News* 64, November 1999.

Pao, Angela C. *No Safe Spaces: Re-Casting Race, Ethnicity, and Nationality in American Theatre*, Ann Arbor, MI: University of Michigan Press, 2010.

Riedel, Michael. "Rough Sledding Ahead," *The New York Post*, January 8, 1999.

Robinson, Danielle. "Oh You Black Bottom! Appropriation, Authenticity, and Opportunity in the Jazz Dance Teaching of 1920s New York." *Dance Research Journal* 38, no. 1 & 2, Summer/Winter 2006: 19–42.

Rothstein, Mervyn. "A Life in the Theatre: Director-Choreographer Graciela Daniele," playbill.com, June 15, 2006.

Rudall, Nicholas. "Introduction," in *La Ronde in a New Translation by Nicholas Rudall*, trans. Nicholas Rudall, Chicago: Ivan R. Dee, 2010.

salaam, kalamu ya, "A Rambling Response to the Play *Marie Christine*." *Lincoln Center Theatre Review* 9, no. 13, Fall 1999: 18–20.

Sandoval-Sánchez, Alberto. *José, Can You See?: Latinos on and off Broadway*, Madison, WI: The University of Wisconsin Press, 1999.

Schudson, Michael. "American Dreams." *American Literary History* 16, no. 3, Autumn 2004: 556–73.

Singer, Barry. *Ever After: The Last Years of Musical Theatre and Beyond*, New York: Applause Books, 2004.

Spindle, Les. "INTERVIEW: Michael John LaChiusa Is a Giant Talent." theatermania.com, May 19, 2012.

Stearns, Marshall Winslow. *Jazz Dance: The Story of American Vernacular Dance*, New York: Da Capo, 1968.

Sternfeld, Jessica, *The Megamusical*. Bloomington, IN: Indiana University Press, 2006.

Steyn, Mark. *Broadway Babies Say Goodnight: Musicals Then and Now*, New York: Routledge, 2000.

Suskin, Steven. "*Heartbreak Country*: Lincoln Center's American Songbook Presents Works of Michael John LaChiusa,"*playbill.com*, February 3, 2014.

Suskin, Steven. "Theater Review: *Giant*," *Variety*, November 16, 2012.

Swain, Susan. *First Ladies: Presidential Historians on the Lives of 45 Iconic American Women*, New York: Perseus Book Group, 2015.

Symonds, Dominic and Millie Taylor. *Gestures of Music Theater: The Performativity of Song and Dance*, Oxford: Oxford University Press, 2014.

Tallant, Robert, *Voodoo in New Orleans*. First Collier Books Edition, New York: Collier Books, 1962.

Taylor, Millie and Dominic Symonds. *Studying Musical Theatre: Theory and Practice*, London: Palgrave Macmillan, 2014.

Teachout, Terry. "A 'Musical' That's Really an Opera," *The New York Times*, January 2nd, 2000.

Teachout, Terry. "A Texas Sized Achievement," *The Wall Street Journal*, November 16th, 2012.

Tommasini, Anthony. "Critic's Notebook; 'Once in Love with Carmen?!' Nope!" *The New York Times*, January 24th, 2000.

Tommasini, Anthony. "Opera? Musical? Please Respect the Difference," *The New York Times*, July 7th, 2011.

Van Gelder, Lawrence. "On the Eve of a New Life, an Untimely Death," *The New York Times*, December 13th, 1996.

Vogel, Shane. "Performance Review," *Theatre Journal* 53, no. 1, March 2001: 145–8.

Walsh, David and Len Platt. *Musical Theater and American Culture*, Westport, CT: Praeger Publishers, 2003.

Warner, Rebecca Applin. *The Musical Theatre Composer as Dramatist: A Handbook for Collaboration*, London: Methuen Drama, 2023.

Wolf, Stacy Ellen. *Changed for Good*, New York: Oxford University Press, 2011.

Wolf, Stacy Ellen. *A Problem Like Maria: Gender and Sexuality In the American Musical*, Ann Arbor, MI: University of Michigan Press, 2002.

Woll, Allen. *Black Musical Theatre: From Coontown to Dreamgirls*, Baton Rouge, LA: Louisiana State University Press, 1989.

Wollman, Elizabeth L. *The Theater Will Rock: A History of the Rock Musical: From Hair to Hedwig*, Ann Arbor, MI: University of Michigan Press, 2006.

Wong, Curtis M. "A Musical Look at the Women of the White House As You've Never Seen Them," *Huffington Post*, November 17, 2015. https://www.huffingtonpost.com/entry/michael-john-lachiusa-first-daughter-suite_us_5644eefee4b06037734843a1. (Accessed May 24, 2024.)

Young, Harvey. *Embodying Black Experience: Stillness, Critical Memory and the Black Body*, Ann Arbor, MI: University of Michigan Press, 2010.